Handbook of Inspirational and Motivational Stories, Anecdotes and Humor

Winston K. Pendleton

Parker Publishing Company, Inc.
West Nyack, New York

© 1982, by

PARKER PUBLISHING COMPANY, INC.

West Nyack, N. Y.

All Biblical quotations are from the King James version.

Library of Congress Cataloging in Publication Data

Pendleton, Winston K.
    Handbook of inspirational and motivational
stories, anecdotes, and humor.

    Includes index.
    1. Public speaking--Handbooks, manuals, etc.
2. Quotations, English. 3. Anecdotes. I. Title.
PN4193.I5P43   082   82-2279

ISBN 0-13-378604-8

ISBN 0-13-378612-9 (PBK)

Printed in the United States of America

How This Book Can Add Zip, Zing, and Sparkle to Your Next Speech

Opening the pages of this handbook is like stepping into a public speaker's department store. Here you will find everything under one roof.

This is the kind of book I have wanted myself for more than 30 years. One of my great frustrations as a writer and public speaker has been the difficulty of finding a variety of material for my talks. If I needed a serious illustration, I would search through a stack of anthologies and books of quotations. For humor, I had to turn to still other books.

So, to help others with the same problem, I have selected some of the best quotations and bits of humor from notes and papers I have been clipping and saving and stuffing into file drawers since my school days.

In this *Handbook of Inspirational and Motivational Stories, Anecdotes and Humor,* you never know exactly what you will find. It might be a bit of ancient wisdom by Aristotle, a spur to action by Woodrow Wilson, or a humorous remark by Phyllis Diller. Variety has been called the spice of life, and this handbook has plenty of it.

I hope you will find my selections useful. In every case where known, I have given credit to the author.

HOW THE BOOK IS ARRANGED

1. You will find the items listed alphabetically by more than 600 categories.
2. Under most categories, you will find numbers that lead to other items on a closely related subject.
3. A Thematic Index at the end of the book lists still other subjects.
4. In the section in the back of the book titled, "Authors Who Are

Quoted," all those who are quoted in the book are identified. Reference numbers show where to find each of their quotes.

HOW TO USE THIS BOOK—A WORKING EXAMPLE

In order to make this example concrete and practical, let's play the game of make-believe. Pretend that you have been invited to speak to the annual Installation of Officers banquet of the Jaycees or Rotaract.

You hope to inspire and motivate these young men and women to "work and achieve" during their new year. You have decided to cover two main points: working together, yet not overlooking the importance of the individual's contribution. As you begin to put your speech together, you look for help in this handbook.

First, to attract the attention of your audience and relax them—and incidentally yourself—why not open with a laugh or two? Turn to the section headed *Humorous Openers*. There you will find a dozen ways to get started with a laugh. You might chose Numbers 2373 and 2375. Put them together and open your speech like this: "Thank you, Mr. Chairman, for that gracious and flattering introduction. About the only thing you didn't say about me was that I was born in a log cabin. And you were right. I wasn't born in a log cabin. But my family did move into one as soon as they could afford it." Then move into your next funny story by gently touching the microphone and saying, "I'm glad this thing is steady. The other night when I started to speak, the microphone dropped down. I pushed it up, but it dropped down again. After that had happened three or four times, the program chairman jumped up with a dime in his hand and began to tighten a set screw. As he worked on it, he said, 'Don't worry folks, nothing's the matter except I think our speaker has a screw loose.' "

Next, you work into the main body of your speech. When you begin to talk about working together, you will find a quotation or two under *Cooperation*. Again, you can combine two or three quotations. If you put Numbers 482, 484, 485, 486, together and shuffle them around, you will come up with an illustration that makes a strong point and also ends with a laugh. This is the way you might say it. "Emerson had a word about cooperation. He said, 'No member of a crew is praised for the rugged individuality of his rowing.' And when you think about it, you will realize that no matter how great a warrior the big chief is, he can't do battle without his Indians backing him up. And on a rainy day, one tiny raindrop might fall unnoticed. But when those tiny raindrops cooperate, you might end up in the middle of a hurricane. And remember this, even when a woman makes a fool out of a man, she can't do it without his cooperation.''

For the windup of your speech, you plan to show that even with cooperation, the responsibility for success ultimately rests with the individual. You can cite some examples of individual accomplishments such as Columbus, Joan of Arc, Alexander the Great (a teenager), Charles Lindbergh. You could end on a high note by reciting this short quotation, Number 1174, which you will find listed under *Individuality*.

> "I am only one, but I am one.
> I cannot do everything,
>   But I can do something.
> And by the Grace of God
>   What I can do, I will do.''

If you want to end with a laugh, you can find this story, 2379, under *Humorous Closers*.

"I would like to close by saying, 'Carbolic acid.' I heard a speaker say that one time and afterward I asked him what he meant by it. And he said, 'I always end my speeches that way. I used to say 'adios' which is goodbye in Spanish. And sometimes I'd say 'au revoir' which is goodbye in French. I even tried 'auf Weidersehen.' That means goodbye in German. So, now I say 'Carbolic acid.' That means goodbye in any language.' ''

Best wishes for much success as you begin looking for the right quotation for the right audience at the right time.

Winston K. Pendleton

Also by the Author:

Complete Speaker's Galaxy of Funny Stories, Jokes and Anecdotes,
  Parker
Pursuit of Happiness, Bethany
How to Stop Worrying—Forever, Pelican
505 Jokes You Can Tell, Bethany
How to Make Money Speaking, Pelican
2121 Funny Stories and How to Tell Them, Bethany
How to Win Your Audience with Humor, Simon & Schuster

Content

Look Here 1

The more than 600 categories in this book ... ...sy to find a quote, anecdote or joke to fit your speech.

How This Book Can Add Zip, Zing and Sparkle to Your Next Speech   5.

HERE IS YOUR HANDBOOK OF INSPIRATIONAL
AND HUMOROUS MATERIAL
You Can Use It Five Ways to Find
the Exact Story or Quotation You Need

1. Look for it under its broad subject. You have more than 600 categories to choose from, listed alphabetically.
2. Refer to the numbers that you will find under some of the categories. They will lead you to other related items.
3. Look in the Thematic Index at the back of the book for still other related listings.
4. Refer to the "Authors Who Are Quoted" section to find the correct identification of the person you are quoting.
5. If you are looking for a quotation from a specific person look for the reference number in "Authors Who Are Quoted."

ABILITY

1. A man's ability cannot possibly be of one sort and his soul of another. If his soul be well-ordered, serious, and restrained, his ability also is sound and sober. Conversely, when the one is degenerated the other is contaminated.

—Seneca

2. Every person is responsible for all the good within the scope of his abilities, and for no more, and none can tell whose sphere is the largest.

—Gail Hamilton

3. Man is a rope stretched between the animal and the superman—a rope over an abyss.

—Friedrich Nietzsche

4. As we advance in life, we learn the limits of our abilities.

—James Anthony Froude

5.   And unto one man he gave five talents, to another, two, and to another, one; to every man according to his several ability.

—*Matthew 25:15*

6.   The neighborhood was celebrating the 100th birthday of their beloved elder citizen. Among other exciting events, he was being interviewed on television. "You look pretty healthy," the young reporter said, "Are you able to get around and walk very much these days?"

"Why certainly," the old man said with a grin, "I can walk a lot better today than I could a hundred years ago."

11, 912, 1359, 1629, 1634, 1752.

ACCIDENT

7.   A youngster rushed into the country store and shouted, "My dad was fixing the roof and the ladder slipped out from under him and he is hanging from the eaves."

The manager of the store said, "Okay, son, we'll rescue him." Then he yelled at all the fellows sitting around the store. "Hey, let's go. On the double, everybody, before he gets too tired and has to turn loose."

But before they could move, the youngster said, "Before you run too fast, will you please help me put some film in my camera?"

746, 948, 1275, 1781.

ACHIEVEMENT

8.   The ideal life is in our blood and never will be still. Sad will be the day for any man when he becomes contented with the thoughts he is thinking and the deeds he is doing—where there is not forever beating at the doors of his soul some great desire to do something larger, which he knows that he was meant and made to do.

—*Phillips Brooks*

9.   Why should we call ourselves men, unless it be to succeed in everything, everywhere? Say of nothing, "This is beneath me," nor feel that anything is beyond our powers. Nothing is impossible to the man who can will.

—*Mirabeau*

10. Unswerving loyalty to duty, constant devotion to truth, and a clear conscience will overcome every discouragement and surely lead the way to usefulness and high achievement.

—Grover Cleveland

11. It is true that I have never learned to sing, not even to play the lyre, but I know how to make a small and obscure city rich and great.

—Themistocles

12. Unless a man undertakes more than he possibly can do, he will never do all he can do.

—Henry Drummond

13. Even a mistake may turn out to be the one thing necessary to a worthwhile achievement.

—Henry Ford

14. Rest satisfied with doing well and leave others to talk of you as they please.

—Pythagoras

15. Satisfaction does not come from indulgence or satiety; it comes from achievement.

—Calvin Coolidge

16. It is not the going out of port, but the coming in, that determines the success of the voyage.

—Henry Ward Beecher

17. Something attempted, something done,
Has earned a night's repose.

—Henry Wadsworth Longfellow

18. If you want a thing well done, do it yourself.

—Charles Haddon Spurgeon

19. Thou shalt ever joy at eventide if thou spend the day fruitfully.

—Thomas A. Kempis

20. In the sweat of thy face shalt thou eat bread.

—Genesis 3:19

21. There is nothing so fatal to character as half-finished tasks.

—David Lloyd George

22.   You never have read anything about the "plans and objectives" of the Apostles. The title of the book is "The Acts of the Apostles."

—Author unknown

23.   I try all things; I achieve what I can.

—Herman Melville

24.   I would rather be sick than idle.

—Seneca

25.   By their fruits ye shall know them.

—Matthew 7:20

26.   A kid in our neighborhood has been making good money mowing lawns on Saturdays. When he first went into business, he followed the old idea of the "early bird gets the worm" and began calling on people at 8:00 a.m. For the first few Saturdays, he didn't get any business at all and by 10:00 a.m. he would give up and go home. Then he made a discovery that brought him all the business he could handle. "I quit going out so early," he said. "Instead, I didn't look for any business until about 11:00. Then I ran into lots of men who were half through mowing their own lawns and they would hire me to finish up for them."

A Few Proverbs from Here and There

27.   Who begins too much accomplishes little.

28.   It is not good enough to aim; you must hit.

29.   The world is divided into men who accomplish things and those who get all the credit.

30.   There is no limit to the good a man can do if he doesn't care who gets the credit.

31.   Yesterday's hits won't win today's ball game.

32.   With God you can go to the moon—without him you had better not walk out your front door.

33.   Take off your hat to your yesterdays; take off your coat for your tomorrows.

34.   God gives the birds their food, but He does not throw it into their nests.

35. Better to be proficient in one art than a smatterer in a hundred.
224, 595, 910, 1018, 1055, 1635, 1654, 1814, 1837, 2014.

ACQUAINTANCE
36. If a man does not make new acquaintances, as he advances through life he will soon find himself left alone. A man, Sir, should keep his friendships in constant repair.

—*Samuel Johnson*

828, 1045.

ACTION
37. The people's instincts are still right. You see them come to the rescue of someone—a child who falls down a well—hundreds of people rush to help, and labor and equipment are volunteered without any thought of who's going to pay for it. This is a basic feeling in Americans. They don't stand back in such a circumstance and ask what the government's going to do about it.

—*Ronald Reagan*

38. How little can we foresee the consequence either of wise or unwise action, of virtue or of malice! Without this measureless and perpetual uncertainty, the drama of human life would be destroyed.

—*Sir Winston Churchill*

39. When Demosthenes was asked what was the first part of oratory, he answered, "Action;" and which was the second, he replied, "Action;" and which was the third, he still answered, "Action."

—*Plutarch*

40. What a man knows should find its expression in what he does; the value of superior knowledge is chiefly in that it leads to a performing manhood.

—*Christian N. Bovee*

41. The chiefest action for a man of spirit is never to be out of action; the soul was never put in the body to stand still.

—*John Webster*

42. However brilliant an action may be, it should not be accounted great when it is not the result of great purpose.

—Francois De La Rochefoucauld

43. Get action. Do things; be sane, don't fritter away your time; create, act, take a place wherever you are and be somebody; get action.

—Theodore Roosevelt

44. Verily, when the day of judgment comes, we shall not be asked what we have read, but what we have done.

—Thomas A. Kempis

45. Actions are right in proportion as they tend to promote happiness; wrong as they tend to produce the reverse of happiness.

—John Stuart Mill

46. Every man feels instinctively that all the beautiful sentiments in the world weigh less than a single lovely action.

—James Russell Lowell

47. Never do today what you can do tomorrow. Something may occur to make you regret your premature action.

—Aaron Burr

48. As I grow older, I pay less attention to what men say. I just watch what they do.

—Andrew Carnegie

49. All human actions have one or more of these causes: chance, nature, compulsion, habit, reason, passion, desire.

—Aristotle

50. If you're going to do something tonight that you'll be sorry for tomorrow morning—sleep late.

—Henny Youngman

51. It is difficult to retain the knowledge one has acquired, without putting it into practice.

—Pliny the Younger

52. Everywhere in life, the true question is not what we gain, but what we do.

—Thomas Carlyle

53. The best way to keep good acts in memory is to refresh them with new.

—Cato

54. I have always thought the actions of men the best interpreters of their thoughts.

—John Locke

55. What the Puritans gave the world was not thought, but action.

—Wendell Phillips

56. Life does not consist of thinking, it consists in acting.

—Woodrow Wilson

57. The great aim of education is not knowledge but action.

—Herbert Spencer

58. It is better to wear out than to rust out.

—Bishop Cumberland

59. No sooner said than done, so acts your man of worth.

—Ennius

60. Heaven never helps the man who will not act.

—Sophocles

61. Action is the proper Fruit of Knowledge.

—Thomas Fuller

62. Whatsoever thy hand findeth to do, do it with thy might.

—Ecclesiastes, 9:10

63. A prison guard rushed into the warden's office and said, "Excuse me for interrupting your work, but I want to report that nine prisoners have broken out."

"Quick," the warden shouted. "Sound the alarm. Call the State Police. Call the National Guard."

"Before we do that," the guard said, "I think we ought to call a doctor. I think it's the measles."

A Few Proverbs from Here and There
64. Last year's actions are like last year's calendar.

65. Actions speak louder than words.

81, 126, 255, 558, 1026, 1036, 1233, 1585, 1791, 1826.

ACTRESS
66. Actress: "I'm looking forward to my 40th birthday."
Friend: "But, you're facing the wrong direction."

ADJUSTMENT
67. Fit thyself into the environment that thou findest on earth, and love the men with whom thy lot is cast.

—Marcus Aurelius

68. Be content with your lot; one cannot be first in everything.

—Aesop

ADMIRATION
69. We always love those who admire us, but we do not always love those whom we admire.

—Francois De La Rochefoucauld

70. All things are admired either because they are new or because they are great.

—Francis Bacon

601, 1180, 1265, 2050.

ADVANTAGE
71. A cowardly act! What do I care about that? You may be sure that I should never fear to commit one if it were to my advantage.

—Napoleon Bonaparte

561, 1547.

ADVERSITY
72. Adversity is a severe instructor, set over us by one who knows us better than we do ourselves, as he loves us better too. He that wrestles with us strengthens our nerves and sharpens our skill.

—Edmund Burke

73. Adversity is sometimes hard upon a man, but for the one man who can stand prosperity there are a hundred who will stand adversity.

—Thomas Carlyle

74. He knows not his own strength that hath not met adversity.

—Ben Jonson

75. If adversity purifies men, why not nations?

—Jean Paul Richter

76. In adversity a man is saved by hope.

—Menander

85, 1092, 1426, 1461, 1744, 1745, 1942, 2141.

ADVICE

77. When in reading we meet with any maxim that may be of use, we should take it for our own, and make an immediate application of it, as we would of the advice of a friend whom we have purposely consulted.

—Charles Caleb Colton

78. Advice is not disliked because it is advice; but because so few people know how to give it.

—Leigh Hunt

79. Let no man presume to give advice to others that has not first given good counsel to himself.

—Seneca

80. I give myself sometimes admirable advice, but I am incapable of taking it.

—Lady Mary Wortley Montagu

81. Get good counsel before you begin; and when you have decided, act promptly.

—Sallust

82. Many receive advice; only the wise profit by it.

—Publilius Syrus

A Few Proverbs from Here and There

83. Advice is least heeded when most needed.

84. Never advise anyone to go to war or to marry.

85. Counsels in wine seldom prosper.

86.   The well-fed give better counsel than the hungry.

87.   It is easy when we are well to give good advice to the sick.

88.   A business man was giving his son some advice as he was preparing to go away to college. "I think it is fine that you are going to study business administration. One thing I would suggest. Be sure to take at least one course in business law."

"Why is that?" his son asked, "I'm going into business, not law."

"Well," his father said, "in business, honesty always is the best policy. Above all, you must be honest. And if you take a course in business law, you will learn all sorts of clever things you can do—and still be honest."

1889, 2044, 2283.

AFFECTION

89.   Affection can withstand very severe storms of vigor, but not a long polar frost of indifference.

—Sir Walter Scott

90.   My affections are first for my own country, and then, generally, for all mankind.

—Thomas Jefferson

AGE

91.   Nobody dies of old age. Whenever a life ends it is because of injury or illness from which recovery has proved impossible. It is as silly to say someone died because he was very old as to say he was born because he was very young.

—Hugh Downs

92.   Old age has a great sense of calm and freedom; when the passions relax their hold. . .we are freed from the grasp not of one mad master only, but of many.

—Plato

93.   What find you better or more honorable than age?. . .Take the pre-eminence of it in everything; in an old friend, in old wine, in an old pedigree.

—Shakerley Marion

94.   Age is not all decay; it is the ripening, the swelling, of the fresh life within, that withers and bursts the husk.

—George Macdonald

95.   The harvest of old age is the memory and rich store of blessings laid up earlier in life.

—Cicero

96.   Old wood best to burn, old wine to drink, old friends to trust, and old authors to read.

—Francis Bacon

97.   Childhood is ignorant, boyhood is lightheaded, youth is rash, and old age is ill-humored.

—Luis De Granada

98.   We do not count a man's years until he has nothing else to count.

—Ralph Waldo Emerson

99.   The ultimate evil is to leave the company of the living before you die.

—Seneca

100.   When saving for old age, be sure to put away a few pleasant thoughts.

—Ancient proverb

101.   A seventy-year-old millionaire had fallen in love with a sweet little 23-year-old. He was talking to a long-time friend about her and asked his advice. "I want to marry her. Do you think I would have a better chance if I told her I was sixty instead of seventy?"

"Your best bet," his friend said, "is to tell her you are eighty."
190, 466, 740, 986, 1436, 1443, 1718, 1854, 1918, 1954.

AGREEMENT

102.   If men would consider not so much wherein they differ, as wherein they agree, there would be far less uncharitableness and angry feeling in the world.

—Joseph Addison

103.   Ah, don't say you agree with me. When people agree with me I always feel that I must be wrong.

—Oscar Wilde

104.   The highest compact we can make with our fellow is—"Let there be truth between us two forevermore."

—*Ralph Waldo Emerson*

AMBITION

105.   Ambition is like choler, which is a humor that maketh man active, earnest, full of alacrity and stirring, if it be not stopped. But if it be stopped, and cannot have its way, it becometh a dust, and thereby malign and venomous.

—*Francis Bacon*

106.   The passion of ambition is the same in a courtier, a soldier, or an ecclesiastic; but, from their different educations and habits, they will take very different methods to gratify it.

—*Lord Chesterfield*

107.   I had ambition not only to go farther than any man had ever been before, but as far as it was possible for a man to go.

—*Captain James Cook*

108.   The ambitious climbs up high and perilous stairs, and never cares how to come down; the desire of rising hath swallowed up his fear of a fall.

—*Thomas Adams*

109.   The noble Brutus
Hath told you Caesar was ambitious:
If it were so, it was a grievous fault;
And grievously hath Caesar answered it.

—*William Shakespeare*

110.   Ambition, like a torrent, ne'er looks back;
And is a swelling, and the last affection
A high mind can put off.

—*Ben Jonson*

111.   I commend you to the goddess of ambition. She teaches the great virtues of labor, aggression and perseverance.

—*John Peter Altgeld*

112.   I maintain what I have said: If Bonaparte remained an artillery Lieutenant, he would still be on the throne.

—Henri Monnier

113.   Ambition often puts men upon doing the meanest offices: so climbing is performed in the same posture with creeping.

—Jonathan Swift

114.   Or mad Ambition's gory hand,
    Sending, like bloodhounds from the slip,
Woe, want, and murder o'er the land.

—Robert Burns

115.   The greatest evil which fortune can inflict on men is to endow them with small talents and great ambition.

—Marquis De Vauvenargues

116.   One often passes from love to ambition, but one rarely returns from ambition to love.

—Francois De La Rochefoucauld

117.   Most people would succeed in small things if they were not troubled with great ambitions.

—Henry Wadsworth Longfellow

118.   Those who are believed to be most abject and humble are usually most ambitious and envious.

—Benedict De Spinoza

119.   The same ambition can destroy or save,
And make a patriot as it makes a knave.

—Alexander Pope

120.   Ambition is a commendable attribute, without which no man succeeds. Only inconsiderate ambition imperils.

—Warren G. Harding

121.   Ambition, in a private man a vice,
Is, in a prince, the virtue.

—Philip Massinger

122.   'Tis a laudable Ambition, that aims at being better than his Neighbors.

—*Benjamin Franklin*

123.   To take a soldier without ambition is to pull off his spurs.

—*Francis Bacon*

124.   Ambition is a vice, but it may be the father of virtue.

—*Quintilian*

125.   Lord, grant that I may always desire more than I can accomplish.

—*Michelangelo*

126.   Ambition and love are the wings of great actions.

—*Goethe*

127.   Too low they build who build beneath the stars.

—*Edward Young*

128.   What village priest would not like to be Pope?

—*Voltaire*

129.   Every scarecrow has a secret ambition to terrorize.

—*Stanislaus J. Lescynski*

130.   Ambition and suspicion always go together.

—*Georg Christoph Lichtenberg*

131.   All women are ambitious naturally.

—*Christopher Marlowe*

132.   Ambition has no rest.

—*Bulwer-Lytton*

133.   Ambition destroys its possessor.

—*The Talmud*

A Few Proverbs from Here and There

134.   Every eel hopes to become a whale.

135.   You cannot climb a ladder by pushing others down.

136.   Where ambition ends happiness begins.

137.   He who would leap high must take a long run.

148, 186, 249, 569, 710, 906, 913, 918, 1377, 1938, 2248.

AMERICA

138.   If I were an American, as I am an Englishman, while a foreign troop was landed in my country I never would lay down my arms,—never! never! never!

—*William Pitt*

139.   Sometimes people call me an idealist. Well, that is the way I know I am an American. America is the only idealistic nation in the world.

—*Woodrow Wilson*

140.   Intellectually I know that America is no better than any other country; emotionally I know she is better than every other country.

—*Sinclair Lewis*

811, 978, 1219, 1608.

AMUSEMENT

141.   Amusement is the happiness of those who cannot think.

—*Alexander Pope*

1805.

ANCESTORS

142.   Whoever serves his country well has no need of ancestors.

—*Voltaire*

143.   The man who has not anything to boast of but his illustrious ancestors is like a potato—the only good belonging to him is underground.

—*Sir Thomas Overbury*

144.   Our ancestors are very good kind of folks; but they are the last people I should choose to have a visiting acquaintance with.

—*Richard B. Sheridan*

145.   I make little account of genealogical trees. Mere family never made a man great. Thought and deed, not pedigree, are the passports to enduring fame.

—*General Skobeleff*

146.   'Tis happy for him that his father was born before him.

—Jonathan Swift

292, 1069, 1480, 1909.

ANGELS

147.   I charge thee, fling away ambition:
By that sin fell the angels.

—William Shakespeare

148.   Men would be angels, angels would be gods.

—Alexander Pope

ANGER

149.   Anybody can become angry—that is easy; but to be angry with the right person, and to the right degree, and at the right time, and for the right purpose, and in the right way—that is not within everybody's power and is not easy.

—Aristotle

150.   I never work better than when I am inspired by anger. When I am angry I can write, pray, and preach well; for then my whole temperament is quickened, my understanding sharpened, and all mundane vexations and temptations depart.

—Martin Luther

151.   Anger wishes that all mankind had only one neck; love, that it has only one heart; grief, two tear-glands; and pride, two bent knees.

—Jean Paul Richter

152.   Two things a man should never be angry at: what he can help, and what he cannot help.

—Thomas Fuller

153.   He that is slow to anger is better than the mighty; and he that ruleth his spirit than he that taketh a city.

—Proverbs 16:23

154.   Be ye angry, and sin not: Let not the sun go down upon your wrath.

—Ephesians, 4:26

155. When angry, count four; when very angry, swear.

— *Mark Twain*

159, 1576.

ANGLER
156. As no man is born an artist, so no man is born an angler.

— *Izaak Walton*

ANIMALS
157. I have seen the hippopotamus, both asleep and awake; and I can assure you that, awake or asleep, he is the ugliest of the works of God.

— *Thomas Macaulay*

158. A cow is a very good animal in the field; but we turn her out of a garden.

— *Samuel Johnson*

ANSWER
159. A soft answer turneth away wrath: but grievous words stir up anger.

— *Proverbs 15:1*

ANTICIPATION
160. I would not anticipate the relish of any happiness, nor feel the weight of any misery, before it actually arrives.

— *Joseph Addison*

161. What we anticipate seldom occurs, what we least expected generally happens.

— *Benjamin Disraeli*

ANXIETY
162. Take therefore no thought for the morrow: for the morrow shall take thought for the things of itself.

— *Matthew 6:34*

1089, 1453.

APPEARANCE

163.   It is only shallow people who do not judge by appearances.

—Oscar Wilde

164.   It is easier to appear worthy of a position one does not hold, than of the office which one fills.

—Francois De La Rochefoucauld

1215.

APPETITE

165.   Once when the power went off at the elementary school, the cook couldn't serve a hot meal in the cafeteria. She had to feed the children something, so at the last minute she whipped up great stacks of peanut-butter-and-jelly sandwiches.

As one little boy filled his plate, he said, "It's about time. At last—a home cooked meal."

289, 784, 1121, 1255.

APPLAUSE

166.   Applause is the spur of noble minds, the end and aim of weak ones.

—Charles Caleb Colton

167.   The silence that accepts merit as the most natural thing in the world, is the highest applause.

—Ralph Waldo Emerson

168.   The applause of a single human being is of great consequence.

—Samuel Johnson

APPRECIATION

169.   The deepest principle in human nature is the craving to be appreciated.

—William James

170.   Blessed are they who have the gift of making friends, for it is one of God's best gifts. It involves many things, but above all, the power of going out of one's self, and appreciating whatever is noble and loving in another.

—*Thomas Hughes*

ARGUMENT

171.   There is no good in arguing with the inevitable. The only argument available with an east wind is to put on your overcoat.

—*James Russell Lowell*

172.   Arguments out of a pretty mouth are unanswerable.

—*Joseph Addison*

173.   The supermarket was crowded. People were shoving and pushing each other all around, especially at the meat counter. Finally, the boss noticed one of the clerks arguing with a woman customer. Suddenly, she left in a huff.

"What was the matter?" the boss asked.

"Oh, she was complaining about the long wait," he said. "You just can't please that woman. Yesterday, she was complaining about the short weight."

548, 1830.

ART

174.   To a person uninstructed in natural history, his country or seaside stroll is a walk through a gallery filled with wonderful works of art, nine-tenths of which have their faces turned to the wall.

—*Thomas Henry Huxley*

175.   I can look for a whole day with delight upon a handsome picture, though it be but of an horse.

—*Sir Thomas Browne*

176.   Love of beauty is Taste. . .The creation of beauty is Art.

—*Ralph Waldo Emerson*

177.   All the arts are brothers; each one is a light to the others.

—*Voltaire*

178.   If people knew how hard I have had to work to gain my mastery, it wouldn't seem wonderful at all.

—Michelangelo

179.   A room hung with pictures is a room hung with thoughts.

—Sir Joshua Reynolds

180.   Two friends were visiting an art exhibit. One painting that had won a blue ribbon showed a down-and-out panhandler sitting dejectedly on a street corner. "How do you like that?" the first visitor said. "There he sits, too broke to buy something to eat or decent clothes, yet he spends all that money to have his portrait painted."

579, 768, 1158, 1394, 1487, 1512, 1694, 1870, 2221, 2223.

ASPIRATIONS

181.   Far away there in the sunshine are my highest aspirations. I may not reach them, but I can look up and see their beauty, believe in them, and try to follow where they lead.

—Louisa May Alcott

182.   When you are aspiring to the highest place, it is honorable to reach the second or even the third rank.

—Cicero

125.

ASSISTANCE

183.   No degree of knowledge attainable by man is able to set him above the want of hourly assistance.

—Samuel Johnson

ATTEMPT

184.   It is not because things are difficult that we do not dare to attempt them, but they are difficult because we do not dare to do so.

—Seneca

ATTITUDE

185.   Speak softly and carry a big stick; you will go far.

—Theodore Roosevelt

186.   He who attends to his greater self becomes a great man, and he who attends to his smaller self becomes a small man.

—*Mencius*

938, 1698, 1729.

AUTHOR
187.   I am always at a loss to know how much to believe of my own stories.

—*Washington Irving*

188.   I don't want to be a doctor, and live by men's diseases; nor a minister to live by their sins; nor a lawyer to live by their quarrels. So I don't see there's anything left for me but to be an author.

—*Nathaniel Hawthorne*

290, 891, 1563, 1760, 1853, 2257.

AUTHORITY
189.   For He taught them as one having authority, and not as the scribes.

—*Matthew 7:29*

BALANCE
190.   To love playthings well as a child, to lead an adventurous and honorable youth, and to settle when the time arrives, into a green and smiling age, is to be a good *artis en life* and deserve well of yourself and your neighbor.

—*Robert Louis Stevenson*

67.

BANKER
191.   The banker had called the man in to talk about his account. "Your financial affairs are in a mess. Your wife constantly overdraws your account. She is behind in her charge accounts at the department store, and her check stubs are all added wrong. Why don't you talk to her about it?"

"Because," said the man, "I would rather argue with you than with her."

1084.

BEAUTY

192.   O beautiful human life! Tears come to my eyes as I think of it.
So beautiful, so inexpressibly beautiful!. . .The song should never be
silent, the dance never still, the laugh should sound like water which
runs forever.

—*Richard Jefferies*

193.   Plain women know more about men than beautiful ones do.
But beautiful women don't need to know about men. It's the men who
have to know about the beautiful women.

—*Katharine Hepburn*

194.   Beauty does not lie in the face. It lies in the harmony between
man and his industry. Beauty is expression. When I paint a mother I try
to render her beautiful by the mere look she gives her child.

—*Jean Francois Millet*

195.   When I am working on a problem, I never think about beauty.
I think only of how to solve the problem. But when I have finished, if
the solution is not beautiful, I know it is wrong.

—*Buckminster Fuller*

196.   The longer I live the more my mind dwells upon the beauty
and the wonder of the world. I hardly know which feeling leads, won-
derment or admiration.

—*John Burroughs*

197.   Nature is painting for us, day after day, pictures of infinite
beauty if only we have the eyes to see them.

—*John Ruskin*

198.   Our Lord has written the promise of the Resurrection, not in
books alone, but in every leaf in springtime.

—*Martin Luther*

199.   Don't waste yourself in rejection, nor bark against the bad,
but chant the beauty of the good.

—*Ralph Waldo Emerson*

200.   Beauty is God's handwriting. Welcome it in every fair face,
every fair sky, every fair flower.

—*Charles Kingsley*

201. The saying that beauty is but skin deep is but a skin deep saying.

—*John Ruskin*

202. It's a good thing that beauty is skin deep, or I'd be rotten to the core.

—*Phyllis Diller*

203. Great perils have this beauty, that they bring to light the fraternity of strangers.

—*Victor Hugo*

204. Nothing is more beautiful than the loveliness of the woods before sunrise.

—*George Washington Carver*

205. Modesty is the citadel of beauty and of virtue.

—*Demades*

206. When beauty fires the blood, how love exalts the mind!

—*John Dryden*

207. Beauty is truth, truth beauty.

—*John Keats*

A Few Proverbs from Here and There
208. It is the beautiful bird which gets caged.

209. What worth has beauty if it be not seen?

210. An ass is beautiful to an ass, and a pig to a pig.

211. Beauty is a good letter of introduction.

172, 174, 176, 181, 783, 904, 969, 973, 1020.

BED
212. The bed comprehends our whole life, for we were born in it, we live in it, and we shall die in it.

—*Guy De Maupassant*

213. The bed has become a place of luxury to me! I would not exchange it for all the thrones in the world.

—*Napoleon Bonaparte*

214.   Arise, take up thy bed, and walk.

—*Mark 2:9*

BEE
215.   Nature's confectioner, the bee.

—*John Cleveland*
239.

BEGGARS
216.   Beggars, actors, buffoons, and all that breed.

—*Horace*

BEGINNING
217.   "Where shall I begin, please your Majesty?" he asked.
"Begin at the beginning," the King said, very gravely, "and go on till you come to the end: then stop."
—Lewis Carroll

BEHAVIOR
218.   We must suit our behavior to the occasion.

—*Cervantes*

BELIEF
219.   I believe that a personal relationship with the hero of the Bible, Jesus Christ, can provide the foundation for a life of purpose, for it is Christ who said, "I came that they may have and enjoy life, and have it in abundance—to the full, till it overflows."

—*Mark O. Hatfield*

220.   We mortals are on board a fast-sailing, never-sinking world-frigate, of which God was the ship-wright; and she is but one craft in a Milky-Way fleet, of which God is the Lord High Admiral. The port we sail from is always astern.

—*Herman Melville*

221.   I am proud of the revolutionary beliefs for which our forebears fought. . .the belief that the rights of man come not from the generosity of the state but the hands of God.

—John F. Kennedy

222.   Believe one who knows: you will find something greater in woods than in books. Trees and stones will teach you that which you can never learn from masters.

—St. Bernard of Clairvaux

223.   Everything that science has taught me—and continues to teach me—strengthens my belief in the continuity of our spiritual existence after death.

—Werner von Braun

224.   They can conquer who believe they can. It is he who has done the deed once who does not shrink from attempting it again.

—Ralph Waldo Emerson

225.   Believe nothing against another but on good authority; nor report what may hurt another, unless it be a greater hurt to conceal it.

—William Penn

226.   Be not afraid of life. Believe that life is worth living and your belief will help create the fact.

—William James

227.   It is not necessary to believe things in order to reason about them.

—Pierre Caron De Beaumarchais

228.   The beliefs for which men have been willing to suffer martyrdom came from religion.

—Calvin Coolidge

229.   I believe the promises of God enough to venture an eternity on them.

—Isaac Watts

230.   To believe with certainty we must begin with doubting.

—Stanislaus J. Lescynski

231.   The practical effect of a belief is the real test of its soundness.

—*James Anthony Froude*

232.   Nothing is so firmly believed as what we least know.

—*Michel Eyquem Montaigne*

233.   What ardently we wish, we soon believe.

—*Edward Young*

234.   For they conquer who believe they can.

—*Virgil*

235.   A politician and his wife were having dinner at a fashionable restaurant. Since he was well known, a great many people stopped at their table and shook hands and spoke. Each time, the politician would tell his friends about his recent fishing trip.

After awhile his wife whispered to him, "I think it's nice that so many people stop to speak to you. And I see nothing wrong with you telling them about your fishing trip. But, each time you tell about the fish you caught, you change the size of the fish and the number. Why in the world do you do that?"

"Well," he said to his wife. "I know all of those people. They are voters and I want them to trust me and take me at my word. So, I make a practice never to tell them more than I think they will believe."
187, 434, 607, 609, 787, 921, 1166.

BENEFIT
236.   A benefit consists not in what is done or given, but in the intention of the giver or doer.

—*Seneca*

237.   If you count the sunny and cloudy days through a year, you will find that sunshine predominates.

—*Ovid*

238.   It is disgraceful not to be able to return a benefit as well as an injury.

—*Socrates*

239.   That which is not good for the swarm, neither is good for the bee.

—*Marcus Aurelius*

246.

BEST

240.   Act so as to elicit the best in others and thereby in thyself.

—Felix Adler

BIBLE

241.   My mother's influence in molding my character was conspicuous. She forced me to learn daily long chapters of the Bible by heart. To that discipline and patient, accurate resolve I owe not only much of my general power of taking pains, but the best of my taste for literature.

—John Ruskin

242.   Unless we form the habit of going to the Bible in bright moments as well as in trouble, we cannot fully respond to its consolations because we lack equilibrium between light and darkness.

—Helen Keller

243.   The Bible is God's chart for you to steer by, to keep you from the bottom of the sea, and to show you where the harbor is, and how to reach it without running on rocks and bars.

—Henry Ward Beecher

244.   England has two books, one which she has made and one which has made her: Shakespeare and the Bible.

—Victor Hugo

245.   The Bible is no mere book, but a Living Creature, with power that conquers all that oppose it.

—Napoleon Bonaparte

246.   The Bible is the greatest benefit which the human race has ever experienced.

—Immanuel Kant

247.   No sciences are better attested than the religion of the Bible.

—Isaac Newton

248.   The municipal garbage truck had just made a pickup at a church. When the garbage collector returned the empty containers, he knocked on the door of the minister's study.

     When the minister opened the door, the man said, "Excuse me, but do you have a Bible handy that I could read for a few minutes?"

The minister handed him a copy of the Bible that he kept on his desk and the man began to look through it slowly and with rapt attention.

"Can I help you find something?" the minister asked.

"Yes," the man said. "I want to find out how to spell Nehemiah. That's the name of my bootlegger and I want to leave him a note."

721, 1088, 1129.

BIRD
249.   No bird soars too high, if he soars with his own wings.

—William Blake

BIRTH
250.   It is as natural to die as to be born, and to a little infant perhaps the one is as painful as the other.

—Francis Bacon

542.

BIRTH CONTROL
251.   A well-known politician was being interviewed on television. As usual, the interviewer asked questions about various subjects; taxes, international trade, law and order, food stamps and the energy crisis. Finally he asked this question: "What do you think about birth control?"

"I'm glad you asked that question," he said, "because whenever anybody mentions the subject, I always remind myself that I have three brothers and two sisters older than I am."

BIRTHDAY
252.   The man asked his wife what she wanted for her birthday and she said, "Not to be reminded of it."

66, 897.

BLIND
253.   In the country of the blind the one-eyed man is king.

—Desiderius Erasmus

254.   What matters it to a blind man that his father could see?

—*Ancient proverb*

BOLDNESS
255.   Are you in earnest? Seize this very minute:
What you can do, or dream you can, begin it;
Boldness has genius, power, and magic in it.
Only engage and the mind grows heated;
Begin and then the work will be completed.

—*Goethe*

256.   Men of principle are always bold, but bold men are not always men of principle.

—*Confucius*

617, 799.

BOOKS
257.   What a place to be in is an old library! It seems as if all the souls of all the writers that had bequeathed their labors to these Bodleians were reposing here as in some dormitory, or middle state. I do not want to handle, to profane the leaves, their winding-sheets. I could as soon dislodge a shade. I seem to inhale learning, walking amid their foliage; and the odor of their old moth-scented coverings is fragrant as the first bloom of these sciential apples which grew amid the happy orchard.

—*Charles Lamb*

258.   The library is not a shrine for the worship of books. It is not a temple where literary incense must be burned or where one's devotion to the bound book is expressed in ritual. A library, to modify the famous metaphor of Socrates, should be the delivery room for the birth of ideas—a place where history comes to life.

—*Norman Cousins*

259.   Except a living man there is nothing more wonderful than a book! A message to us from the dead—from human souls we never saw, who lived, perhaps thousands of miles away. And yet these, in those little sheets of paper, speak to us, arouse us, terrify us, teach us, comfort us, open their hearts to us as brothers.

—Charles Kingsley

260.   I have ever gained the most profit, and the most pleasure also, from the books which have made me think the most; and, when the difficulties have once been overcome, these are the books which have struck the deepest root, not only in my memory and understanding, but likewise in my affections.

—A. W. Hare

261.   Books are delightful when prosperity happily smiles; when adversity threatens, they are inseparable comforters. They give strength to human compacts, nor are grave opinions brought forward without books. Arts and sciences, the benefits of which no mind can calculate, depend upon books.

—Richard Aungerville

262.   Books are the food of youth, the delight of old age; the ornament of prosperity, the refuge and comfort of adversity; a delight at home, and no hindrance abroad; companions by night, in traveling, in the country.

—Cicero

263.   When a book raises your spirit and inspires you with noble and manly thoughts, seek for no other test of its excellence. It is good and made by a good workman.

—Jean De La Bruyere

264.   The first time I read an excellent book, it is to me as if I had gained a new friend. When I read over a book I have perused before, it resembles a meeting with an old one.

—Oliver Goldsmith

265.   Books are the legacies that a great genius leaves to mankind, which are delivered down from generation to generation, as presents to the posterity of those who are yet unborn.

—Joseph Addison

266.   If I have not read a book before, it is, to all intents and purposes, new to me, whether it was printed yesterday or three hundred years ago.

—William Hazlitt

267. I conceive that a knowledge of books is the basis on which all other knowledge rests.

—George Washington

268. Books must follow sciences, and not sciences books.

—Francis Bacon

269. All that Mankind has done, thought, gained or been, is lying as a magic preservation in the pages of books. They are the chosen possession of men.

—Thomas Carlyle

270. A book is a friend whose face is constantly changing. If you read it when you are recovering from an illness, and return to it years after, it is changed surely, with the change in yourself.

—Andrew Lang

271. No matter what his rank or position may be, the lover of books is the richest and happiest of the children of men.

—John Alford Langford

272. Things printed can never be stopped; they are like babies baptized, they have a soul from that moment, and go on forever.

—George Meredith

273. He who loveth a book will never want a faithful friend, a wholesome counselor, a cheerful companion, or an effectual comforter.

—Isaac Barrow

274. A good book is the precious life-blood of a master-spirit, embalmed and treasured up on purpose to a life beyond life.

—John Milton

275. That is a good book which is opened with expectation and closed with profit.

—Louisa May Alcott

276. A great thing is a great book; but a greater thing than all is the talk of a great man.

—Benjamin Disraeli

277. Read the best books first, or you may not have a chance to read them at all.

—Henry David Thoreau

278.   Books are the ever-burning lamps of accumulated wisdom.
—*George William Curtis*

279.   As you grow ready for it, somewhere or other you will find what is needful for you in a book.
—*George Macdonald*

280.   A house without books is like a room without windows.
—*Horace Mann*

281.   The cloak that I left at Troas with Carpus, when thou comest bring with thee, and the books, but especially the parchments.
—*II Timothy 4:13*

282.   A family doctor who still made house calls, shouted to his nurse, "Quick, get my hat and coat and bag, I've got a rush call."

"Is it a terrible accident or something?" she cried.

"No," said the doctor. "it's worse than that. Mrs. Smartwon just called. Her little boy is sick. I don't know what is wrong with him, but she has one of those books that tells what to do until the doctor arrives, and I want to get there before she does it."

245, 704, 771, 1074.

BOREDOM
283.   The secret of being tiresome is telling everything.
—*Voltaire*

284.   A bore is one who, when you ask him, "How are you?" tells you.

BOYS

A Few Proverbs from Here and There
285.   An angelic boyhood becomes a satanic old age.

286.   God takes care of boys and Irishmen.

287.   One boy is more trouble than a dozen girls.

288.   A growing boy has a wolf in his belly.

289.   A boy is an appetite with a skin pulled over it.

BRAGGING
290.   The author who speaks about his own books is almost as bad as a mother who talks about her own children.

—Benjamin Disraeli

291.   A Texan in his ten gallon hat and driving an oversized limosine, stopped for gasoline in a tiny village in the Tennessee mountains. While the attendant was servicing his car, the Texan struck up a conversation with an old fellow sitting on an overturned nail keg.

"You live around here?" the Texan asked.

"Yep," the man said, "That's my farm just across the road."

"How many acres you got?" the Texan asked.

"Eighty acres, more or less," the man said.

"Only eighty acres?" the Texan said. "Let me tell you about my farm. Why, I get in my car at six o'clock in the morning and I start driving in a straight line and by noon I haven't reached the other side of my farm."

"I know what you mean," the man said. "I've got a car exactly like that myself."

962.

BRAVERY
292.   The brave are born from the brave and good. In steers and in horses is to be found the excellence of their sires; nor do savage eagles produce a peaceful dove.

—Horace

293.   A brave captain is as a root, out of which as branches, the courage of his soldiers doth spring.

—Sir Philip Sidney

294.   The hero is no braver than an ordinary man, but he is brave five minutes longer.

—Ralph Waldo Emerson

295.   Every man thinks meanly of himself for not having been a soldier.

—Samuel Johnson

296.   It is easy to be brave from a safe distance.

—Aesop

297.   None but the brave deserves the fair.

—John Dryden

298.   The fireman had rushed into a burning building and rescued a beautiful young lady who was clad only in the top half of her baby-doll nightgown. He had carried her in his arms down three flights of stairs.

As they arrived safely outside the building, she looked at him with great admiration and said, "Oh, you are wonderful. It must have taken great courage to rescue me the way you did."

"Yes it did," the fireman admitted. "I had to fight off three other fireman who were trying to get to you."

493.

BREAD
299.   Half a loaf is better than no bread.

—John Ray

300.   I am the bread of life.

—John 6:35

301.   Give us this day our daily bread.

—Matthew 6:11

1076.

BRUTALITY
302.   Brutality to an animal is cruelty to mankind—it is only the difference in the victim.

—Alphonse De Lamartine

BUSINESS
303.   The business of America is business.

—Calvin Coolidge

304.   The propensity to truck, barter, and exchange one thing for another. . .is common to all men, and to be found in no other race of animals.

—Adam Smith

388.

CALAMITY

305. Calamity is the perfect glass wherein we truly see and know ourselves.

—Sir William D'Avenant

CANDOR

306. I do not belong to the amiable group of "men of compromise." I am in the habit of giving candid and straightforward expression to the convictions which a half-century of serious and laborious study has led me to form. If I seem to you an iconoclast, I pray you to remember that the victory of pure reason over superstition will not be achieved without a tremendous struggle.

—Ernst Haeckel

CAPITAL

307. Each needs the other; capital cannot do without labor, nor labor without capital.

—Pope Leo XIII

CARE

308. If we had paid no more attention to our plants than we have to our children, we would now be living in a jungle of weeds.

—Luther Burbank

309. Willy had just been vaccinated, and the doctor was getting ready to put a stick-on bandage on his arm.

"Please put it on the other arm," Will pleaded.

"Why do that?" the doctor asked. "This will let everyone know you have been vaccinated and they won't hit your sore arm."

"Please put it on my other arm! Please!" Willy said. "You don't know those kids at school."

1165.

CAT

310. A man was visiting his niece and noticed that after being married for ten years, her children now had a cat as a family pet. "I see you finally got a cat for the children," he said.

"Yes," his niece said. "One day he wandered in, discovered that we had mice and air-conditioning and decided to stay."

CAUSE
311.   A cause may be inconvenient, but it's magnificent. It's like champagne or high shoes, and one must be prepared to suffer for it.

—*Arnold Bennett*

49, 328, 668, 707, 711.

CAUTION
312.   The coward calls himself cautious.

—*Publilius Syrus*

A Few Proverbs from Here and There
313.   Don't take any wooden nickels.

314.   A wise man does not put all his eggs in one basket.

315.   Forewarned is forearmed.

316.   If you can't be good, be careful.

317.   It is always best to moor your ship with two anchors.
599, 675, 799.

CENSORSHIP
318.   Censorship, like charity, should begin at home; but unlike charity, it should end there.

—*Clare Boothe Luce*

319.   Every burned book enlightens the world.

—*Ralph Waldo Emerson*

CENSURE
320.   Few persons have sufficient wisdom to prefer censure, which is useful to them, to praise, which deceives them.

—*Francois De La Rochefoucauld*

CHANCE

321. There is many a slip "twixt the cup and the lip."

—Richard Harris Barham

322. He who trusts all things to chance, makes a lottery of his life.

—Ancient proverb

364, 366, 880.

CHANGE

323. Today is not yesterday; we ourselves change; how can our Works and Thoughts, if they are always to be the fittest, continue always the same? Change, indeed, is painful; yet ever needful; and if Memory have its force and worth, so also has Hope.

—Thomas Carlyle

324. The basis of our political systems is the right of the people to make and to alter their constitutions of government. But the constitution which at any time exists, until changed by an explicit and authentic act of the whole people, is sacredly obligatory upon all.

—George Washington

325. A woman changes when she loves and is loved. When there is nobody who cares for her she loses her spirits and the charm is gone. Love draws out what is in her and on it her development decidedly depends.

—Vincent van Gogh

326. There is nothing more difficult to take in hand, more perilous to conduct or more uncertain in its success than to take the lead in the introduction of a new order of things.

—Niccolo Machiavelli

327. Constitutions should consist only of general provisions; the reason is that they must necessarily be permanent, and that they cannot calculate for the possible change of things.

—Alexander Hamilton

328. Christians are supposed not merely to endure change, nor even to profit by it, but to cause it.

—Harry Emerson Fosdick

329. All things change, and you yourself are constantly wasting away. So, also, is the universe.

—*Marcus Aurelius*

330. No well-informed person has declared a change of opinion to be inconstancy.

—*Cicero*

331. The most distinguishing hallmark of the American society is and always has been—change.

—*Eric Severeid*

332. Everybody thinks of changing humanity and nobody thinks of changing himself.

—*Leo Tolstoy*

333. All great alterations in human affairs are produced by compromise.

—*Sydney Smith*

334. The absurd man is the one who never changes.

—*Auguste Marseille Barthelemy*

A Few Proverbs from Here and There
335. Never swap horses crossing a stream.

336. It's a long road that has no turning.

337. The more it changes, the more it remains the same.
449.

CHARACTER
338. The prosperity of a country depends, not on the abundance of its revenues, nor on the strength of its fortifications, nor on the beauty of its public buildings, but it consists in the number of its men of enlightenment and character.

—*Martin Luther*

339. In acquiring knowledge there is one thing equally important, and that is character. Nothing in the. . .world is worth so much, will last so long, and serve its possessor so well as good character.

—*William McKinley*

340.   America has furnished to the world the character of Washington, and if our American institution had done nothing else, that alone would have entitled them to the respect of mankind.

—Daniel Webster

341.   In men of the highest character and noblest genius there is to be found an insatiable desire for honor, command, power, and glory.

—Cicero

342.   I would rather be adorned by beauty of character than by jewels. Jewels are the gift of fortune, while character comes from within.

—Plautus

343.   In this world a man must either be anvil or hammer.

—Henry Wadsworth Longfellow

344.   I am a thorough believer in the American test of character. He will not build high who does not build for himself.

—Benjamin Harrison

345.   It is not the brains that matter most, but that which guides them—character, the heart, generous qualities, progressive ideas.

—Dostoevsky

346.   The higher the character or rank, the less the pretense, because there is less to pretend to.

—Bulwer-Lytton

347.   Character is a by-product; it is produced in the great manufacture of daily duty.

—Woodrow Wilson

348.   Take care that the divinity within you has a creditable charge to preside over.

—Marcus Aurelius

349.   The measure of a man's real character is what he would do if he knew he would never be found out.

—Thomas Macauley

350.   No civilization is complete which does not include the dumb and defenseless of God's creatures within the sphere of charity and mercy.

—Queen Victoria

21, 415, 562, 635.

CHARITY

351.   He who receives a benefit should never forget it; he who bestows should never remember it.

—Pierre Charron

352.   There is as much greatness of mind in acknowledging a good turn, as in doing it.

—Seneca

353.   Did universal charity prevail, earth would be heaven, and hell a fable.

—Charles Caleb Colton

318, 1064.

CHEERFULNESS

354.   The men whom I have seen succeed best in life have always been cheerful and hopeful men, who went about their business with a smile on their faces, and took the changes and chances of this mortal life like men, facing rough and smooth alike as it came.

—Charles Kingsley

355.   Health and cheerfulness mutually beget each other.

—Joseph Addison

356.   Cheerfulness and content are great beautifiers and are famous perservers of youthful looks.

—Charles Dickens

357.   It is not fitting, when one is in God's service, to have a gloomy face or a chilling look.

—St. Francis of Assisi

358.   Those who bring sunshine into the lives of others cannot keep it from themselves.

—Sir James Matthew Barrie

929, 1159.

CHILDREN

359.   I love children. They do not prattle of yesterday: their interests are all of today and the tomorrows—I love children.

—Richard Mansfield

360. Raising kids is part joy and part guerrilla warfare.

—*Edward Asner*

361. "Our marriage would have broken up years ago if it hadn't been for the children," a woman said to her friend. "We can't get a divorce because he won't take them and neither will I."
308, 1016.

CHOICE

362. A liberated woman is one who feels confident in herself, and is happy in what she is doing. She is a person who has a sense of self. . .It all comes down to freedom of choice.

—*Betty Ford*

363. Were it offered to my choice, I should have no objection to a repetition of the same life from its beginning, only asking the advantages authors have in a second edition to correct some faults of the first.

—*Benjamin Franklin*

364. Destiny is not a matter of chance, it is a matter of choice; it is not a thing to be waited for, it is a thing to be achieved.

—*William Jennings Bryan*

365. God offers to every mind its choice between truth and repose. Take which you please—you can never have both.

—*Ralph Waldo Emerson*

366. Chance makes our parents, but choice makes our friends.

—*Jacques Delille*

367. A young lady, a stranger in town, asked the owner of the Country Store, "Do you sell powder?"

"Yes, we do," he said. "Which kind do you want—washing, baking, rat, headache, face, tooth, teething, insect, or gun?"
442, 1011.

CHRISTIANITY

368. There's not much practical Christianity in the man who lives on better terms with angels and seraphs, than with his children, servants and neighbors.

—*Henry Ward Beecher*

CHRISTMAS

369.   If Christmas didn't already exist, man would have had to invent it. There has to be at least one day in the year to remind us we're here for something else besides our general cussedness.

—*Eric Severeid*

370.   Happy, happy, Christmas, that can win us back to the delusions of our childish days, recall to the old man the pleasures of his youth, and transport the traveler back to his own fireside and quiet home!

—*Charles Dickens*

371.   On the day following Christmas, half a dozen cars were waiting in line for the traffic light to change. Just as it turned green, an obnoxious horn-tooter began blasting away. A lady in a car alongside his, yelled at him and said, "What else did Santa Claus bring you?"

CIRCUMSTANCES

372.   The circumstances of others seem good to us, while ours seem good to others.

—*Publilius Syrus*

373.   Circumstances! I make circumstances!

—*Napoleon Bonaparte*

374.   I endeavor to subdue circumstances to myself, and not myself to circumstances.

—*Horace*

CIVILIZATION

375.   A civilization which develops only on its material side, and not in corresponding measure on its mental and spiritual side, is like a vessel with a defective steering gear, which gets out of control at a constantly accelerating pace, and drifts toward catastrophe.

—*Albert Schweitzer*

376.   Civilization is a movement and not a condition, a voyage and not a harbor.

—*Arnold Toynbee*

377.   Man by nature is a civic animal.

—Aristotle

CLARITY
378.   As soon as a true thought has entered our mind, it gives a light which makes us see a crowd of other objects which we have never perceived before.

—Francois Chateaubriand

379.   He that will write well in any tongue must follow this counsel of Aristotle, to speak as the common people do, to think as wise men do.

—Roger Ascham

380.   The spectacles of experience; through them you will see clearly a second time.

—Henrik Ibsen

381.   In language clearness is everything.

—Confucius

382.   A nationally known author was delivering the graduation speech at a large university. It was well written and was being delivered in a most inspiring manner. The theme was one of optimism and hope for the future.

Two foreign students were in the audience. One of them said to the other, who understood English, "What is he saying?"

"School is out," said the other.

CLEANLINESS
383.   Above all things, keep clean. It is not necessary to be a pig in order to raise one.

—Robert Ingersoll

COMFORT
384.   Thy rod and thy staff they comfort me.

—Psalms 23:4

904, 1044.

COMMAND

385.   No man is fit to command another that cannot command himself.

—William Penn

386.   It is a fine thing to command, even if it only be a herd of cattle.

—Cervantes

COMMENTARY

387.   Of all commentaries upon the Scriptures, good examples are the best and the liveliest.

—John Donne

COMMERCE

388.   Free trade, one of the greatest blessings which a government can confer on a people, is in almost every country unpopular.

—Thomas Macaulay

COMMON SENSE

389.   Common sense, (which in truth, is very uncommon) is the best sense I know of.

—Lord Chesterfield

390.   Common sense isn't as common as it used to be.

—Will Rogers

885.

COMMUNICATION

391.   Conversation is an art in which a man has all mankind for his competitors, for it is that which all are practicing every day while they live.

—Ralph Waldo Emerson

392.   Look in the face of the person to whom you are speaking if you wish to know his real sentiments, for he can command his words more easily than his countenance.

—Lord Chesterfield

393.   The patrolman had stopped a woman who was speeding. He asked to see her driver's license and said, "Lady, you were going 50 miles an hour in a 35 mile-an-hour zone."

As she handed him her license, she said, "Before you begin writing that ticket, I think we should get our priorities straight. Are you supposed to advise me of my constitutional rights first, or am I supposed to tell you that my son is head of the State highway patrol?"
699.

COMPANION
394.   Tell me what company thou keepest, and I'll tell thee what thou art.

—Cervantes

395.   No possession is gratifying without a companion.

—Seneca

769, 843.

COMPANY
396.   Lay aside the best book whenever you can go into the best company; and depend upon it, you change for the better.

—Lord Chesterfield

770, 852.

COMPARISON
397.   Nothing is good or bad but by comparison.

—Thomas Fuller

398.   A man said to his friend: "How is your wife?"
His friend said: "Compared to what?"

1000.

COMPASSION
399.   Half the misery of human life might be extinguished if men would alleviate the general curse they lie under by mutual offices of compassion, benevolence, and humanity.

—Joseph Addison

982.

COMPETITION

400.   Every child of the Saxon race is educated to wish to be first. It
is our system; and a man comes to measure his greatness by the regrets,
envies, and hatreds of his competitors.

—*Ralph Waldo Emerson*

401.   No man lives without jostling and being jostled; in all ways he
has to elbow himself through the world, giving and receiving offense.

—*Thomas Carlyle*

402.   The earth cannot tolerate two suns, nor Asia two kings.

—*Alexander the Great*

483.

COMPLAINT

403.   Those who make the worst use of their time are the first to
complain of its shortness.

—*Jean De La Bruyere*

404.   A man was complaining to a friend about a used car he had
just bought. ''I don't say it is falling apart, but the only part that doesn't
make a noise is the horn.''

COMPLIMENTS

405.   Compliments cost nothing, yet many pay dear for them.

—*Thomas Fuller*

COMPROMISE

406.   The word ''right'' is one of the most deceptive of pitfalls.
Most rights are qualified.

—*Oliver Wendell Holmes*

407.   Please all, and you will please none.

—*Aesop*

A Few Proverbs from Here and There
408.   If you cannot beat them, join them.

409.   If you would have a hen lay, you must bear with her cackling.

410.   A lean compromise is better than a fat lawsuit.

CONCEIT
411.   He was like a cock who thought the sun had risen to hear him crow.

—George Eliot

657.

CONCERN
412.   A man was reading the morning paper and said to his wife, "Hey, listen to this. The cashier at the bank has absconded with $60,000. Not only that, he stole one of the bank's executive limousines and ran off with the bank president's wife."

"My, that's awful," said his wife, "I wonder who they will get to teach his Sunday school class next week?"
414.

CONDUCT
413.   Conduct thyself toward thy parents as thou wouldst wish thy children to conduct themselves toward thee.

—Isocrates

414.   Conduct is three-fourths of our life and its largest concern.

—Matthew Arnold

415.   Our characters are the result of our conduct.

—Aristotle

CONFESSION
416.   It is not our wrong actions which it requires courage to confess, so much as those which are ridiculous and foolish.

—Jean-Jacques Rousseau

CONFIDENCE
417.   We shall not flag or fail. We shall fight in France, we shall fight on the seas and oceans, we shall fight with growing confidence and growing strength in the air, we shall defend our island, whatever the cost may be, we shall fight on the beaches, we shall fight on the landing grounds, we shall fight in the fields and in the streets, we shall fight in the hills; we shall never surrender.

—Sir Winston Churchill

418.   I see before me the statue of a celebrated minister, who said that confidence was a plant of slow growth. But I believe, however gradual may be the growth of confidence, that of credit requires still more time to arrive at maturity.

—Benjamin Disraeli

419.   It is vain to wait for money, or temporize. The great desiderata are public and private confidence. No country in the world can do without them. . .The circulation of confidence is better than the circulation of money. . .Confidence produces the best effects.

—James Madison

420.   Confidence is that feeling by which the mind embarks in great and honorable courses with a sure hope and trust in itself.

—Cicero

421.   Peace is not an absence of war, it is a virtue, a state of mind, a disposition for benevolence, confidence, justice.

—Benedict Spinoza

422.   Confidence is a thing not to be produced by compulsion. Men cannot be forced into trust.

—Daniel Webster

423.   Lack of confidence is not the result of difficulty; the difficulty comes from lack of confidence.

—Seneca

424.   The man who trusts men will make fewer mistakes than he who distrusts them.

—Cavour

425.   By mutual confidence and mutual aid, great deeds are done, and great discoveries made.

—Homer

426.   Confidence, like the soul, never returns whence it has once departed.

—Publilius Syrus

427.   Confidence in other's honesty is no light testimony to one's own integrity.

—Michel Eyquem Montaigne

428.   Confidence is a plant of slow growth in an aged bosom.

—William Pitt

429.   Confidence does more to make conversation than wit.

—Francois De La Rochefoucauld

430.   Confidence placed in another often compels confidence in return.

—Livy

431.   They can do all because they think they can.

—Virgil

432.   The calm confidence of a Christian with four aces.

—Mark Twain

433.   Skill and confidence are an unconquered army.

—George Herbert

434.   They can conquer who believe they can.

—John Dryden

435.   Doubt whom you will, but never yourself.

—Christian N. Bovee

436.   And this is the confidence that we have in Him, that, if we ask anything according to His will, He heareth us.

—I John 5:14

A Few Proverbs from Here and There
437.   Never confide in women or servants.

438.   Confidence is keeping your chin up; overconfidence is sticking your neck out.

439.   Confidence is the feeling you have before you understand the situation.
488, 611, 702, 731, 760, 783.

CONFLICT
440.   Taken to the streets, conflict is a destructive force; taken to the courts, conflict can be a creative force.

—Richard M. Nixon

CONFUSION

441.   Order governs the world. The Devil is the author of confusion.

—*Jonathan Swift*

CONQUEST

442.   When we conquer enemies by kindness and justice we are more apt to win their submission than by victory in the field. In the one case, they yield only to necessity; in the other, by their own free choice.

—*Polybius*

443.   So long as man's courage endures he will conquer; upon the courage in his heart all things depend.

—*H. G. Wells*

CONSCIENCE

444.   For nothing reaches the heart but what is from the heart, or pierces the conscience but what comes from a living conscience.

—*William Penn*

445.   Conscience was born when man had shed his fur, his tail, his pointed ears.

—*Sir Richard Burton*

446.   A clear conscience needeth no excuse, nor feareth any accusation.

—*John Lyly*

447.   Labor to keep alive in your breast that little spark of celestial fire, called conscience.

—*George Washington*

448.   Conscience is God's presence in man.

—*Emanuel Swedenborg*

487.

CONSERVATISM

449.   There is danger in reckless change, but greater danger in blind conservatism.

—*Henry George*

511, 995.

CONSOLATION

450. Education is a controlling grace to the young, consolation to the old, wealth to the poor, and ornament to the rich.

—Diogenes

CONSTANCY

451. Without constancy there is neither love, friendship, nor virtue in the world.

—Joseph Addison

CONSTITUTION

452. We may be tossed upon an ocean where we can see no land—nor, perhaps, the sun or stars. But there is a chart and a compass for us to study, to consult, and to obey. That chart is the Constitution.

—Daniel Webster

324, 327.

CONTEMPT

453. A woman who considered herself to be a careful driver was stopped for speeding. She insisted that she had not been driving more than 35 miles an hour. The patrolman said he had clocked her at 55 miles an hour. A heated argument developed and in the end, the woman lost her temper and called the patrolman a "stupid, dumb jackass."

In court the patrolman told the judge about the argument and the judge said to the lady, "I'm going to fine you $25.00 for speeding. And I warn you that you'll be held in contempt of court if you go around calling patrolmen, 'stupid, dumb jackasses.'"

"I'm sorry, your honor," the lady said, "I didn't know it was against the law to call a policeman names. Would it also be against the law if I called a stupid, dumb jackass, a policeman?"

The judge thought about that for a moment and said, "No, I would not consider that against the law."

"Thank you for clearing up that point," the lady said. Then as she left the courtroom, she turned to the officer who had arrested her and shouted, "Goodbye, Policeman."

CONTENTMENT

454.   We shall be made truly wise if we be made content; content, too, not only with what we can understand, but content with what we do not understand—the habit of mind which theologians call, and rightly, faith in God.

—Charles Kingsley

455.   The utmost we can hope for in this world is contentment; if we aim at anything higher, we shall meet with nothing but grief and disappointment.

—Joseph Addison

456.   With only plain rice to eat, with only water to drink, and with only an arm for a pillow, I am still content.

—Confucius

457.   Of the blessings set before you, make your choice and be content.

—Samuel Johnson

458.   The wisdom of life consists of eliminating the non-essentials, and of finding contentment in those things closest to us.

—Lin Yutang

459.   When we cannot find contentment in ourselves; it is useless to seek it elsewhere.

—Francois De La Rochefoucauld

460.   My crown is in my heart, not on my head. . .my crown is called content.

—William Shakespeare

461.   Fortify yourself with contentment, for this is an impregnable fortress.

—Epictetus

462.   With a few flowers in my garden, half a dozen pictures and some books, I live without envy.

—Lope de Vega

463.   Where there is content there will be no revolution.

—Confucius

464. I have learned in whatsoever state I am, therewith to be content.

—Philippians 4:11

68, 356.

CONTROVERSY

465. When a thing ceases to be a subject of controversy, it ceases to be a subject of interest.

—William Hazlitt

775.

CONVERSATION

466. It gives me great pleasure to converse with the aged. They have been over the road that all of us must travel, and know where it is rough and difficult and where it is level and easy.

—Plato

467. For good or ill, your conversation is your advertisement. Every time you open your mouth, you let me look into your mind.

—Bruce Barton

468. Silence is one great art of conversation. He is not a fool who knows when to hold his tongue.

—William Hazlitt

469. The more the bodily pleasure decreases, the greater grows the desire for the pleasure of conversation.

—Plato

470. The true spirit of conversation consists in building on another man's observation, not overturning.

—Bulwer-Lytton

471. Conversation teaches more than meditation.

—Henry George Bohn

472. "My goodness," a fellow said to his friend, "what happened to your face? I never saw such a mess."

"Well," his friend said, "you have been hearing all this stuff about how you should talk to your plants. I decided to try it. Yesterday I

had a long and intimate conversation with that honeysuckle vine that is growing up the oak tree in my back yard. When we were saying goodbye to each other and I was telling it I would see it again today, it said to me, "Oh, by the way. I'm not a honeysuckle. I'm a poison ivy."
391, 429, 1070, 1111.

CONVICTION
473.   The only faith that wears well and holds its color in all weathers is that which is woven of conviction and set with the sharp mordant of experience.

—James Russell Lowell

474.   The men who succeed best in public life are those who take the risk of standing by their own convictions.

—James A. Garfield

475.   I will listen to anyone's convictions, but pray keep your doubts to yourself.

—Goethe

487, 1030.

COOKING

A Few Proverbs from Here and There
476.   To make a stew, first catch your rabbit.

477.   He is a sorry cook that may not lick his own finger.

478.   Too many cooks spoil the broth.

COOPERATION
479.   We are made for cooperation, like feet, like hands, like eyelids, like the rows of the upper and lower teeth. To act against one another then is contrary to Nature, and it is acting against one another to be vexed and turn away.

—Marcus Aurelius

480.   According to the Spanish proverb, four persons are wanted to make a good salad: a spendthrift for the oil, a miser for vinegar, a counsellor for salt, and a madman to stir it all up.

—Abraham Hayward

481.   The race of mankind would perish from the earth did they cease to aid each other.

—*Sir Walter Scott*

482.   No member of a crew is praised for the rugged individuality of his rowing.

—*Ralph Waldo Emerson*

483.   Cooperation, and not Competition, is the life of trade.

—*William C. Fitch*

A Few Proverbs from Here and There
484.   On a rainy day, one tiny raindrop might fall unnoticed. But when those tiny raindrops cooperate you might end up in the middle of a hurricane.

485.   No matter how great a warrior the big chief is, he can't do battle without his Indians backing him up.

486.   Even when a woman makes a fool out of a man, she can't do it without his cooperation.
566.

COURAGE
487.   Last, but by no means least, courage—moral courage, the courage of one's convictions, the courage to see things through. The world is in a constant conspiracy against the brave. It's the age-old struggle—the roar of the crowd on one side and the voice of your conscience on the other.

—*General Douglas MacArthur*

488.   You gain strength, courage and confidence by every experience in which you really stop to look fear in the face. You are able to say to yourself, "I lived through this horror. I can take the next thing that comes along.". . .You must do the thing you think you cannot do.

—*Eleanor Roosevelt*

489.   Have courage for the great sorrow of life and patience for the small one; and when you have laboriously accomplished your daily task, go to sleep in peace. God is awake.

—*Victor Hugo*

490.   Whether you be man or woman you will never do anything in this world without courage. It is the greatest quality of the mind next to honor.

—*James Lane Allen*

491.   God, grant me the serenity to accept things I cannot change, courage to change things I can, and wisdom to know the difference.

—*Reinhold Niebuhr*

492.   Courage is almost a contradiction in terms: it means a strong desire to live taking the form of readiness to die.

—*Gilbert Keith Chesterton*

493.   The bravest thing—the courage we desire and prize—is not the courage to die decently, but to live manfully.

—*Thomas Carlyle*

494.   It is curious—curious that physical courage should be so common in the world and moral courage so rare.

—*Mark Twain*

495.   True courage is to do without witnesses everything that one is capable of doing before all the world.

—*Francois De La Rochefoucauld*

496.   Courage is doing what you're afraid to do. There can be no courage unless you're scared.

—*Eddie Rickenbacker*

497.   Courage and perseverance have a magical talisman, before which difficulties disappear and obstacles vanish into air.

—*John Quincy Adams*

498.   In sport, in courage, and the sight of heaven, all men meet on equal terms.

—*Sir Winston Churchill*

499.   The greatest test of courage on earth is to bear defeat without losing heart.

—*Robert G. Ingersoll*

500.   It isn't life that matters, it's the courage you bring to it.

—*Sir Hugh Walpole*

501.   Keep your fears to yourself, but share your courage with others.

—Robert Louis Stevenson

502.   Courage is the thing. All goes if courage goes.

—Sir James Matthew Barrie

503.   Many men would be cowards if they had courage enough.

—Thomas Fuller

504.   A newspaper reporter was interviewing the lion tamer of the circus that was performing in a small town.

"I saw you perform today," the reporter said. "You are a brave man to enter that cage with all of those ferocious lions. Would you say that your job is the most dangerous in the world?"

"Oh, it's dangerous," the lion tamer said, "but not nearly as dangerous as the job I had before this one."

"More dangerous than a cage of lions," the reporter said. "what sort of work was that?"

"I drove a school bus," the lion tamer said.

A Few Proverbs from Here and There

505.   It takes courage to stand up and speak out. It takes just as much courage to sit down and listen.

506.   It is better to live one day as a lion than a hundred years as a sheep.

507.   History shows, time and time again, that a curageous minority is more powerful than a cowardly majority.

443, 532, 550, 599, 718, 755, 758, 767.

COURTESY

508.   If a man be gracious and courteous to strangers, it shows he is a citizen of the world.

—Francis Bacon

509.   The greater the man, the greater courtesy.

—Alfred Lord Tennyson

510.   All doors open to courtesy.

—Thomas Fuller

1004.

COWARDICE

511.   A conservative is a man who is too cowardly to fight and too fat to run.

—Elbert Hubbard

512.   Cowards die many times before their deaths;
             The valiant never taste of death but once.

—William Shakespeare

513.   To see the right and not do it is cowardice.

—Confucius

71, 312, 503, 758.

CREATOR

514.   Here is my creed. I believe in one God, Creator of the Universe. That He governs it by His providence. That He ought to be worshipped. That the most acceptable service we render Him is doing good to His other children.

—Benjamin Franklin

CREED

515.   A man's action is only a picture of his creed.

—Ralph Waldo Emerson

CRITICISM

516.   I would rather be attacked than unnoticed. For the worst thing you can do to an author is to be silent as to his works.

—Samuel Johnson

517.   There is probably no hell for authors in the next world—they suffer so much from critics and publishers in this.

—Christian N. Bovee

518.   It is much easier to be critical than to be correct.

—Benjamin Disraeli

519.   A young playwright gave a special invitation to a highly regarded critic to watch his new play. The critic came to the play, but slept through the entire performance.

The young playwright was indignant and said, "How could you sleep when you knew how much I wanted your opinion?"

"Young man," the critic said, "sleep is an opinion."

757.

CROWN

520.   The royal crown cures not the headache.

—Benjamin Franklin

1866.

CRUELTY

521.   Scarcely anything awakens attention like a tale of cruelty. The writer of news never fails to tell how the enemy murdered children and ravished virgins; and if the scene of action be somewhat distant, scalps half the inhabitants of a province.

—Samuel Johnson

CULTURE

522.   Television is the first democratic culture—the first culture available to everyone and entirely governed by what the people want. The most terrifying thing is what people do want.

—Clive Barnes

523.   No one is so savage that he cannot become civilized, if he will lend a patient ear to culture.

—Horace

CURIOSITY

524.   Curiosity is free-wheeling intelligence. It endows the people who have it with a generosity in argument and a serenity in their own mode of life which spring from the cheerful willingness to let life take the forms it will.

—Alistair Cooke

525. What we have to do is to be forever curiously testing new opinions and courting new impressions.

—Walter Pater

CUSTOM
526. Have a place for everything and keep the thing somewhere else. This is not advice, it is merely custom.

—Mark Twain

527. Men's customs change like leaves on the bough; some go and others come.

—Dante

528. Custom is the plague of wise men and the idol of fools.

—Thomas Fuller

CYNICISM
529. I hate cynicism a great deal worse than I do the devil; unless, perhaps, the two were the same thing?

—Robert Louis Stevenson

530. The cynic is one who never sees a good quality in a man, and never fails to see a bad one. He is the human owl, vigilant in darkness, and blind to light, mousing for vermin, and never seeing noble game.

—Henry Ward Beecher
725.

DAILY TASK
531. A man came home from work one day to find his house in a shambles. The beds hadn't been made, the kitchen sink was filled with dirty dishes, the children's clothes and toys and books were scattered throughout the house. Besides that, dinner wasn't ready.

"What in the world happened?" the man asked his wife when he saw the mess.

"Nothing," she said, "absolutely nothing. You are always wondering what I do all day long. Well, take a look. Today, I didn't do it."
489.

DANGER

532. No man can answer for his courage who has never been in danger.

—Francois De La Rochefoucauld

533. Those who play with cats must expect to be scratched.

—Cervantes

534. As soon as there is life there is danger.

—Ralph Waldo Emerson

535. Live dangerously and you live right!

—Goethe

203, 764, 1249, 1455, 1498, 2252.

DARKNESS

536. Darkness is more productive of sublime ideas than light.

—Edmund Burke

1811.

DAY

537. One day well spent is to be preferred to an eternity of error.

—Cicero

A Few Proverbs from Here and There

538. Better the day, better the deed.

539. The day has eyes; the night has ears.

540. Wait till it is night before saying it has been a fine day.

541. Count that day lost whose low descending sun
Views from thy hand no noble action done.

DEATH

542. If thou grievest for the dead, mourn also for those who are born into the world; for as the one thing is of nature, so is the other too of nature.

—St. John Chrysostom

543.   Let us not lament too much the passing of our friends. They are not dead, but simply gone before us along the road which all must travel.

—Antiphanes

544.   Death is not the greatest loss in life. The greatest loss is what dies inside us while we live.

—Norman Cousins

545.   The nice part about owning a cemetery plot is, it takes all the worry out of dying.

—Bob Orben

546.   Is death the last sleep? No, it is the last and final awakening.

—Sir Walter Scott

547.   The fear of death is more to be dreaded than death itself.

—Publilius Syrus

DEBATE
548.   To strive with an equal is a doubtful thing to do; with a superior, a mad thing; with an inferior a vulgar thing.

—Seneca

549.   To be able to argue, men must first understand each other.

—Honore de Balzac

550.   A member of a high school debating team was talking to his friend about his next big debate.

"This will be the most important debate of the year," he said. "This will be a real battle of wits."

"How courageous of you," his friend said, "to enter the battle only half prepared."
2187.

DEBT
551.   The man who starts out with the notion that the world owes him a living generally finds that the world pays its debt in the penitentiary or the poorhouse.

—William Graham Sumner

552. There is none so rich but he sometimes owes. There is none so poor but one may sometimes borrow of him.

—Francois Rabelais

553. A trifling debt makes a man your debtor, a large one makes him your enemy.

—Seneca

647, 1432.

DECEIT

554. You can fool some of the people all of the time, and all of the people some of the time, but you cannot fool all of the people all of the time.

—Abraham Lincoln

DECISIONS

555. Making decisions is simple: get the facts, seek God's guidance; form a judgment; act on it; worry no more.

—Charles E. Bennett

556. Men must be decided on what they will *not* do, and then they are able to act with vigor *in what they ought to do*.

—Mencius

557. We learn how to make decisions by making decisions.

—Ancient proverb

DEEDS

558. He fills his lifetime with deeds, not with inactive years.

—Ovid

44, 1002.

DEFEAT

559. He who fears being conquered is sure of defeat.

—Napoleon Bonaparte

499, 2204.

DEFENSE
560.   God grants liberty only to those who love it, and are always ready to guard and defend it.

—Daniel Webster

DELIGHT
561.   The whole fruit of friendship is in the love itself, for it is not the advantage, procured through a friend, but his love that gives delight.

—Cicero

1053.

DEMOCRACY
562.   It is for this that we love democracy: for the emphasis it puts on character; for its tendency to exalt the purposes of the average man to some high level of endeavor; for its just principle of common assent in matters in which all are concerned; for its ideals of duty and its sense of brotherhood.

—Woodrow Wilson

563.   Democracy is more than a form of political organization, it is a human faith. True democracy is not and cannot be imperialistic. The brotherhood of this faith is the guarantee of good will.

—Herbert Hoover

564.   Democracy may not prove in the long run to be as efficient as other forms of government, but it has one saving grace; it allows us to know and say that it isn't.

—Bill Moyers

565.   Democracy is a charming form of government, full of variety and disorder, and dispensing a sort of equality to equals and unequals alike.

—Plato

566.   To define democracy in one word, we must use the word "cooperation."

—Dwight D. Eisenhower

567.   "I'm glad I live in a democracy," the man said. "I can do anything I please as long as I get permission from my boss, my doctor,

my banker, my lawyer, the IRS, the state, the city, and my wife and kids."
1338, 1852.

DENTIST
568. The dentist said to his patient, "I've got good news and bad news. Which do you want first?"

"Give me the bad news first," his patient said, "Then maybe the good news will cheer me up."

So the dentist told him the bad news. "You need a root canal operation and a whole lower bridgework. That will cost about $1800."

"Okay," the patient said. "Now what's the good news?"

"The good news," the dentist said, "is that I shot a hole-in-one yesterday."
965.

DESIRES
569. It seems to me we can never give up longing and wishing while we are thoroughly alive. There are certain things we feel to be beautiful and good, and we must hunger after them.

—George Eliot

570. The desire of knowledge, like the thirst of riches, increases ever with the acquisition of it.

—Laurence Sterne

571. Man seeks his own good at the whole world's cost.

Robert Browning

572. Temperance is the moderating of one's desires in obedience to reason.

—Cicero

573. No man is born without ambitious worldly desires.

—Thomas Carlyle

574. Women wish to be loved without a why or wherefore; not because they are pretty, or good, or well-bred, or graceful, or intelligent, but because they are themselves.

—Henri-Frederic Amiel

575.   Love and desire are the spirit's wings to great deeds.

—Goethe

576.   He begins to die that quits his desires.

—George Herbert

577.   Can one desire too much of a good thing?

—Cervantes

578.   All men by nature desire to know.

—Aristotle

579.   Art is the desire of a man to express himself, to record the reactions of his personality to the world he lives in.

—Amy Lowell

341, 1368, 1922, 2207.

DESTINY

580.   The oak grows silently in the forest a thousand years; only in the thousandth year, when the axeman arrives with his axe, is there heard an echoing through the solitudes; and the oak announces itself when, with far-sounding crash, it falls.

—Thomas Carlyle

581.   Fame comes only when deserved, and then is as inevitable as destiny, for it is destiny.

—Henry Wadsworth Longfellow

582.   Destiny waits in the hand of God, not in the hands of statesmen.

—T. S. Eliot

583.   One's destiny is determined, not by what he possesses, but by what possesses him.

—Ancient proverb

364.

DIET

584.   You know it is time to diet when you nod one chin and two others second the motion.

DIFFERENCE

585.   It is not best that we should all think alike; it is difference of opinion that makes horse races.

—*Mark Twain*

586.   The difference between landscape and landscape is small, but there is great difference in the beholders.

—*Ralph Waldo Emerson*

587.   Though all men were made of one metal, yet they were not cast all in the same mold.

—*Thomas Fuller*

102.

DIFFICULTY

588.   There is nothing so easy that at first is not difficult to believe, nothing so wonderful that in time men will not cease to marvel at it.

—*Lucretius*

589.   The greater the difficulty, the greater the glory.

—*Cicero*

590.   Settle one difficulty and you keep a hundred others away.

—*Ancient proverb*

423, 466, 497, 1533, 1643, 1845, 1889.

DIGNITY

591.   Dignity is like a perfume: those who use it are scarcely conscious of it.

—*Queen Christina of Sweden*

DILIGENCE

592.   Few things are impossible to diligence and skill.

—*Samuel Johnson*

DISAGREEMENT

593.   "It was a lousy date," the high school senior said. "She disagreed with my bumper sticker and I disagreed with her T-shirt."

DISCIPLINE

594.   For the artist, life is always a discipline, and no discipline can be without pain. That is so even of dancing, which of all the arts is most associated in the popular mind with pleasure. To learn to dance is the most austere of disciplines.

—Havelock Ellis

595.   I don't wait for moods. You accomplish nothing if you do that. Your mind must know it has got to get down to earth.

—Pearl Buck

596.   Discipline is the soul of an army. It makes small numbers formidable, procures success to the weak, and esteem to all.

—George Washington

597.   My son Hannibal will be a great general, because of all my soldiers he best knows how to obey.

—Barca Hamilcar

DISCOVERY

598.   The tourist with a camera around his neck had stopped beside a tumbled-down shack on a mountain road. Sitting on the porch in a rocking chair was the perfect picture of a rugged old mountaineer.

"May I take your picture?" the tourist asked.

"All right with me," the man said. "Go ahead."

After he had made two or three exposures the tourist said, "I've always wondered how you mountain people live to such a ripe old age. What is your secret?"

"No secret how I live," he said. "Everybody around here knows. I drink a quart of home-made whiskey every day, smoke a half a dozen cigars that I make myself from my own home-grown tobacco and I chase after all the neighborhood gals. I catch most of 'em, too."

"That seems like a rather strenuous life for a man of your age," the tourist said. "Just how old are you anyway?"

"I'll be thirty-two, come October," the man said.

425.

DISCRETION
599.   Three lions had escaped from the circus one night as it was setting up for a performance in a small Alabama town. Within half an hour the chief of police had organized a group of twenty-five or thirty men to try to round up the lions.

When he had finished briefing the men on how they were going to search for the lions, the chief said, "Men, it looks as though we're going to have a long night ahead of us so before we get started, how about stepping in the bar across the street and I'll buy all of you a couple of drinks."

"Not for me, thanks," said a man standing next to him.

"Why not, Harry?" the chief said. "I've seen you take a drink."

"Oh, I take a drink," Harry said, "but not when I'm starting on a lion hunt. Two shots of whiskey might give me too much courage."

DISPOSITION
600.   There is nothing so advantageous to a man as a forgiving disposition.

—Terence

DISTANCE
601.   Distance is a great promoter of admiration.

—Denis Diderot

DIVINITY
602.   Blessed be His name for shining upon so dark a heart as mine.

—Oliver Cromwell

DIVORCE
603.   For some reason, we see divorce as a signal of failure despite the fact that each of us has a right and an obligation to rectify any other mistake we make in life.

—Dr. Joyce Brothers

361.

DOCTOR

604.   The country doctor parked his twenty year-old car in front of the Post Office while he ran an errand. When he returned, a group of small boys were gathered around it making fun of it. "That sure is a beat-up old rattletrap you've got," one of them said.

"Yes it is," the doctor said. "But it is paid for." Then pointing to several of the children he said, "But you're not, and you're not, and you're not."
309, 2059.

DOG

605.   During a county-wide drive to round up all unlicensed dogs, a patrolman signaled a car to pull over to the curb. When the driver asked why he had been stopped, the officer pointed to the big dog sitting on the seat beside him. "Does your dog have a license?" he asked.

"Oh, no," the man said, "He doesn't need one. I always do the driving."
1859, 2185.

DOING

606.   Our grand business undoubtedly is, not to *see* what lies dimly at a distance, but *do* what lies clearly at hand.

—Thomas Carlyle

DOUBT

607.   The sun, with all those planets moving around it, can ripen the smallest bunch of grapes as if it had nothing else to do. Why then should I doubt His power?

—Galileo

608.   If a man will begin with certainties, he will end with doubts; but if he will be content to begin with doubts, he shall end in certainties.

—Francis Bacon

609.   One does not have to believe everything one hears.

—Cicero

610.   Who never doubted never half believed.

—*Philip James Bailey*

230, 435, 475, 1147, 1892, 1935.

DREAMS

611.   Go confidently in the direction of your dreams! Live the life you've imagined! As you simplify your life, the laws of the universe will be simpler, solitude will not be solitude, poverty will not be poverty, nor weakness weakness.

—*Henry David Thoreau*

612.   Your old men shall dream dreams, and your young men shall see visions.

—*Joel 2:28*

DRINK

613.   The owner of a sheet metal shop, who was a teetotaler, returned from a trip and found the assistant foreman in charge. "Where's the foreman?" he asked the assistant.

"He's on one of those binges of his," said the assistant.

"Where's the welder, then?" the boss asked.

"He's over at Bill's Tavern drunk," he said.

"I didn't see the stock clerk when I came through the stockroom. Where's he?"

"Oh, he's at the gym getting a steam bath to cure a hangover."

The boss dropped into a chair, shaking his head sadly. "Well," he said, "for a man who never touches a drop, I seem to suffer more from the effects of alcohol than any man in this town."

1712.

DRUG

614.   Words, of course, are the most powerful drug used by mankind.

—*Rudyard Kipling*

DUTY

615. We live in a world which is full of misery and ignorance, and the plain duty of each and all of us is to make the little corner he can influence somewhat less miserable and somewhat less ignorant than it was before he entered it.

—Thomas Huxley

616. My fellow Americans, ask not what your country can do for you; ask what you can do for your country. My fellow citizens of the world, ask not what America will do for you, but what together we can do for the freedom of man.

—John F. Kennedy

617. It is wonderful what strength of purpose and boldness and energy of will are aroused by the assurance that we are doing our duty.

—Sir Walter Scott

618. To let oneself be bound by a duty from the moment you see it approaching is part of the integrity that alone justifies responsibility.

—Dag Hammarskjold

619. Only aim to do your duty, and mankind will give you credit where you fail.

—Thomas Jefferson

620.   He gives only the worthless gold
                    Who gives from a sense of duty.

—James Russell Lowell

621. In doing what we ought we deserve no praise, because it is our duty.

—St. Augustine

10, 347, 1089.

EARS

622. What a mercy it would be if we were able to open and close our ears as easily as we open and close our eyes!

—Georg Christoph Lichtenberg

1053, 1361.

EASE

623. All work, even cotton-spinning, is noble; work is alone noble. . .A life of ease is not for any man, nor for any god.

—Thomas Carlyle

ECONOMY

624. Any government, like any family, can for a year spend a little more than it earns. But you and I know that a continuance of that habit means the poorhouse.

—Franklin D. Roosevelt

625. A terrible thing happened to me last week. I tried to live within my means and was picked up for vagrancy.

—Bob Orben

626. The salesman was trying to sell a home freezer. "You'll save enough on your food bill to pay for it," he said.

"I can understand that," the husband said, "but we're paying for our car on the busfare we save, and on our washing machine on the laundry money we save and on our house on the rent we save. Right now our monthly payments are so high that we just can't afford to save any more money."
1479, 1522, 2326.

EDUCATION

627. I believe that education lies at the heart of American experience. It is the engine which, in a climate of freedom, has made possible the upward social and economic mobility which is the hallmark of American history. That mobility, demonstrated in millions of private lives, has been the driving force behind all that America has done: its success as a self-governing society, its unprecedented economic growth, its enhancement of the quality of life in a thousand ways.

—Howard H. Baker, Jr.

628. Education is a companion which no misfortune can depress, no crime can destroy, no enemy can alienate, no despotism can enslave. At home a friend, abroad an introduction, in solitude a solace, and in society an ornament. It chastens vice, it guides virtue, it gives, at once,

grace and government to genius. Without it, what is man? A splendid
slave, a reasoning savage.

—Joseph Addison

629.　Education does not mean teaching people what they do not
know. It means teaching them to behave as they do not behave. It is not
teaching the youth the shapes of letters and the tricks of numbers, and
then leaving them to turn their arithmetic to roguery, and the literature
to lust. It means, on the contrary, training them into the perfect exercise
and kingly continence of their bodies and souls. It is a painful, continual
and difficult work to be done by kindness, by watching, by warning, by
precept, and by praise, but above all—by example.

—John Ruskin

630.　The sheet-anchor of the Ship of State is the common school.
Teach, first and last, Americanism. Let no youth leave the school without being thoroughly grounded in the history, the principles, and the incalculable blessings of American liberty. Let the boys be the trained soldiers of constitutional freedom, the girls the intelligent lovers of
freemen.

—Chauncey M. Depew

631.　State a moral case to a ploughman and a professor. The former
will decide it as well, and often better than the latter, because he has not
been led astray by artificial rules.

—Thomas Jefferson

632.　Let mental culture go on advancing, let the natural sciences
progress in ever greater extent and depth, and the human mind widen
itself as much as it desires; beyond the elevation and moral culture of
Christ's way as it shines forth in the Gospels, it will not go.

—Goethe

633.　Be not forgetful of prayer. Every time you pray, if your prayer
is sincere, there will be new feeling and new meaning in it, which will
give you fresh courage, and you will understand that prayer is an
education.

—Dostoevsky

634. The aim of reading is gradually to create an ideal life, a sort of secret, precious life, a refuge, a solace, an eternal source of inspiration in the soul of the reader.

—Arnold Bennett

635. Learn to know yourself to the end that you may improve your powers, your conduct, your character. This is the true aim of education and the best of all education is self-education.

—Rutherford B. Hayes

636. I call a complete and generous education that which fits a man to perform justly, skillfully, and magnanimously all the offices, both private and public, of peace and war.

—John Milton

637. I am not so lost in lexicography as to forget that words are the daughters of earth, and that things are the sons of heaven.

—Samuel Johnson

638. I have no technical and no university education, and have just had to pick up a few things as I went along.

—Sir Winston Churchill

639. As a general proposition, colleges are best administered by administrators, next best by faculty, and most worst by students.

—William F. Buckley, Jr.

640. If you wish to appear agreeable in society you must consent to be taught many things which you know already.

—Johann Kaspar Lavater

641. Finally, education alone can conduct us to that enjoyment which is, at once, best in quality and infinite in quantity.

—Horace Mann

642. It is the vice of scholars to suppose that there is no knowledge in the world but that of books.

—William Hazlitt

643. When you educate a man you educate an individual; when you educate a woman you educate a whole family.

—Charles D. McIver

644.   Education makes a people easy to lead, but difficult to drive: easy to govern, but impossible to enslave.

—Lord Brougham

645.   Education makes a greater difference between man and man, than nature has made between man and brute.

—John Adams

646.   The classroom—not the trench—is the frontier of freedom now and forevermore.

—Lyndon B. Johnson

647.   Education—A debt due from present to future generations.

—George Peabody

648.   Study without thought is vain; thought without study is dangerous.

—Confucius

649.   The nation that has the schools has the future.

—Bismarck

650.   I grow old learning something new every day.

—Solon

651.   Only the educated are free.

—Epictetus

652.   Although the little boy was only three, he already had learned the alphabet. His proud parents were showing off his accomplishment to his visiting grandparents.

"My, you're a smart young man," said his grandmother. "And what is the first letter?"

"A," said the little boy.

"That's right," said his proud grandmother, "and what comes after A?"

"All the rest of them," said the little boy.

57, 450, 1088, 1315, 1411, 1534, 1746, 1858, 1891, 2200.

EFFECT

653.   The work an unknown good man has done is like a vein of water flowing hidden underground, secretly making the ground green.

—Thomas Carlyle

654.   The rotten apple spoils his companions.

—*Benjamin Franklin*

708.

EGG
655.   All the goodness of a good egg cannot make up for the badness of a bad one.

—*Charles Anderson Dana*

656.   You can't unscramble scrambled eggs.

—*Ancient proverb*

314.

EGO
657.   Conceit is the most incurable disease that is known to the human soul.

—*Henry Ward Beecher*

ELECTION
658.   A straw vote only shows which way the air blows.

—*O. Henry*

2281.

ELOQUENCE
659.   In a country and government like ours, eloquence is a powerful instrument, well worthy of the special pursuit of our youth.

—*Thomas Jefferson*

660.   He is an eloquent man who can treat humble subjects with delicacy, lofty things impressively and moderate things temperately.

—*Cicero*

661.   He who has put a good finish to his undertaking is said to have placed a golden crown to the whole.

—*Eustachius*

1057, 1082, 1360, 1675, 2058.

ENDURANCE
662.   The sum of the whole matter is this: If our civilization is to survive materially, it must be redeemed spiritually.

—*Woodrow Wilson*

663.   The first thing a child should learn is how to endure. It is what he will have most need to know.

—*Jean-Jacques Rousseau*

755, 1585.

ENERGY
664.   Genius is mainly an affair of energy.

—*Matthew Arnold*

886, 2309.

ENLIGHTENMENT
665.   A tourist was visiting a small town and asked a man in front of the Post Office if there was a movie or other entertainment in the town.

"No," the native said, "but if you're looking for entertainment why don't you drop in at the Country Store. We've got a freshman home from college."

338.

ENTHUSIASM
666.   The best thing that history yields us is the enthusiasm it generates.

—*Goethe*

667.   Nothing great was ever achieved without enthusiasm.

—*Ralph Waldo Emerson*

668.   Enthusiasm for a cause sometimes warps judgment.

—*William Howard Taft*

879, 1932, 2309.

EQUALITY
669.   We hold these truths to be self-evident—that all men are created equal; that they are endowed by their Creator with certain unalien-

able rights; that among these are life, liberty, and the pursuit of happiness.

—Declaration of Independence

670. You cannot possibly have a broader basis for any government than that which includes all the people, with all their rights in their hands, and with an equal power to maintain their rights.

—William Lloyd Garrison

671. It is not true that equality is a law of nature. Nature knows no equality. Its sovereign law is subordination and dependence.

—Marquis De Vauvenargues

672. He sendeth the rain on the just and on the unjust.

—Matthew 5:45

1219, 1294, 1338, 1339, 2381.

ERROR

673. A man should never be ashamed to say he has been in the wrong, which is but saying in other words that he is wiser today than he was yesterday.

—Alexander Pope

674. A man protesting against error is on the way toward uniting himself with all men that believe in the truth.

—Thomas Carlyle

675. It is better to err on the side of daring than the side of caution.

—Alvin Toffler

798, 1205, 1464, 1467, 2151.

ESTEEM

676. The new janitor had reported to work about ten or fifteen minutes late each morning. After a week of his tardiness, the boss called him in and said, "We hired you for this job because you are a veteran. I would like to know what they did in the army when you showed up ten minutes late every morning."

"Oh, whenever I was late," the janitor said, "everybody stood up and the captain would salute and say, 'Good morning, Colonel.' "

596, 1441.

ETERNITY

677.   The truest end of life is to know the Life that never ends.

—*William Penn*

229, 1428.

EVIL

678.   A bad man is wretched amidst every earthly advantage; a good man—troubled on every side, yet not distressed; perplexed, but not in despair; persecuted, but not forsaken; cast down, but not destroyed.

—*Plato*

679.   The evil that men do lives after them;
                   The good is oft interred with their
                          bones.

—*William Shakespeare*

680.   There are thousands hacking at the branches of evil to one who is striking at the root.

—*Henry David Thoreau*

681.   All that is necessary for the triumph of evil is that good men do nothing.

—*Edmund Burke*

682.   You may be as orthodox as the Devil, and as wicked.

—*John Wesley*

EXAMPLE

683.   Our nation can be strong abroad only if it is strong at home, and we know that the best way to enhance freedom in other lands is to demonstrate here that our democratic system is worthy of emulation.

—*Jimmy Carter*

684.   Few things are harder to put up with than the annoyance of a good example.

—*Mark Twain*

685.   A good example is the best sermon.

—*Benjamin Franklin*

387, 629, 1113, 1508, 1901.

EXCELLENCE

686. The society which scorns excellence in plumbing because plumbing is a humble activity and tolerates shoddiness in philosophy because it is an exalted activity will have neither good plumbing nor good philosophy. Neither its pipes nor its theories will hold water.

—John W. Gardner

687. I assure you I had rather excel others in the knowledge of what is excellent, than in the extent of my power and dominion.

—Alexander the Great

EXCESS

688. Every reform, however necessary, will by weak minds be carried to an excess which will itself need reforming.

—Samuel Taylor Coleridge

EXCUSE

689. I never knew a man who was good at making excuses who was good at anything else.

—Benjamin Franklin

EXISTENCE

690. No man is in true health who cannot stand in the free air of heaven, with his feet on God's free turf, and thank his Creator for the simple luxury of physical existence.

—T. W. Higginson

EXPECTATIONS

691. Live your life, every day of it, with great expectations and great things will happen in your life, daily.

—Art Fettig

692. It is idle to wait for your ship to come in unless you have sent one out.

—Allen Drury

161.

EXPERIENCE

693.   The world is a country which no one yet ever knew by description; one must travel it oneself to be acquainted with it. . .Courts and camps are the only place to learn the world in.

—Lord Chesterfield

694.   Experience is the oracle of truth; and where its responses are unequivocal, they ought to be conclusive and sacred.

—James Madison

695.   I have but one lamp by which my feet are guided, and that is the lamp of experience.

—Patrick Henry

696.   No man's knowledge, here, can go beyond his experience.

—John Locke

697.   A whale ship was my Yale College and my Harvard.

—Herman Melville

698.   The little girl had been listening to her grandfather read the story of Noah's Ark. After he had finished, she looked at his wrinkled old face and said, "Granddaddy, were you in Noah's Ark?"

"No, I wasn't," he said.

"Then why weren't you drowned?"

380, 1181, 1531, 1534, 1636.

EXPRESSION

699.   Strong emotion—love, despondency, patriotic fervor, sympathy, anger—will sometimes lead a man to express himself in the form of a poem or song or essay. If, that is, the man is a poet, composer or essayist.

—Steve Allen

700.   A hopeless young actor had been given a part in a Broadway play because he was a nephew of the man who was backing the show financially. He was given a simple part with only one line to say. In scene three someone was supposed to rush on stage and shoot him.

His one line was, "My God, I am shot."

In spite of all the coaching he could give the young fellow, the director couldn't teach him to say the line properly.

"Say it right," the director would say. "My God, I am *shot*."

And the young fellow would either speak his words in a non-excited monotone or with the wrong emphasis such as, "My God, *I* am shot."

Finally, in desperation the director figured out a trick. On opening night, he would put rubber bullets in the gun so that the man would be shot, but not hard enough to hurt him. He figured that in his surprise the young man might speak naturally—and of course say his lines correctly.

Came the big night. The big scene. The shot. And the actor said, "My God, I *am* shot."

194, 579.

FACE
701. The face of a man gives us fuller and more interesting information than his tongue, for his face is the summary of all he will ever say.

—Arthur Schopenhauer

702. Nature has written a letter of credit upon some men's faces which is honored wherever presented. You cannot help trusting such men; their very presence gives confidence.

—William Makepeace Thackery

703. If a good face is a letter of recommendation, a good heart is a letter of credit.

—Bulwer-Lytton

704. Your face is a book where men may read strange matters.

—William Shakespeare

FACTS
705. Get your facts first, and then you can distort 'em as much as you please.

—Mark Twain

1247, 1445, 2157, 2200.

FAILURE

706. There are some who want to get rid of their past, who if they could, would begin all over again. . .but you must learn, you must let God teach you, that the only way to get rid of your past is to get a future out of it.

—Phillips Brooks

707. The probability that we may fail in the struggle ought not to deter us from the support of a cause we believe to be just.

—Abraham Lincoln

708. It is hard to fail, but it is worse never to have tried to succeed. In this life we get nothing save by effort.

—Theodore Roosevelt

709. They fail, and they alone, who have not striven.

—Thomas Bailey Aldrich

710. I would sooner fail than not be among the greatest.

—John Keble

711. They never fail who die in a great cause.

—Lord Byron

712. Not failure, but low aim, is crime.

—James Russell Lowell

713. Too far is no better than not far enough.

—Confucius

714. No good thing is failure and no evil thing success.

—Ancient proverb

1467, 1841, 2220, 2033.

FAIRNESS

715. What man dislikes in his superiors, let him not display in the treatment of his inferiors.

—Ancient proverb

716. A man was telling a friend about a new business operation. "I'm taking in a partner," he said. "It's going to be a 50-50 deal."

"Are you both putting up the same amount of capital?" his friend asked.

"No," the man said. "Not to start with. He's putting up the capital and I'm putting up the experience. But within five or six years that should change. By then I will have the capital and he will have the experience."

FAITH

717.   I have now disposed of all my property to my family. There is one thing more I wish I could give them and that is faith in Jesus Christ. If they had that and I had not given them one shilling, they would have been rich; and if they had not that, and I had given them all the world, they would be poor indeed.

—Patrick Henry

718.   I have lived eighty-six years. I have watched men climb to success, hundreds of them, and of all the elements that are important for success, the most important is faith. No great thing comes to any man unless he has courage.

—James Cardinal Gibbons

719.   I do not believe there is a problem in this country or the world today which could not be settled if approached through the teaching of the Sermon on the Mount.

—Harry S. Truman

720.   Christian faith is a grand cathedral, with divinely pictured windows. Standing without, you can see no glory, nor can imagine any, but standing within, every ray of light reveals a harmony of unspeakable splendors.

—Nathaniel Hawthorne

721.   I am profitably engaged reading the Bible. Take all of this Book upon reason that you can, and the balance on faith, and you will live and die a better man.

—Abraham Lincoln

722.   I believe in Christ like I believe in the sun, not just because I see it, but because by it I can see everything else.

—C. S. Lewis

723.   Faith is to believe what we do not see, and the reward of this faith is to see what we believe.

—*St. Augustine*

724.   Faith is a gift of God which man can neither give nor take away by promise of rewards or menace of torture.

—*Thomas Hobbes*

725.   It is cynicism and fear that freeze life; it is faith that thaws it out, releases it, sets it free.

—*Harry Emerson Fosdick*

726.   'Tis not the dying for a faith that's so hard. . .'tis the living up to it that's difficult.

—*William Makepeace Thackeray*

727.   Faith is an assurance inwardly prompted, springing from the irrepressible impulse to do, to fight, to triumph.

—*George Santayana*

728.   I gather the rose from the thorn, the gold from the earth, the pearl from the oyster.

—*St. Jerome*

729.   Faith takes up the cross, love binds it to the soul, patience bears it to the end.

—*Bonard*

730.   Men grow in stature only as they daily rededicate themselves to a noble faith.

—*Dwight D. Eisenhower*

731.   If you think you can win, you can win. Faith is necessary to victory.

—*William Hazlitt*

732.   The only limit to our realization of tomorrow will be our doubts of today. Let us move forward with strong and active faith.

—*Franklin D. Roosevelt*

733.   All work that is worth anything is done in faith.

—*Albert Schweitzer*

734. You cannot have faith and tension at the same time.

—Mahatma Gandhi

735. If ye have faith as a grain of mustard seed, ye shall say unto this mountain, "Remove hence to yonder place;" and it shall remove; and nothing shall be impossible unto you.

—Matthew 17:20

736. Yea, though I walk through the valley of the shadow of death, I will fear no evil; for thou art with me.

—Psalms 23:4

737. I have fought a good fight, I have finished my course, I have kept the faith.

—II Timothy 4:7

738. Faith is the substance of things hoped for, the evidence of things not seen.

—Hebrews 11:1

739. Faith without works is dead.

—James 2:26

473, 563, 760, 1159, 1694, 2132.

FAITHFULNESS

740. Young men want to be faithful and are not; old men want to be faithless and cannot.

—Oscar Wilde

FAME

741. If a man love the labor of any trade, apart from any question of success or fame, the gods have called him.

—Robert Louis Stevenson

742. I'll make thee glorious by my pen, and famous by my sword.

—Marquis of Montrose

743. Nothing arouses ambition so much in the heart as the trumpet-clang of another's fame.

—Baltasar Gracian

744.   Literary fame is the only fame of which a wise man ought to be ambitious, because it is the only lasting living fame.

—Robert Southey

745.   The less people speak of their greatness the more we think of it.

—Francis Bacon

746.   Fame, we may understand, is no sure test of merit, but only a probability of such: it is an accident, not a property of man.

—Thomas Carlyle

747.   Fame usually comes to those who are thinking about something else.

—Oliver Wendell Holmes

748.   To be occasionally quoted is all the fame I care for.

—Alexander Smith

749.   Familiarity, truly cultivated, can breed love.

—Dr. Joyce Brothers

581, 1316, 1784, 1814, 1970.

FARMER
750.   The farmer stood in his chicken yard watching hundreds of baby chicks running here and there. He kept pointing to them and trying to count them. "One, two, three, four, five, six. . .oh, no. . ." then he would start over, "one, two, three, four, and. . .oh, no." Then, he'd start over again.

Finally he gave up. "I give up," he said. "They say don't count your chickens before they hatch but it sure is easier to do that than it is to count them after they hatch."

2321.

FASHION
751.   Those who seem to lead the public taste, are, in general, merely outrunning it in the direction it is spontaneously following.

—Thomas Macaulay

752. Fashion is a form of ugliness so intolerable that we have to alter it every six months.

—Oscar Wilde

753. Every generation laughs at the old fashions, but follows religiously the new one.

—Henry David Thoreau

754. Fashion is gentility running away from vulgarity, and afraid of being overtaken by it.

—William Hazlitt

FATE

755. Fate gave to man the courage of endurance.

—Ludwig van Beethoven

109.

FAULT

756. It is not alone what we do, but also what we do not do, for which we are accountable.

—Moliere

757. Men count up the faults of those who keep them waiting.

—Ancient proverb

FEAR

758. Courage is resistance to fear, mastery of fear—not absence of fear. Except a creature be part coward it is not a compliment to say it is brave.

—Mark Twain

759. Quiet minds cannot be perplexed or frightened, but go on in fortune or misfortune at their own private pace, like a clock during a thunderstorm.

—Robert Louis Stevenson

760. Don't be afraid to take a big step if one is indicated. You can't cross a chasm in two small jumps.

—David Lloyd George

761.   Fear God and where you go men will think they walk in hallowed cathedrals.

—Ralph Waldo Emerson

762.   The only thing we have to fear is fear itself.

—Franklin D. Roosevelt

763.   Fear makes men ready to believe the worst.

—Quintus Curtius Rufus

764.   Dangers bring fears, and fears more dangers bring.

—Richard Baxter

765.   No one loves the man whom he fears.

—Aristotle

766.   Fear knocked at the door. Faith answered. No one was there.

—Ancient proverb

767.   There is no fear in love; but perfect love casteth out fear: because fear hath torment. He that feareth is not made perfect in love.

—I John 4:18

108, 488, 501, 547, 1080, 1307, 1498, 1666, 1740, 1872.

FEELING

768.   Art is not a handicraft, it is the transmission of feeling the artist has experienced.

—Leo Tolstoy

FELLOWSHIP

769.   Fellowship is Heaven, and lack of fellowship is Hell; fellowship is life, and lack of fellowship is death; and the deeds that ye do upon the earth, it is for fellowship's sake that ye do them.

—William Morris

770.   He that goeth to bed with dogs ariseth with fleas.

—James Sandford

769.

FICTION

771. The most influential books, and the truest in their influence, are works of fiction. . .They repeat, they rearrange, they clarify the lessons of life; they disengage us from ourselves, they constrain us for the acquaintance of others; and they show us the web of experience, but with a singular change—that monstrous consuming ego of our being, for the nonce, struck out.

—Robert Louis Stevenson

772. Fictions meant to please should be close to the real.

—Horace

1331, 1767.

FIDELITY

773. If I were to select a watchword that I would have every young man write above his door and on his heart, it would be that good word "fidelity."

—Benjamin Harrison

774. Fidelity bought with money is overcome by money.

—Seneca

1401.

FIGHT

775. I am quite certain that there is nothing which draws so good, or at least so large a congregation as a fight in the pulpit.

—Bolton Hall

776. Most sorts of diversion in men, children, and other animals, are in imitation of fighting.

—Johnathan Swift

777. When a man begins to fight within himself, he's worth something.

—Robert Browning

417, 1699, 1722, 1871, 2230.

FIRESIDE

778.   You are a King by your own Fireside, as much as any Monarch on His Throne.

—*Cervantes*

FLAG

779.   If it were my destiny to die for the cause of liberty I would die upon the tomb of the Union, the American flag as my winding sheet.

—*Andrew Johnson*

780.   The things that the flag stands for were created by the experiences of a great people. Everything that it stands for was written by their lives. The flag is the embodiment, not of sentiment, but of history. It represents the experiences made by men and women, the experiences of those who do and live under that flag.

—*Woodrow Wilson*

781.   I pledge allegiance to the flag of the United States of America and to the republic for which it stands, one nation under God, indivisible, with liberty and justice for all.

—*The Pledge of Allegiance to the Flag*

FLOWERS

782.   Flowers have an expression of countenance as much as men or animals. Some seem to smile; some have a sad expression; some are pensive and diffident; others again are plain, honest and upright, like the broadfaced sunflower and the hollyhock.

—*Henry Ward Beecher*

783.   A seed catalog is the first step toward having a home filled with spectacularly beautiful flowers. You take it down to the florist and point at what you want.

—*Bob Orben*

200, 1398, 1980.

FOOD

784.   Some people have food, but no appetite; others have appetite, but no food; I have both. The Lord be praised!

—*Oliver Cromwell*

785.   The way to a man's heart is through his stomach.

—Fanny Fern

FOOL
786.   The most difficult character in comedy is that of a fool, and he must be no simpleton who plays the part.

—Cervantes

787.   He that does not believe that God is above all, is either a fool or has no experience of life.

—Statius

788.   Any man may make a mistake; none but a fool will persist in it.

—Cicero

789.   The foolish and dead alone never change their opinion.

—James Russell Lowell

790.   If there were fewer fools, knaves would starve.

—Isaac Asimov

486, 1250, 1984, 2030, 2202, 2244, 2283.

FORCE
791.   One fact stands out in bold relief in the history of men's attempts for betterment. That is that when compulsion is used, only resentment is aroused, and in the end is not gained. Only through moral suasion and appeal to men's reason can a movement succeed.

—Samuel Gompers

792.   A man without passion is only a latent force, only a possibility, like a stone waiting for the blow from the iron to give forth sparks.

—Henri-Frederic Amiel

793.   There is no force so democratic as the force of an ideal.

—Calvin Coolidge

794.   By persuasion, not by force of arms.

—Plutarch

422, 1133, 1223, 1370.

FOREBEARS

795.   I don't know who my grandfather was; I am much more concerned to know what his grandson will be.

—*Abraham Lincoln*

221.

FORGIVENESS

796.   "I can forgive, but I cannot forget," is only another way of saying, "I cannot forgive."

—*Henry Ward Beecher*

797.   They who forgive most shall be most forgiven.

—*Philip James Bailey*

798.   To err is human, to forgive divine.

—*Alexander Pope*

600.

FORTUNE

799.   It takes a great deal of boldness, mixed with a vast deal of caution, to acquire a great fortune; but then it takes ten times as much wit to keep it after you have got it as it took to make it.

—*Meyer A. Rothschild*

800.   Let the man who has to make his fortune remember this maxim: Attacking is the only secret. Dare, and the world always yields; or if it beat you sometimes, dare it again and it will succumb.

—*William Makepeace Thackeray*

801.   Here is a rule to remember in future, when anything tempts you to feel bitter: not, "This is a misfortune," but, "To bear this worthily is good fortune."

—*Marcus Aurelius*

802.   I do not value fortune. The love of labor is my sheet-anchor. I work that I may forget, and forgetting, I am happy.

—*Stephen Girard*

803.   The only sure thing about luck is that it will change.

—*Bret Harte*

804. Every man is the architect of his own fortune.

—Appius Claudius

115, 1016, 1404, 2037, 2269.

FORWARD
805. I will go anywhere, provided it be forward.

—David Livingstone

FOUNDATION
806. Upon a good foundation a good building may be raised, and the best foundation in the world is money.

—Cervantes

807. That Book, sir, is the rock on which this Republic rests.

—Andrew Jackson

219, 1540.

FREEDOM
808. In the cause of freedom we have to battle for the rights of people with whom we do not agree; and whom, it many cases, we may not like . . . If we do not defend their rights, we endanger our own.

—Harry S. Truman

809. Freedom from fear and injustice and oppression will be ours only in the measure that men who value such freedom are ready to sustain its possession—to defend it against every thrust from within or without.

—Dwight D. Eisenhower

810. Since the general civilization of mankind, I believe there are more instances of the abridgment of the freedom of the people by gradual and silent encroachments of those in power than by violent and sudden usurpations.

—James Madison

811. The genius of America has been its incredible ability to improve the lives of its citizens through a unique combination of governmental and free citizen activity.

—Gerald R. Ford

812.   That this nation, under God, shall have a new birth of freedom, and that government of the people, by the people, for the people, shall not perish from the earth.

—*Abraham Lincoln*

813.   None who have always been free can understand the terrible fascinating power of the hope of freedom to those who are not free.

—*Pearl Buck*

814.   The basic freedoms: the freedom to worship, the freedom to choose your occupation, the freedom to try and fail and, if need be, to try again, the freedom to make mistakes and to do things others might consider stupid.

—*Ronald Reagan*

815.   Everything that is really great and inspiring is created by the individual who can labor in freedom.

—*Albert Einstein*

816.   Those who expect to reap the blessings of freedom, must, like man, undergo the fatigue of supporting it.

—*Thomas Paine*

817.   There can be no freedom or beauty about a home life that depends on borrowing and debt.

—*Henrik Ibsen*

818.   Freedom has a thousand charms to show, that slaves, howe'er contented, never know.

—*William Cowper*

819.   Who knows what women can be when they are finally free to become themselves?

—*Betty Friedan*

820.   In health there is freedom. Health is the first of all liberties.

—*Henry-Frederic Amiel*

821.   Three hostile newspapers are more to be feared than a thousand bayonets.

—*Napoleon Bonaparte*

822. Let us remember that revolutions do not always establish freedom.

—*Millard Fillmore*

823. We live under a government of men and morning newspapers.

—*Wendell Phillips*

824. The cause of freedom is the cause of God.

—*William Lisle Bowles*

92, 627, 651, 1335, 1443, 1548, 1618, 1896, 1967, 2155.

FRIENDSHIP

825. We are all travelers in what John Bunyan calls the wilderness of this world, and the best that we find in our travels is an honest friend. He is a fortunate voyager who finds many. We travel indeed to find them. They are the end and the reward of life. They keep us worthy of ourselves; and when we are alone, we are only nearer to the absent.

—*Robert Louis Stevenson*

826. The world is so empty if one thinks only of mountains, rivers and cities; but to know someone here and there who thinks and feels with us, and who, though distant, is close to us in spirit, this makes the earth for us an inhabited garden.

—*Goethe*

827. Blessed are they who have the gift of making friends, for it is one of God's best gifts. It involves many things, but above all, the power of going out of one's self, and appreciating whatever is noble and loving in another.

—*Thomas Hughes*

828. If a man does not make new acquaintances as he advances through life, he will soon find himself left alone. A man, sir, should keep his friendships in constant repair.

—*Samuel Johnson*

829. You can make more friends in two months by becoming interested in other people than you can in two years by trying to get other people interested in you.

—*Dale Carnegie*

830.   The proper office of a friend is to side with you when you are wrong. Nearly anybody will side with you when you are in the right.

—*Mark Twain*

831.   It is a good thing to be rich, and a good thing to be strong, but it is a better thing to be beloved of many friends.

—*Euripides*

832.   The things which our friends do with and for us, form a portion of our lives; for they strengthen and advance our personality.

—*Goethe*

833.   True friendship is a plant of slow growth, and must undergo and withstand the shocks of adversity before it is entitled to the appellation.

—*George Washington*

834.   Life often seems like a long shipwreck of which the debris are friendship, glory, and love. The shores of existence are strewn with them.

—*Madame De Stael*

835.   I find friendship to be like wine, raw when new, ripened with age, the true old man's milk and restorative cordial.

—*Thomas Jefferson*

836.   The firmest friendships have been formed in mutual adversity, as iron is most strongly united by the fiercest flame.

—*Charles Caleb Colton*

837.   A friend will be sure to act the part of an advocate before he will assume that of a judge.

—*Robert Southey*

838.   Friendship is a strong and habitual inclination in two persons to promote the good and happiness of one another.

—*E. Budgell*

839.   The best way to keep your friends is to never owe them anything and never lend them anything.

—*Paul De Kock*

840.   It is in the character of very few men to honor without envy a friend who has prospered.

—*Aeschylus*

841. The most I can do for my friend is simply to be his friend.

—*Henry David Thoreau*

842. A brother may not be a friend, but a friend will always be a brother.

—*Benjamin Franklin*

843. The company of just and righteous men is better than wealth and a rich estate.

—*Euripides*

844. Without friends, no one would choose to live, though he had all other goods.

—*Aristotle*

845. If you have one true friend you have more than your share.

—*Thomas Fuller*

846. There is nothing so great that I fear to do it for my friend; nothing so small that I will disdain to do it for him.

—*Sir Philip Sidney*

847. This communicating of a man's self to his friend works two contrary effects; for it redoubleth joys, and cutteth griefs in half.

—*Francis Bacon*

848. Real friendship is shown in times of trouble; prosperity is full of friends.

—*Euripides*

849. A friend should bear his friend's infirmities.

—*William Shakespeare*

850. A friend should be a master at guessing and keeping still.

—*Friedrich Nietzsche*

851. Friendship is the highest degree of perfection in society.

—*Michel Eyquem Montaigne*

852. It is better to be alone than in ill company.

—*George Pettie*

853. Prosperity makes friends. Adversity tries them.

—*Publilius Syrus*

854. Friendships multiply joys, and divide griefs.

—*Henry George Bohn*

855. The only way to have a friend is to be one.

—Ralph Waldo Emerson

856. A faithful friend is beyond price; his worth is more than money can buy.

—Ecclesiasticus 6:15

857. Greater love hath no man than this, that a man lay down his life for his friends.

—John 15:13

858. A man that hath friends, must show himself friendly.

—Proverbs 18:24

859. What sweetness is left in life, if you take away friendship? Robbing life of friendship is like robbing the world of the sun.

—Cicero

860. Every man should keep a fair-sized cemetery in which to bury the faults of his friends.

—Henry Ward Beecher

A Few Proverbs from Here and There

861. The real friend is the person who is still your friend when you don't deserve a friend.

862. Friendship is a plant that we must water often.

863. Everybody's friend is nobody's friend.

864. A genuine friend walks in when everybody else walks out.

865. Do not remove a fly from your friend's forehead with a hatchet.

866. A friend is someone who dislikes the same people you do.

867. Friendship is like two clocks keeping time.

868. A real friend laughs at your jokes when they aren't very funny, and sympathizes with your problems when they aren't very serious.

869. Friendships often are strengthened when both friends have the same problem—like arthritis.

870.   No family ever realizes how many friends they have until they put a swimming pool in the back yard.

871.   If you want to win friends, you have to learn to lose arguments.

872.   Forget an injury. Never forget a kindness.

873.   Two men were playing golf together when the name of a mutual acquaintance came up. "You're a good friend of Wilbur's aren't you?" the first golfer said.

"I should say I am," the man said. "We went to school together. There's nothing in this world I wouldn't do for Wilbur and there's nothing in the world he wouldn't do for me. In fact, we've gone through life together for nearly fifty years doing absolutely nothing for each other."

874.   Two men were talking about a friend. "Since Joe lost all of his money," the first friend said, "half of his friends have deserted him. They won't even speak to him."

"What about the other half?" the second friend asked.

"Oh," said the first friend, "they haven't heard that he lost it."

875.   Two neighbors were gossiping over a cup of coffee. "Those two," one gossip said, "how in the world do you think they ever came to get married?"

"Oh," said the other gossip, "you know how those things happen. They started out to be good friends and then changed their minds."
36, 170, 366, 561, 1298, 1376, 1423, 1744, 1813.

FUTURE

876.   For my part, I think that a knowledge of the future would be a disadvantage.

—Cicero

877.   No one regards what is before his feet; we all gaze at the stars.

—Ennius

878.   The empires of the future are empires of the mind.

—Sir Winston Churchill

879.   Members of the family were helping grandfather celebrate his eightieth birthday. One of his granddaughters said to him, "You look so happy today. Doesn't it bother you to grow old?"

"Bother me?" he said. "Heck no, it doesn't bother me. I enjoy it. I look forward to getting older and older and older. Because the very moment I quit getting older, I'm dead."
162, 706, 1212, 1301, 1453, 1665, 1715, 1825, 2128, 2245.

FUTURE SHOCK
880.   Man has a limited biological capacity for change. When this capacity is overwhelmed, the capacity is in future shock.

—Alvin Toffler

GENEALOGY
881.   A genealogist is someone who traces back your family tree as far as your money will go.

GENEROSITY
882.   The teacher said to the first grader, "If your mother gave you a big apple and a little apple and told you to give one to your brother, which apple would you give him—the big apple or the little apple?

The little boy thought for a moment and then said, "Do you mean my big brother or my little brother?"
345, 1222.

GENIUS
883.   When a man of genius is in full swing, never contradict him, set him straight or try to reason with him. Give him a free field. A listener is sure to get a greater quantity of good, no matter how mixed, than if the man is thwarted. Let Pegasus bolt—he will bring you up in a place you know nothing about.

—Linnaeus

884.   There is no work of genius which has not been the delight of mankind, no word of genius to which the human heart and soul have not, sooner or later, responded.

—James Russell Lowell

885. If a man can have only one kind of sense, let him have common sense. If he has that and uncommon sense too, he is not far from genius.

—Henry Ward Beecher

886. Genius is mainly an affair of energy, and poetry is mainly an affair of genius; therefore a nation characterized by energy may well be eminent in poetry.

—Matthew Arnold

887. When I hear a young man spoken of as giving promise of great genius, the first question I ask about him always is, "Does he work?"

—John Ruskin

888. When nature has work to be done, she creates genius to do it.

—Ralph Waldo Emerson

889. Genius is the power of lighting one's own fire.

—John Foster

890. How quickly the visions of genius become the canned goods of the intellectuals.

—Saul Bellow

891. No author is a man of genius to his publisher.

—Heinrich Heine

892. There is no great genius without a mixture of madness.

—Aristotle

893. Originality is the supreme evidence of genius.

—Marquis De Vauvenargues

255, 664, 1593, 1649, 1844, 1932, 2012, 2054, 2164, 2336.

GENTLEMAN

894. A man asked to define the essential characteristics of a gentleman—using the term in its widest sense—would presumably reply: "The will to put himself in the place of others; the horror of forcing others into positions from which he would himself recoil; the power to do what seems to him to be right, without considering what others may say or think."

—John Galsworthy

895.   It is almost a definition of a gentleman to say he is one who never inflicts pain.

—*John Henry, Cardinal Newman*

GENTLENESS
896.   It is only people who possess firmness who can possess true gentleness. Those who appear gentle generally possess nothing but weakness, which is readily converted into harshness.

—*Francois De La Rochefoucauld*

1109, 1111.

GIFT
897.   A teenager said to her mother, "I've got to get a birthday present for Cousin Edith. If you were 17, what would you like?"

"Just that," her mother said. "Just that and nothing more."

351, 1492, 2194.

GIVING
898.   You give but little when you give of your possessions. It is when you give of yourself that you truly give.

—*Kahil Gibran*

899.   What is given by the gods more desirable than a happy hour?

—*Catullus*

900.   Take heed that ye do not your alms before men, to be seen of them . . .But when thou doest alms, let not thy left hand know what thy right hand doeth.

—*Matthew 6:1-3*

901.   He gives twice who gives quickly.

—*Ancient proverb*

902.   The delightful and friendly custom of handing out a gift to help you celebrate a special event is becoming more widespread. Like the eight-year old who took a bag of bubble gum to school. As he passed it out to his friends he said, "I just became a brother yesterday."

903.   And the young lady who gave everyone where she worked a bright red carnation. When they asked her why, she showed them a sparkling new diamond engagement ring and said, "It's a boy, six feet tall and 175 pounds."
620.

GLORY
904.   All His glory and beauty come from within, and there He delights to dwell. His visits there are frequent, His conversations sweet, His comforts refreshing, and His peace passing all understanding.

—Thomas A. Kempis

905.   Glorious indeed is the world of God around us, but more glorious the world of God within us. There lies the land of song; there lies the poet's native land.

—Henry Wadsworth Longfellow

906.   The noblest spirit is most strongly attracted by the love of glory.

—Cicero

907.   For all may have, if they dare try, a glorious life, or grave.

—George Herbert

908.   Our greatest glory is not in never failing but in rising every time we fall.

—Confucius

909.   The greater the obstacle, the more glory in overcoming it.

—Moliere

910.   Whatsoever ye do, do all to the glory of God.

—I Corinthians 10:31

911.   The heavens declare the glory of God.

—Psalms 19:1

341, 589, 742, 834.

GOALS

912.   Every man who can be a first-rate something—as every man
can be who is a man at all—has no right to be a fifth-rate something; for
a fifth-rate something is no better than a first-rate nothing.

—J. G. Holland

913.   To all our means of culture is added the powerful incentive to
personal ambition . . .No post of honor is so high but the poorest may
hope to reach it.

—James A. Garfield

914.   Hitch your wagon to a star. Let us not lag in paltry works
which serve our pot and bag alone.

—Ralph Waldo Emerson

915.   To be what we are, and to become what we are capable of becoming, is the only end of life.

—Robert Louis Stevenson

916.   Let us be resolute in prosecuting our ends, and mild in our
methods of so doing.

—Aquaviva

917.   The true worth of a man is to be measured by the objects he
pursues.

—Marcus Aurelius

918.   If you wish to reach the highest, begin at the lowest.

—Publilius Syrus

919.   What shall it profit a man, if he shall gain the whole world,
and lose his own soul?

—Mark 8:36

GOD

920.   It takes no brains to be an atheist. Any stupid person can deny
the existence of a supernatural power because man's physical senses
cannot detect it. But there cannot be ignored the influence of conscience, the respect we feel for moral law, the mystery of first life on
what once must have been a molten mass, or the marvelous order in
which the universe moves about us on this earth. All of these evidence

the handiwork of a beneficent Deity. For my part, that Deity is the God of the Bible and of Christ, his Son.

—Dwight D. Eisenhower

921. He who believes in God is not careful for the morrow, but labors joyfully and with a great heart. "For He giveth His beloved as in sleep." They must work and watch, yet never be careful or anxious, but commit all to Him, and live in serene tranquillity; with a quiet heart, as one who sleeps safely and quietly.

—Martin Luther

922. The Kingdom of God is a society of the best men, working for the best ends, according to the best methods. Its law is one word—loyalty; its gospel one message—love. If you know anything better, live for it; if not, in the name of God and of humanity, carry out Christ's plan.

—Henry Drummond

923. We are intelligent beings; and intelligent beings cannot have been formed by a blind, brute, insensible being. There is certainly some difference between a clod and the ideas of Newton. Newton's intelligence came from some greater Intelligence.

—Voltaire

924. I thank God for the honesty and virility of Jesus's religion which makes us face the facts and calls us to take a man's part in the real battle of life.

—Henry Van Dyke

925. If I can put one touch of a rosy sunset into the life of any man or woman, I shall feel that I have worked with God.

—Henry David Thoreau

926. To us also, through every star, through every blade of grass, is not God made visible if we will open our minds and eyes?

—Thomas Carlyle

927. An instinctive taste teaches men to build their churches with spire steeples which point as with a silent finger to the sky and stars.

—Samuel Taylor Coleridge

928.   If Shakespeare should come amongst us we should all rise, but if He should appear we should all kneel.

—*Charles Lamb*

929.   The Lord has turned all our sunsets into sunrises.

—*Clement of Alexandria*

220, 514, 719, 910, 1062, 1066, 1101, 1370, 1516, 2244.

GOLF

Because the presentation of golf trophies is a part of so many luncheons and banquets, this special section of golf stories has been included.

930.   If there is any reward I treasure most, it is the way that the game of golf has responded to my inner drives, to the feeling we all have that—in those moments that are so profoundly a challenge to man himself—he has done his best. That—win or lose—nothing more could have been done.

—*Arnold Palmer*

931.   In Australia the aborigines perform an ancient custom of beating the ground with clubs and uttering wild and terrifying sounds. According to anthropologists, this is a manifestation of primitive self-expression. When the same practice takes place in the United States, we have another name for it—GOLF!

932.   The world's lowest golf score was made by a golfer in the nudist colony. He went around 18 holes in nothing.

933.   Late one Saturday afternoon, the locker-room boy at the country club answered the telephone. A woman's voice said she wanted to know if her husband was there.

"No, lady," he said. "He isn't here."

"How can you say he isn't there?" she screamed. "I haven't even told you my name yet."

"It doesn't matter, lady," he said. "There ain't never anybody's husband here on Saturday afternoon."

934.   "My wife told me a month ago that if I didn't give up golf she was going to pack up and leave me."

"My, that's terrible."

"Yes it is. It sure is lonesome around the house at night."

935. GOLF: The miracle that took the cow out of the pasture and let the bull in.

936. A young man wanted his new girl friend to learn to play golf. He was explaining the game to her. "The idea of the game," he said, "is to knock a ball into a hole with as few strokes as possible."

"Oh," she said demurely, "that sounds exciting. Sort of like basketball. And are you supposed to try to stop me?"

937. The rich duffer joined a foursome on the first tee. Two caddies stood behind him.

"Why did you bring two caddies?" one of his friends asked.

"Oh," the duffer said, "I always have to send one back to the club house for laughing."

938. Every golfer is a combination of good attributes and bad. When you play golf, you should be kind and gracious to your opponent and think only of his sterling qualities. You should try to overlook any slight flaw in his character. Remember that he too is a human being with the same frustrations and disappointments and problems that you have. You should not make harsh judgments just because he happens to be a dirty low-down rascal who is three up on you.

939. An irate man came screaming out of his home which faced the golf course; "Hey, there! Look what you did. You hooked your drive and the ball broke my big picture window. What are you going to do about it?"

The golfer looked at him earnestly and said, "I think I'll try a more relaxed grip and maybe hold my elbow in a little closer."

940. Two young fellows were chatting. "I have been thinking about getting a job as a caddy at the country club," the first one said. "Do you know what sort of pay you get for caddying?"

"I don't know how much you get for caddying," his friend said, "but I understand the tipping is good when you back up the lies of the man you are caddying for."

941. The caddy was suffering from a severe case of hiccups. He was making a nervous wreck of the golfer he was caddying for. On the eighth hole, the golfer missed a birdie putt by three inches. He couldn't control himself any longer. He turned to the caddy and shouted, "You and your hiccups! See what you caused me to do?"

"But," said the caddy, "I didn't hiccup when you were putting."

"I know it," cried the golfer, "but I allowed for it."

942.   Two duffers were playing together. After the first hole, one said to the other. "What did you take on that hole?"

"I took a seven," the second duffer said. "What did you take?"

"I took a six," his friend said.

After they had finished the second hole, the first duffer said, "What did you. . .?"

"Hey, not so fast," his friend said. "It's my turn to ask first."

943.   One golfer said to another, "Look at that foursome ahead of us. That's sure going to be a battle of wits."

"What do you mean, it's going to be a battle of wits? How can a game of golf be a battle of wits?"

"Look who's playing," his friend said. "Horowitz, Muscowitz, Shimkowitz and Lefkowitz."

944.   A duffer complained to his friend, "Don't ever play golf with Wilhoyt. Yesterday, he wouldn't even concede a two foot putt."

"Why fuss about it?" his friend asked.

"Because it cost me three strokes, that's why," the first golfer said.

945.   One woman explained why more women don't play golf. "We have more important things to lie about."

946.   A typical beach bum was curled up asleep underneath some shrubbery near the tee on a swank Miami golf course. The club secretary and the pro were playing an early round together when they found the sleeping man. The club secretary woke him up with a swift kick. "Get up," he shouted. "You aren't supposed to sleep here."

"Who do you think you are," the bum asked, "waking me out of a comfortable nap?"

"I'm the club secretary and chairman of the membership committee," the man said. "That's who I am."

"Well," the bum said, "all I can say is, that's a lousy way to try to get new members."

947.   Two women were chatting about their husbands. "My husband almost lost his mind over golf," the first woman said. "All he thought about was golf, golf, golf. He never played less than three days a week. His problem is so bad that he now visits a psychiatrist about it."

"Is the psychiatrist helping him?" her friend asked.

"I think he must be," the first woman said, "because he and my husband play golf together every Tuesday, Thursday and Saturday."

948.   A golfer was talking to his friend. "You know how late it was when we left the club house yesterday? Well, when I got home my wife didn't say a word about me being late. She had dinner waiting for me and after that she wouldn't even let me help with the dishes. She made me sit in the living room and she brought my pipe and slippers and told me to be comfortable while I read the evening paper."

"How much damage," his friend asked, "had she done to the car?"

949.   A man was playing golf with his wife who was in a talkative mood. He finally turned to her in disgust, "Please don't talk so much. You are driving me out of my mind."

"That's no drive," she said. "That's just a short putt."

950.   "What sort of game of golf does Willard play?" a man asked his friend.

"I'd say he plays a fair game—when you watch him," his friend said.

951.   A man was showing his friend a new set of matched golf clubs he had just bought. "Doctor's orders," the man told his friend. "My wife and I have been gaining too much weight and we went to see the doctor about it. He said we needed more exercise, so I joined the country club and bought myself this set of golf clubs."

"What about your wife?" the friend asked. "What did you buy her?"

"A new lawn mower," the golfer said.

952.   "How much are your rooms?" a man asked the clerk at the motel.

"Twenty-six dollars up," the clerk said.

"That seems to me to be a little high," the man said. "Don't you have another rate? I'm a golf pro."

"In that case," the clerk said, "it will be twenty-six dollars down."

953.   A successful man is a fellow who can hire somebody to mow his lawn so he will have time to play golf—for exercise.

954.   The duffer had been invited to play with three of the best players in the club. They were men who usually shot in the low 70's. The duffer was invited to tee off first. In his embarrassment at playing in such illustrious company, he completely missed his ball on his first swing. Trying even harder on his second swing, he missed in the same way. Feeling that he had to say something, he turned to the others and said: "Tough course, isn't it?"

955.   The expectant mother who was being rushed to the hospital didn't quite make it. Instead, she gave birth to her baby on the hospital lawn. Later, the father received a bill listing the delivery room fee as $50. Disturbed about it, he complained to the hospital bookkeeping department. He reminded them that his wife gave birth to the baby on the front lawn.

By return mail he received a corrected bill which read, "Greens fee, $65.00."

956.   The veteran golfer sat down to his Saturday night supper. His wife smiled as she said, "I think Junior was smart to get a job as a caddy at the country club. He tells me that he caddied for you this afternoon."

"By George," the golfer said, "I thought I'd seen that kid somewhere before."

957.   Spring had come. At breakfast the golfer's wife said, "Now just because the weather is pretty today, don't think you're going to sneak off and play golf all day."

"Now, honey," he said, "Don't get upset. Golf is the furthest thing from my mind. Would you please pass the toast and putter?"

958.   A golfer was playing with friends at a course where he had never played before. His first swing missed the ball completely. His second swing, even harder than the first, missed exactly like the first. He was terribly embarrassed and felt he had to make some sort of excuse. He looked at his friends and said: "Boy, what do you think about that? This course is two inches lower than the one I usually play on."

959.   First golfer: "My wife doesn't mind me playing golf every Wednesday afternoon just as long as I get home by six-thirty."

Second golfer: "I have to be home by six. My wife's a half-hour meaner than yours."

960.   A man was on the verge of a nervous breakdown. His psychiatrist advised him to take up golf to get his mind off his business. Six months later the doctor advised him to take up business in order to get his mind off golf.

961.   A golfer rushed up to the foursome ahead of him and said, "Do you mind if I play through? I just had an urgent message. My wife was injured in an automobile accident and has been rushed to the hospital."

962.   The record for bragging goes to a Texan who had graduated from Harvard, served two years in the Marines, had six grandchildren, and had just made a hole-in-one at his local country club.

963.   A golf pro was teaching a new pupil how to swing his club.

"Now that you have the right idea," the pro said, "just go through the motions without hitting the ball."

"I can already do that," the pupil said. "I want you to teach me how to hit it."

964.   A golfer had been hit on the head by a long drive and was lying in the center of the fairway with a small crowd around him. As he began to regain consciousness, one of the other players was trying to question him. "Are you married?" he asked the injured man.

"No," the fellow said, "this is the worst situation I've ever been in."

965.   Just as the dentist was leaving his office to meet a friend for golf, the phone rang. His secretary answered it and called to the dentist, "It's a woman with a toothache. She wants to know if she can come in right away."

"Tell her I won't be available," the dentist said. "Tell her I already have an appointment to fill 18 cavities this afternoon."

966.   The duffer was slicing and hooking his way around the course. He felt embarrassed about his play and said to a member of his foursome, "I'm just not playing my usual game today."

And with a straight face, his friend asked, "And what game do you usually play?"

967.   A golfer was sitting at the bar in the club house complaining about the poor day he had. "I fell into bad company today," he said. "I had a quart of whiskey in my golf bag and all of the other fellows in my foursome were teetotalers."

GOODNESS
968.   Do all the good you can,
                           By all the means you can,
                           In all the ways you can,
                           In all the places you can,
                           At all the times you can,
                           To all the people you can,
                           As long as ever you can.

                                                        —*John Wesley*

969.   The ideals which have always shone before me and filled me with the joy of living are goodness, beauty, and truth.

                                                        —*Albert Einstein*

970.   In nothing do men more nearly approach the gods than in doing good to their fellow men.

                                                        —*Cicero*

971.   The most acceptable service of God is doing good to men.

                                                        —*Benjamin Franklin*

972.   They're only truly great who are truly good.

                                                        —*George Chapman*

973.   What is beautiful is good, and who is good will soon be beautiful.

                                                        —*Sappho*

974.   No good deed goes unpunished.

                                                        —*Clare Boothe Luce*

975.   All things work together for good to them that love God.

                                                        —*Romans 8:28*

577, 678, 679, 1380, 1449, 2047, 2149.

GOSSIP

976. There is only one thing in the world worse than being talked about, and that is not being talked about.

—*Oscar Wilde*

977. The small town minister was chiding one of his members for missing church the previous two Sundays.

"This is Spring planting time," the man said. "I had to get my crops in. But, I was careful to work on the back forty so that people couldn't see me working on Sunday."

"Yes," the minister said, "but God could see you."

"I know that," the farmer said, "but he doesn't gossip like the members of this church do."

225, 875, 922.

GOVERNMENT

978. America is not manipulated by a few people behind the scenes. I've been behind the scenes and it's so crowded you can hardly move around. It's like Times Square on New Year's Eve.

—*John W. Gardner*

979. A good government produces citizens distinguished for courage, love of justice, and every other good quality; a bad government makes them cowardly, rapacious, and the slaves of very foul desire.

—*Dionysius of Halicarnassus*

980. We admit of no government by divine right. . .the only legitimate right to govern is an express grant of power from the governed.

—*William Henry Harrison*

981. That is the best government which desires to make the people happy, and knows how to make them happy.

—*Thomas Macaulay*

982. Our government must at the same time be both competent and compassionate.

—*Jimmy Carter*

983. Men will either be governed by God or ruled by tyrants.

—*William Penn*

984. The government is us; we are the government, you and I.

—*Theodore Roosevelt*

985. What is the best government?
That which teaches us to govern ourselves.

—*Goethe*

564, 624, 670, 812, 1232, 1306, 1540, 1731, 2145, 2354.

GRACE

986. When grace is joined with wrinkles, it is adorable. There is an unspeakable dawn in happy old age.

—*Victor Hugo*

1266.

GRATITUDE

987. He who receives a benefit with gratitude, repays the first installment on his debt.

—*Seneca*

988. A thankful heart is not only the greatest virtue, but the parent of all the other virtues.

—*Cicero*

989. There is not a more pleasing exercise of the mind than gratitude.

—*Joseph Addison*

990. O Lord, that lends me life, lend me a heart replete with thankfulness.

—*William Shakespeare*

991. Into the well which supplies thee with water, cast no stone.

—*The Talmud*

992. Gratitude is the sign of noble souls.

—*Aesop*

993. It is a good thing to give thanks unto the Lord.

—*Psalms 92:1*

994. The little boy had been taken for a trip to the zoo by his grandfather and later to a snack shop for some ice cream. When he came

home, his mother said, "Did you thank your grandfather for taking you
to the zoo?"

There wasn't any answer. She asked him a second time and still he
didn't answer.

"Jimmie," she said. "Answer me! Did you thank your
grandfather?"

"Yes," the little boy said, "but he said 'don't mention it!' "
238, 1704, 2078.

GREATNESS

995.   All great peoples are conservatives; slow to believe in novel-
ties; patient of much error in actualities; deeply and forever certain of
the greatness that is in law, in custom once solemnly established, and
now long recognized as just and final.

—Thomas Carlyle

996.   There is no such thing as a little country. The greatness of people is no more determined by their number than the greatness of a man is
determined by his height.

—Victor Hugo

997.   Greatness is a spiritual condition worthy to excite love, interest, and admiration; and the outward proof of possessing greatness is,
that we excite love, interest, and admiration.

—Matthew Arnold

998.   The nearer we come to great men the more clearly we see that
they are only men. They rarely seem great to their valets.

—Jean De La Bruyere

999.   The way to greatness is the path of self-reliance, independence and steadfastness in time of trial and stress.

—Herbert Hoover

1000.   The superiority of some men is merely local. They are great
because their associates are little.

—Samuel Johnson

1001.   Great men are meteors designed to burn so that the earth may
be lighted.

—Napoleon Bonaparte

1002.   A great life never dies. Great deeds are imperishable; great names immortal.

—*William McKinley*

1003.   No man was ever great without divine inspiration.

—*Cicero*

1004.   The greater the man, the greater courtesy.

—*Alfred, Lord Tennyson*

1005.   Great hopes make great men.

—*Thomas Fuller*

1006.   He that is least among you all, the same shall be great.

—*Luke 9:48*

745, 1167, 1803, 2074.

GRIEF
1007.   There are people who can endure personal tragedies and private griefs exacted by the nation only if they feel the nation itself is worthy.

—*Bill Moyers*

847.

GROWTH
1008.   You cannot force the growth of human life and civilization, any more than you can force these slow-growing trees. That is the economy of Almighty God, that all good growth is slow growth.

—*William J. Gaynor*

1009.   The psychological growth of man must keep pace with his physical powers; every increase in power must be matched by an increase in understanding.

—*Harry Allen Overstreet*

1010.   It is only when men begin to worship that they begin to grow.

—*Calvin Coolidge*

1011.   The strongest principle of growth lies in human choice.

—*George Eliot*

418, 428, 1450.

HABIT

1012. If we have a bad habit we call it a bad habit, but if we have a good habit we call it self-discipline. Essentially the mechanism is the same, however. If you devote a specific amount of time each day to a useful end, you will discover that you are addicted to it. If you try to break the habit, you will find yourself dealing with feelings of guilt. For example, writing one page a day in one hour each day will bring you a complete book manuscript at the end of a year. This concept is applicable to almost any endeavor.

—William Manchester

1013. The man who makes it the habit of his life to go to bed at nine o'clock, usually gets rich and is always reliable. Of course, going to bed does not make him rich—I merely mean that such a man will in all probability be up early in the morning and do a big day's work, so his weary bones put him to bed early. Rogues do their work at night. Honest men work by day. It's all a matter of habit, and good habits in America make any man rich. Wealth is largely a result of habit.

—John Jacob Astor

1014. It seems, in fact, as though the second half of a man's life is made up of nothing but the habits he has accumulated during the first half.

—Dostoevsky

1015. Habit is a cable; we weave a thread of it every day, and at last we cannot break it.

—Horace Mann

1016. A man who gives his children habits of industry provides for them better than by giving them a fortune.

—Archbishop Whately

1017. Nothing so needs reforming as other people's habits.

—Mark Twain

HAPPINESS

1018. Happiness lies not in the mere possession of money, it lies in the joy of achievement, in the thrill of creative effort. The joy and moral stimulation of work no longer must be forgotten in the mad chase of evanescent profits. These dark days will be worth all they cost us if they teach us that our true destiny is not to be ministered unto but to minister to ourselves and to our fellow men.

—*Franklin D. Roosevelt*

1019.   Happiness in this world, when it comes, comes incidentally. Make it the object of pursuit, and it leads us on a wild-goose chase, and is never attained. Follow some other object, and very possibly we may find that we have caught happiness without dreaming of it; but likely enough it is gone the moment we say to ourselves, "Here it is!" like the chest of gold that treasure-seekers find.

—*Nathaniel Hawthorne*

1020.   Happiness itself is sufficient excuse. Beautiful things are right true; so beautiful actions are those pleasing to the gods. Wise men have an inward sense of what is beautiful, and the highest wisdom is to trust this intuition and be guided by it. The answer to the last appeal of what is right lies within a man's own breast. Trust thyself.

—*Aristotle*

1021.   To look fearlessly upon life; to accept the laws of nature, not with meek resignation, but as her sons, who dare to search and question; to have peace and confidence within our souls—there are the beliefs that make for happiness.

—*Maeterlinck*

1022.   Happiness includes chiefly the idea of satisfaction after full honest effort. No one can possibly be satisfied and no one can be happy who feels that in some paramount affair he has failed to take up the challenge of life.

—*Arnold Bennett*

1023.   In order that people may be happy in their work, these three things are needed: They must be fit for it: They must not do too much of it: And they must have a sense of success in it.

—*John Ruskin*

1024.   It is a fact that so far as our happiness is concerned it matters not much where we are, so that we are satisifed with our situation, and whether we will be satisifed or not depends upon ourselves.

—*Franklin Pierce*

1025.   The longer I live the more I am convinced that the one thing worth living for and dying for is the privilege of making someone more happy and more useful. No man who ever does anything to lift his fellows ever makes a sacrifice.

—Booker T. Washington

1026.   The grand essentials to happiness in this life are something to do, something to love, and something to hope for.

—Joseph Addison

1027.   The happiness of life is made up of minute fractions—the little, soon forgotten charities of a kiss or a smile, a kind look or a heartfelt compliment, and the countless infinitesimals of pleasurable and genial feeling.

—Samuel Taylor Coleridge

1028.   In the pursuit of happiness half the world is on the wrong scent. They think it consists in having and getting, and in being served by others. Happiness is really found in giving and serving others.

—Henry Drummond

1029.   To watch the corn grow, or the blossoms set; to draw hard breath over the ploughshare or spade; to read, to think, to love, to pray, are the things that make men happy.

—John Ruskin

1030.   The greatest happiness of life is the conviction that we are loved, loved for ourselves, or rather loved in spite of ourselves.

—Victor Hugo

1031.   The secret of happiness is not in doing what one likes, but in liking what one has to do.

—Sir James Matthew Barrie

1032.   Hope is itself a species of happiness, and, perhaps, the chief happiness which this world affords.

—Samuel Johnson

1033.   A mind always employed is always happy. This is the true secret, the grand recipe, for felicity.

—Thomas Jefferson

1034.   The most delicate, the most sensible of all pleasures, consists in promoting the pleasure of others.

—Jean De La Bruyere

1035.   Most folks are about as happy as they make up their minds to be.

—Abraham Lincoln

1036.   Action may not always bring happiness; but there is no happiness without action.

—Benjamin Disraeli

1037.   Hold him alone truly fortunate who has ended his life in happy well-being.

—Aeschylus

1038.   One is happy in the world only when one forgets the world.

—Anatole France

1039.   Happiness is not what you have, but what you are.

—Winston K. Pendleton

1040.   Employment is nature's physician, and is essential to human happiness.

—Galen

1041.   The ground-work of all happiness is health.

—Leigh Hunt

1042.   True happiness springs from moderation.

—Goethe

1043.   To be happy, memorize something good each day, see something beautiful each day, do something helpful each day.

—Ancient proverb

899, 1171, 1203, 1462, 1472, 2008, 2017, 2137, 2231, 2246.

HARDSHIP

1044.   Most of our comforts grow up between our crosses.

—Edward Young

1987.

HASTE

1045. A sixth-grader rushed home from school one afternoon and headed straight for the telephone and dialed a number.

"Hello," he said. "Betty, can you go with me to the movies tonight?"

After a moment's silence, he said, "O.K., I'll call you tomorrow."

"What was that excitement and rush all about?" his mother wanted to know. "Who is Betty? And, another thing, it isn't right to ask a girl out the same day you call. You should ask her some time in advance."

"But, Mom," the boy said, "I didn't even like her until two hours ago."

955, 1586.

HATRED

1046. In no one else in all history do you find an abiding hatred, an immortal hatred except against Our Lord. . .The hatred against Christ has never weakened even after twenty centuries. . .because He is still an obstacle—an obstacle to sin, to selfishness, to godlessness, and to the spirit of the world.

—Fulton J. Sheen

1047. Always remember others may hate you but those who hate you don't win unless you hate them. And then you destroy yourself.

—Richard M. Nixon

1048. Hating people is like burning down your house to get rid of a rat.

—Harry Emerson Fosdick

1173, 1375.

HEALTH

1049. Health lies in labor, and there is no royal road to it but through toil.

—Wendell Phillips

1050.   Health and appetite impart the sweetness to sugar, bread, and meat.

—Ralph Waldo Emerson

1051.   If you mean to keep as well as possible, the less you think about your health the better.

—Oliver Wendell Holmes

355, 820, 1041, 1194, 2079.

HEARING
1052.   You shall hear from me nothing but the truth.

—Plato

1053.   He that hath ears to hear, let him hear.

—Matthew 11:15

1362, 2062.

HEART
1054.   Best of all is to preserve everything in a pure, still heart, and let there be for every pulse a thanksgiving, and for every breath a song.

—Konrad von Gesner

1055.   My heart bids me do it, if I can, and it is a thing possible to do.

—Homer

1056.   God has two dwellings: one in heaven, and the other in a meek and thankful heart.

—Izaak Walton

1057.   It is the heart which makes men eloquent.

—Quintilian

1058.   Faint heart never won fair lady.

—William Camden

444, 703, 1208, 2139.

HEARTH
1059.   A hearth is no hearth unless a woman sit by it.

—Richard Jefferies

HEAVEN

1060.   Happy the man to whom heaven has given a morsel of bread without laying him under the obligation of thanking any other for it than heaven itself.

—Cervantes

1061.   God who placed me here will do what He pleases with me hereafter, and He knows best what to do.

—Bolingbroke

1062.   Heaven is the soul finding its own perfect personality in God.

—Phillips Brooks

1063.   There is a Land of Pure Delight.

—Isaac Watts

1064.   Every charitable act is a stepping-stone toward Heaven.

—Henry Ward Beecher

1065.   All the way to heaven is heaven.

—Canon Farrar

1066.   Acquaint thyself with God, if thou wouldst taste His works.

—William Cowper

498, 1256, 1685, 1761.

HELP

1067.   He who helps a child helps humanity with an immediateness which no other help given to human creature in any other stage of human life can possibly give again.

—Phillips Brooks

1068.   Be an opener of doors for such as come after thee, and do not try to make the universe a blind alley.

—Ralph Waldo Emerson

183, 481, 1369.

HERITAGE

1069.   I came upstairs into the world; for I was born in a cellar.

—William Congreve

HISTORY

1070.   What man most needs now is to apply his conversion skills to those things that are essential for his survival. He needs to convert facts into logic, free will into purpose, conscience into decision. He needs to convert historical experience into a design for a sane world.

—Norman Cousins

1071.   If men could learn from history, what lessons it might teach us! But passion and party blind our eyes, and the light which experience gives is a lantern on the stern which shines only on the waves behind us.

—Samuel Taylor Coleridge

1072.   History is "the track of God's footsteps through time." It is in His dealings with our forefathers that we may expect to find the laws by which He will deal with us.

—Charles Kingsley

1073.   History is a relentless master. It has no present, only the past rushing into the future. To try to hold fast is to be swept aside.

—John F. Kennedy

1074.   Every school boy and girl who has arrived at the age of reflection ought to know something about the history of the art of printing.

—Horace Mann

1075.   History can be well written only in a free country.

—Cicero

507, 666, 1839, 2025, 2180, 2278.

HOME

1076.   Dry bread at home is better than roast meat abroad.

—George Herbert

778, 1114, 1525, 1617.

HONESTY

1077.   The first of qualities for a great statesman is to be honest. . .I have, and must have, confidence in the possible virtue of human nature. . .To believe all men honest would be folly. To believe not so, is something worse.

—John Quincy Adams

1078.   I hope I shall always possess firmness and virtue enough to maintain (what I consider the most enviable of all titles) the character of an honest man.

—George Washington

1079.   Of more worth is one honest man to society, and in the sight of God, than all the crowned ruffians that ever lived.

—Thomas Paine

1080.   All my fears and cares are of this world; if there is another, an honest man has nothing to fear from it.

—Robert Burns

1081.   Make yourself an honest man, and then you may be sure that there is one rascal less in the world.

—Thomas Carlyle

1082.   Honesty is one part of eloquence. We persuade others by being in earnest ourselves.

—William Hazlitt

1083.   An honest man's the noblest work of God.

—Alexander Pope

1084.   The personnel director of a bank was interviewing applicants for the job of cashier. After talking to a fine-looking fellow, he decided to check his references. He called a man who had been listed as a former employer.

"We are thinking of hiring your former employee as a cashier." the personnel director said. "I wonder if you could tell me whether or not he is perfectly honest."

"Honest," said the voice on the phone. "I should say he is. He has been arrested nine times for embezzlement and he was acquitted each time."

88, 427, 924, 1156, 1171, 2018, 2326.

HONOR

1085.   I had rather men should ask why no statue has been erected in my honor, than why one has been.

—Cato

490, 928, 1126, 1372.

HOPE

1086. Everything that's done in the world is done by hope. No husbandman would sow one grain of corn if he hoped not it would grow up and become seed. . .no merchant or tradesman would set himself to work if he did not hope to reap benefit thereby.

—Martin Luther

1087. In the midst of hope and anxiety, in the midst of fear and anger, believe every day that has dawned to be your last; happiness which comes unexpected will be the more welcome.

—Horace

1088. So great is my veneration for the Bible that the earlier my children begin to read it, the more confident will be my hope that they will prove useful citizens to their country, and respectable members of society.

—John Quincy Adams

1089. Be not anxious about tomorrow. Do today's duty, fight today's temptation, and do not weaken and distract yourself by looking forward to the things which you cannot see, and could not understand if you saw them.

—Charles Kingsley

1090. Hope is the best possession. None are completely wretched but those who are without hope, and few are reduced so low as that.

—William Hazlitt

1091. The setting of a great hope is like the setting of the sun. The brightness of our life is gone.

—Henry Wadsworth Longfellow

1092. Hope and patience are two sovereign remedies for all, the surest reposals, the softest cushions to lean on in adversity.

—Robert Burton

1093. The natural flights of the human mind are not from pleasure to pleasure, but from hope to hope.

—Samuel Johnson

1094. The hours we pass with happy prospects in view are more pleasing than those crowned with fruition.

—Oliver Goldsmith

1095. To the sick, while there is life there is hope.

—Cicero

1096. Hope is the pillar that holds up the world. Hope is the dream of a waking man.

—Pliny

1097. A ship ought not to be held by one anchor, nor life by a single hope.

—Epictetus

1098. He who loses hope, may then part with anything.

—William Congreve

1099. You heart's desires be with you!

—William Shakespeare

1100. Hope is the dream of a waking man.

—Diogenes

1101. The word which God has written on the brow of every man is Hope.

—Victor Hugo

1102. Hope ever urges us on, and tells us tomorrow will be better.

—Albius Tibullus

76, 420, 1005, 1026, 1032, 1105, 1451.

HUMANITY

1103. The measure of a man's humanity is the extent and intensity of his love for mankind.

—Cato

1104. Be ashamed to die until you have won some victory for humanity.

—Horace Mann

332, 399, 1067.

HUMILITY

1105. In our great pride at being the arsenal of democracy we must remember that we are also regarded as the arsenal of hope. Great leadership in such a righteous cause requires that a nation be humble—before God and its fellow men.

—General Omar N. Bradley

1106.   Men cannot be brothers if they are not humble. It is pride, no matter how legitimate it may seem to be, which provokes tension and struggles for prestige, for predominance, colonialism, egoism. That is, pride disrupts brotherhood.

—Pope Paul VI

1107.   There are on earth no actors too humble and obscure not to have a gallery; that gallery which envenoms the play by stealthy jeers, counsels or anger, amused comments, or words of perfidious compassion.

—Joseph Conrad

1108.   The President hears a hundred voices telling him that he is the greatest man in the world. He must listen carefully indeed to hear the one voice that tells him he is not.

—Harry S. Truman

1109.   In order to love people and to be loved by them, one must train oneself to gentleness, humility, the art of bearing with disagreeable people and things.

—Leo Tolstoy

1110.   One must reach the point of not caring two straws about his own status before he can wish wholly for God's kingdom, not his own, to be established.

—C. S. Lewis

1111.   Be humble and gentle in your conversation; and of few words, I charge you; but always pertinent when you speak.

—William Penn

1112.   Sometimes it's difficult to be humble—like a mortician at a $10,000 funeral.

—Will L. Ketner

1113.   No man is so insignificant as to be sure his example can do no hurt.

—Lord Clarendon

1114.   Be it ever so humble, there's no place like home.

—John Howard Payne

1115.   After crosses and losses men grow humbler and wiser.

—Benjamin Franklin

118, 1106, 1253.

HUMOR
1116.   Humor is like the curve at the end of a straight line. A punch line is the curve. And unless we can first think straight, then we cannot identify the curve. Humorless people think in wavy lines.

—Art Fettig

1117.   Humor is a humanizing agent. We will accept almost any allegation of our deficiencies—cosmetic, intellectual, virtuous—save one, the charge that we have no sense of humor.

—Steve Allen

1118.   A good laugh is sunshine in a house.

—William Makepeace Thackeray

1119.   A laugh is worth a hundred groans in any market.

—Charles Lamb

1120.   Men show their character in nothing more than in what they find laughable.

—Ancient proverb

1840.

HUNGER
1121.   The most violent appetites in all creatures are lust and hunger: the first is a perpetual call upon them to propagate their kind, the latter to preserve themselves.

—Joseph Addison

1246.

HYPOCRISY
1122.   Actors are the only honest hypocrites.

—William Hazlitt

IDEALISM

1123.   The power of ideals is incalculable. We see no power in a drop of water. But let it get into a crack in the rock and be turned to ice, and it splits the rock; turned into steam, it drives the pistons of the most powerful engines. Something has happened to it which makes active and effective the power that is latent in it.

—Albert Schweitzer

1124.   You always have a need to make ideals clear to yourself. You always have to be aware of them, even if there does not seem to be any direct path to their realization. Were there no ideals, there would be no hope.

—Andrei Sakharow

1125.   All higher motives, ideals, conceptions, sentiments in a man are of no account if they do not come forward to strengthen him for the better discharge of the duties which devolve upon him in the ordinary affairs of life.

—Henry Ward Beecher

1126.   Show me the kind of man you honor, and I will know what kind of man you are, for it shows me what your ideal of manhood is, and what kind of man you long to be.

—Thomas Carlyle

1127.   Americans have not fully realized their ideals. There are imperfections. But the ideal is right. It is everlastingly right. What our country needs is the moral power to hold to it.

—Calvin Coolidge

1128.   Be such a man, and live such a life, that if every man were such as you, and every life a life like yours, this earth would be God's Paradise.

—Phillips Brooks

1129.   As a nation we are indebted to the Book of Books for our national ideals and representative institutions. Their preservation rests in adhering to its principles.

—Herbert Hoover

1130. The activist cannot be a perfectionist. He's got to be a realist. And he ought to be an idealist.

—*Edmund Muskie*

139, 514, 793, 1902.

IDEAS

1131. Ideas are the only thing in this universe that are immortal. . .Our race has ideas, and because ideas are immortal, if they be true, we build monuments to them.

—*James A. Garfield*

1132. The word is a symbol, and its meaning is constituted by the ideas, images, and emotions, which it raises in the mind of the hearer.

—*Alfred North Whitehead*

1133. Ideas are in truth, forces. Infinite, too, is the power of personality. A union of the two always makes history.

—*Henry James*

1134. Greater than any army with banners is an idea whose time has come.

—*Victor Hugo*

345, 1150, 1446.

IDLENESS

1135. There is always hope in a man who actually and earnestly works. In idleness alone is there perpetual despair.

—*Thomas Carlyle*

1136. Work is no disgrace: it is idleness which is a disgrace.

—*Hesiod*

1137. A lady went into the shoe store and asked the manager, "Do you have any loafers?"

"Yes," he said. "We have several. I'll see if I can get one of them to wait on you."

1642, 2093, 2329.

IGNORANCE

1138.   Pollution is nothing but the resources money makers don't know can be exploited. They allow them to disperse because they have been ignorant of their value.

—Buckminster Fuller

1139.   Tim was so learned that he could name a horse in nine languages. So ignorant that he bought a cow to ride on.

—Benjamin Franklin

1140.   I envy the beasts two things—their ignorance of evil to come, and their ignorance of what is said about them.

—Voltaire

1141.   No man should so act as to make a gain out of the ignorance of another.

—Cicero

1142.   To be conscious that you are ignorant is a great step to knowledge.

—Benjamin Disraeli

1143.   Ignorance is the night of the mind, but a night without moon or star.

—Confucius

1144.   Half of the world knows not how the other half lives.

—George Herbert

1145.   To the ignorant even the words of the wise seem foolishness.

—Euripides

1146.   Everybody is ignorant, only on different subjects.

—Will Rogers

1147.   He that knows nothing doubts nothing.

—George Herbert

1256, 1259, 1263, 1286, 1382, 1861, 2155, 2227.

ILLUSIONS

1148.   Don't part with your illusions. When they are gone you may still exist, but you have ceased to live.

—Mark Twain

IMAGINATION

1149. There are no dead-ends except those that are set up by craven spirits. There are no blind alleys except those that are blocked by lazy minds. Truly, the only limitations on the horizon of tomorrow, is the vigor and vitality of our imagination today.

—Charles Luckman

1150. Most new ideas are a combination of two other ideas. Therefore, if I hope to continue to produce new ideas, then I must keep a constant flow of ideas into my subconscious mind.

—Art Fettig

1151. There are two worlds: the world that we can measure with line and rule, and the world that we feel with our hearts and imagination.

—Leigh Hunt

1152. Whatever strengthens and purifies the affections, enlarges the imagination, and adds spirit to sense, is useful.

—Shelley

1153. The human race is governed by its imagination.

—Napoleon Bonaparte

1154. Imagination is the eye of the soul.

—Joseph Joubert

1155. The little boy in the first grade had drawn a picture of a stagecoach for his art assignment. The teacher looked at it and said, "It's beautiful. It's a work of art. But, you didn't put any wheels on it. What holds it up?"

"Oh," he said after a moment's thought, "the bandits in the black hats."

2221.

IMITATION

1156. When a certain worthy died, one man copied his way of wearing his hat, another his way of carrying his sword, a third the cut of his beard, and a fourth his walk, but not one tried to be the honest man that he was.

—Georg Christoph Lichtenberg

1157.   We are more than half what we are by imitation. The great point is to choose good models and to study them with care.

—*Lord Chesterfield*

1158.   A mere copier of nature can never produce anything great.

—*Sir Joshua Reynolds*

1512.

IMMORTALITY

1159.   There is only one way to get ready for immortality, and that is to love this life and live it as bravely and faithfully, and cheerfully as we can.

—*Henry Van Dyke*

1160.   If I err in my belief that the souls of men are immortal, I err gladly, and I do not wish to lose so delightful an error.

—*Cicero*

1161.   He only is advancing in life whose heart is getting softer, whose blood warmer, whose brain quicker, whose spirit is entering into living space.

—*John Ruskin*

1162.   Life is beautiful when one sees beyond it.

—*Bonnat*

1163.   Life is the childhood of our immortality.

—*Goethe*

543, 1160.

IMPORTANCE

1164.   When you feel too important, remember, the weather determines the size of your funeral.

—*Will L. Ketner*

1165.   If you think nobody cares if you're alive, try missing a couple of car payments.

—*Earl Wilson*

IMPOSSIBLE

1166.   Man can believe the impossible, but man can never believe the improbable.

—Oscar Wilde

1193, 1646.

IMPROVEMENT

1167.   It is great, and there is no other greatness—to make one nook of God's creation more fruitful, better, more worthy of God; to make some human heart a little wiser, manlier, happier—more blessed, less accursed.

—Thomas Carlyle

791.

INACTION

1168.   Iron rusts from disuse, stagnant water loses its purity. . .even so does inaction sap the vigors of the mind.

—Leonardo da Vinci

1186.

INDEPENDENCE

1169.   I do not believe that the way to a better future lies in perpetuating our dangerous dependence on others for strategic materials. Nor do I think it lies in locking up our land and pursuing a quest for the pristine state of nature at home that can only hasten environmental havoc abroad. Nor does it lie in turning our backs on the less fortunate and saying, in effect, "I've got mine. Let's freeze things where they are." Rather, there is a "middle way" of responsible growth and responsible use of our material heritage, and it is this way we must follow if we are to attain comity among nations, amity among peoples and harmony with nature.

—David Rockefeller

1170.   We, therefore, the representatives of the United States of America, in General Congress assembled, appealing to the Supreme

Judge of the world for the rectitude of our intentions, do, in the name and by the authority of the good people of these colonies, solemnly publish and declare that these United Colonies are, and of right ought to be, free and independent states.

—Declaration of Independence

1171.   Let all your views in life be directed to a solid, however moderate, independence; without it no man can be happy, nor even honest.

—Junius

1172.   A typical example of the new generation of completely independent, self-reliant, individualistic young people, age 17, said to his father in no uncertain terms, "Dad, it's time I stood on my own two feet and made my own way. I'm going to buy a car and move into my own apartment. But, I'm never going to be able to do it on my present meager allowance."
990.

INDIFFERENCE
1173.   The worst sin toward our fellow creatures is not to hate them, but to be indifferent to them: that's the essence of inhumanity.

—George Bernard Shaw

89.

INDIVIDUALITY
1174.   I am only one, but I am one
                             I cannot do everything
                                   but I can do something.
                             And by the Grace of God
                                   what I can do, I will do.

—Edward Everett Hale

1175.   The social force in which I am interested is. . .the sole source of progress; it is American individualism.

—Herbert Hoover

1176. The worth of a State in the long run is the worth of the individuals composing it.

—John Stuart Mill

482.

INDUSTRY
1177. Temperance and industry are man's true remedies; work sharpens his appetite and temperance teaches him to control it.

—Jean-Jacques Rousseau

1016, 2055, 2319, 2326.

INFLATION
1178. Inflation has touched everything. Recently a cemetery raised the price of its burial lots and blamed it on "the high cost of living."

—Will L. Ketner

1718.

INFLUENCE
1179. You cannot antagonize and influence at the same time.

—John Knox

1180. No nobler feeling than this, of admiration for one higher than himself, dwells in the breast of man. It is to this hour, and at all hours, the vivifying influence in man's life.

—Thomas Carlyle

615, 654, 771, 1793, 1986.

INFORMATION
1181. Information's pretty thin stuff, unless mixed with experience.

—Clarence Day

1182. A little old lady called on a travel agent and asked him to work out a schedule for a four-week vacation tour. The travel agent spent several hours on a tour that included Yellowstone, Yosemite, the Grand Canyon with a week on the Mississippi River.

He took great care to write down all of the connecting flights and the bus schedules and the names of the hotels with the cost in great detail. The little lady took all of the information with her and said she would let him know.

In about an hour she was back. This time she asked for information on exactly the same tour.

"I just gave you all of that information," the travel agent said, "Why are you asking me for it again?"

"Oh," the little lady said, "This time it's for my sister. She wants to go with me."

1789, 1921, 2024.

INGRATITUDE
1183.   Everyone takes pleasure in returning small obligations; many go so far as to acknowledge moderate ones, but there is hardly anyone who does not repay great ones with ingratitude.

—Francois De La Rochefaucauld

1184.   No favor produces less permanent gratitude than the gift of liberty, especially among people who are ready to make a bad use of it.

—Livy

1185.   Earth produces nothing worse than an ungrateful man.

—Ausonius

INITIATIVE
1186.   Initiative is doing the right things without being told.

—Victor Hugo

INJURY
1187.   Write injuries in dust, benefits in marble.

—Benjamin Franklin

1260.

INJUSTICE
1188.   Whoever does injustice does injustice to himself, for to that extent he makes himself bad.

—Marcus Aurelius

INNOCENCE
1189.   I was innocent myself once, but "live and learn" is an old saying, and a true one.

—*David Garrick*

1204, 1221.

INSPIRATION
1190.   You never have to change anything you got up in the middle of the night to write.

—*Saul Bellow*

1191.   A teacher who is attempting to teach without inspiring the pupil with a desire to learn is hammering on cold iron.

—*Horace Mann*

1192.   A writer is rarely so well inspired as when he talks about himself.

—*Anatole France*

1193.   Man is so made that when anything fires his soul impossibilities vanish.

—*Jean De La Fontaine*

150.

INTELLIGENCE
1194.   Health and intellect are the two blessings of life.

—*Menander*

1195.   The soul of man is divided into three parts, intelligence, reason and passion. Intelligence and passion are possessed by other animals, but reason by man alone. . .Reason is immortal, all else mortal.

—*Pythagoras*

923.

INVENTION
1196.   If a man can write a better book, preach a better sermon, or make a better mouse-trap than his neighbor, though he builds his house in the woods, the world will make a beaten path to his door.

—*Ralph Waldo Emerson*

INVESTMENT
1197.   Search and see if there is not some place where you may invest your humanity.

—*Albert Schweitzer*

JEALOUSY
1198.   "Why did you get fired?" a man asked his friend.

"Jealousy," the man said.

"What do you mean, jealousy? Who was jealous?" his friend asked.

"The foreman," the man said. "You know what a foreman does. He stands around all day watching everybody else work. And my foreman got jealous because all of the workers thought I was the foreman."

JOKE
1199.   A joke loses everything when the joker laughs at himself.

—*Johann Christop Von Schiller*

1200.   A joke's a very serious thing.

—*Charles Churchill*

868.

JOY
1201.   You pray in your distress and in your need; would that you might pray also in the fullness of your joy in the days of abundance.

—*Kahlil Gibran*

1202.   You will give us joy and gladness if you obey what we have written through the Holy Spirit.

—*Clement of Rome*

1203.   Joy is the pizazz in your life.

—*Velma Seawell Daniels*

19, 360, 847, 1416, 1487, 2305.

JUDGMENT
1204.   If we wish to be just judges of all things, let us first persuade ourselves of this: that there is not one of us without fault; no man is

found who can acquit himself; and he who calls himself innocent does so with reference to a witness, and not to his conscience.

—Seneca

1205.   It is only an error of judgment to make a mistake, but it argues an infirmity of character to adhere to it when discovered.

—Christian Nestell Bovee

1206.   Common sense is, of all kinds, the most uncommon. It implies good judgment, sound discretion, and true and practical wisdom applied to common life.

—Tryon Edwards

1207.   You take all the experience and judgment of men over fifty out of the world, and there wouldn't be enough left to run it.

—Henry Ford

1208.   To judge human nature rightly, a man may sometimes have a very small experience, provided he has a very large heart.

—Bulwer-Lytton

1209.   The world at large does not judge us by who we are and what we know; it judges us by what we have.

—Dr. Joyce Brothers

1210.   We judge ourselves by what we feel capable of doing, while others judge us by what we have already done.

—Henry Wadsworth Longfellow

1211.   All men judge the acts of others by what they would have done themselves.

—Dionysius of Halicarnassus

1212.   I know of no way of judging the future but by the past.

—Patrick Henry

1213.   We sometimes see a fool possessed of talent, but never of judgment.

—Francois De La Rochefaucauld

1214.   The more one judges, the less one loves.

—Honore de Balzac

1215.   Judge not according to the appearance.

—John 7:24

1216.   The evidence against the defendant was overwhelming and the judge was certain he would be convicted. But when the jury foreman announced the verdict he said, "Not guilty."

"What?" shouted the judge. "What reason could the jury have for finding this person not guilty?"

"Insanity, Your Honor," said the jury foreman.

"All twelve of you?" shouted the judge.

668, 1254, 1939, 2018.

JUSTICE

1217.   The mistake of the best men through generation after generation has been the great one of thinking to help the poor by almsgiving, and by preaching of patience and hope, and by every other means, emollient or consolatory, except the one thing which God orders for them, justice.

—John Ruskin

1218.   The quality of mercy is not strain'd;
It droppeth as the gentle rain from heaven.
Upon the place beneath: it is twice bless'd;
It blesseth him that gives and him that takes;
'Tis mightiest in the mightiest. . .
And earthly power doth then show likest God's
When mercy seasons justice.

—William Shakespeare

1219.   Equal and exact justice to all men. . .freedom of religion, freedom of the press, freedom of person under the protection of the habeas corpus; and trial by juries impartially selected—these principles form the bright constellation which has gone before us.

—Thomas Jefferson

1220.   Who shall put his finger on the work of justice and say, "It is there?" Justice is like the kingdom of God: it is not without us as a fact; it is within us as a great yearning.

—George Eliot

1221.   In America, an acquittal doesn't mean you're innocent. It means that you beat the rap. My clients lose even when they win.

—F. Lee Bailey

1222.   Abraham Lincoln was as just and generous to the rich and well-born as to the poor and humble—a thing rare among politicians.

—John Hay

1223.   Our whole social life is in essence but a long, slow striving for the victory of justice over force.

—John Galsworthy

1224.   If you say what is just, men will hate you; if you say what is unjust, the gods will.

—Aristotle

1225.   If all the world were just, there would be no need of valour.

—Plutarch

1226.   Justice travels with a leaden heel, but strikes with an iron hand.

—Judge Jeremiah S. Black

1227.   I have always found that mercy bears richer fruits than strict justice.

—Abraham Lincoln

1228.   Man is unjust, but God is just; and finally justice triumphs.

—Henry Wadsworth Longfellow

1229.   Let us remember that justice must be observed even to the lowest.

—Cicero

1230.   There is no virtue so truly great and godlike as justice.

—Joseph Addison

1231.   Though justice moves slowly, it seldom fails to overtake the wicked.

—Horace

1232.   The administration of justice is the foremost pillar of Government.

—George Washington

1233.   Justice is truth in action.

—*Benjamin Disraeli*

1234.   When the defendant's name was called in court, he stood up, to everyone's amazement, in the jury box.

"What are you doing in the jury box?" the judge asked.

"I was called to serve on jury duty," he said.

"But surely you knew that was a mistake. You can't sit on the jury in your own case."

"Well," said the defendant, "I will admit I thought I was getting a lucky break."

442, 974, 1218, 1439, 1598, 1824.

KINDNESS

1235.   I expect to pass through this world but once. Any good therefore that I can do, or any kindness that I can show to any fellow creature, let me do it now. Let me not defer or neglect it, for I shall not pass this way again.

—*Stephen Grellet*

1236.   Life is short, and we have never too much time for gladdening the hearts of those who are traveling the dark journey with us. Oh, be swift to love, make haste to be kind!

—*Henri-Frederic Amiel*

1237.   Life is made up, not of great sacrifices or duties, but of little things in which smiles and kindnesses, and small obligations, given habitually, are what win and preserve the heart.

—*Sir Humphrey Davy*

1238.   He who confers a favor should at once forget it. . .To remind a man of a kindness conferred on him, and to talk of it, is little different from reproach.

—*Demosthenes*

1239.   Kind words. . . They soothe and quiet and comfort the hearer. . . We have not yet begun to use kind words in such abundance as they ought to be used.

—*Blaise Pascal*

1240.   Wherever there is a human being, there is an opportunity for kindness.

—Seneca

1241.   What wisdom can you find that is greater than kindness?

—Jean-Jacques Rousseau

481, 1365, 2006, 2100, 2326.

KNOWLEDGE

1242.   There is knowledge and knowledge: knowledge that resteth in the bare speculation of things, and knowledge that is accompanied with the grace of faith and love, which puts a man upon doing even the will of God from the heart.

—John Bunyan

1243.   Many men are stored full of unused knowledge. Like loaded guns that are never fired off, or military magazines in times of peace, they are stuffed with useless ammunition.

—Henry Ward Beecher

1244.   When you know a thing, to hold that you know it; and when you do not know a thing, to allow that you do not know it; this is knowledge.

—Confucius

1245.   Knowledge is two-fold, and consists not only in an affirmation of what is true, but in the negation of that which is false.

—Charles Caleb Colton

1246.   Knowledge is the food of the soul. Must they not be utterly unfortunate whose souls are compelled to pass through life always hungering.

—Plato

1247.   The degree of one's emotion varies inversely with one's knowledge of the facts—the less you know, the hotter you get.

—Bertrand Russell

1248.   It is far better to know something about everything than to know all about one thing. Universality is the best.

—Blaise Pascal

1249.   If a little knowledge is dangerous, where is the man who has so much as to be out of danger?

—*Thomas Henry Huxley*

1250.   It ain't what man don't know that makes him a fool, but what he does know that ain't so.

—*Josh Billings*

1251.   All things I thought I knew, but now confess, the more I know I know, I know the less.

—*Dr. John Owen*

1252.   Contemplation is to knowledge, what digestion is to food— the way to get life out of it.

—*Tryon Edwards*

1253.   Knowledge is proud that he has learn'd so much; wisdom is humble that he knows no more.

—*William Cowper*

1254.   No man can justly censure or condemn another, because indeed no man truly knows another.

—*Sir Thomas Browne*

1255.   In order that knowledge be properly digested, it must have been swallowed with a good appetite.

—*Anatole France*

1256.   And seeing ignorance is the curse of God,
         Knowledge the wing wherewith we fly to heaven.

—*William Shakespeare*

1257.   There is nothing so minute, or inconsiderable, that I would not rather know it than not.

—*Samuel Johnson*

1258.   If I cannot brag of knowing something, then I brag of not knowing it.

—*Ralph Waldo Emerson*

1259.   The first step to knowledge is to know that we are ignorant.

—*Lord David Cecil*

1260.   A life of knowledge is not often a life of injury and crime.

—*Sidney Smith*

1261.   All I know is just what I read in the papers.

—*Will Rogers*

1262.   We do not know one millionth of one percent about anything.

—*Thomas Edison*

1263.   To be conscious that you are ignorant is a great step to knowledge.

—*Benjamin Disraeli*

1264.   The greater our knowledge increases, the greater our ignorance unfolds.

—*John F. Kennedy*

1265.   There is an admiration which is the daughter of knowledge.

—*Joseph Joubert*

1266.   Knowledge is folly except grace guide it.

—*George Herbert*

1267.   Knowledge comes of learning well retained—unfruitful else.

—*Dante*

1268.   All men naturally desire knowledge.

—*Aristotle*

1269. He who knows not, and knows not that he knows not,
           is a fool, shun him.
    He who knows not, and knows that he knows not,
           is a child, teach him.
    He who knows, and knows not that he knows,
           is asleep, wake him.
    He who knows, and knows that he knows,
           is wise, follow him.

—*Author unknown*

A Few Proverbs from Here and There
1270.   The surest way to get into "Who's Who" is to know what's what.

1271.   It's not what you know, but what you do with what you know.

1272.   There are no national frontiers to learning.

1273.   A specialist knows more and more about less and less, and less and less about more and more.

1274.   The wise carry their knowledge, as they do their watches, not for display, but for their own use.

1275.   The evening meal was finished and Mother was in the kitchen cleaning up and washing dishes with the help of her ten-year old daughter.

Father and the eight-year old boy were in the living room watching television.

Suddenly from the kitchen came the noise of a crash and the sound of shattering glass.

Utter silence for ten seconds, then the little boy whispered to his father, "Mom broke a glass."

"How do you know it was your mother who broke it?" the boy's father asked.

"Because," the boy said, "Nobody said anything."

40, 61, 267, 570, 640, 1142, 1312, 1322, 1444, 1672, 1723, 1849, 1917, 2098, 2200, 2361.

LABOR

1276.   To travel hopefully is a better thing than to arrive, and the true success is to labor.

—Robert Louis Stevenson

1277.   A woman who had worked for a company for ten years without a raise in pay finally got up enough courage to talk to the boss about it. "I think I should have a raise," she said.

"I'm sorry," her boss said. "Business has been bad lately and I can't afford to pay you any more money."

"But," she said, "I'm doing the work of three people."

"Three people," the boss said with great surprise. "I didn't know that. Tell me who the other two are and I'll fire them."

111, 307, 741, 1049, 1914, 2131, 2232, 2325.

LANGUAGE

1278. Millions of Americans are being short-changed, or are short-changing themselves: they are denied the pleasure and satisfaction that come from using the language imaginatively and precisely.

—Edwin Newman

1279. Language is a city to the building of which every human being brought a stone.

—Ralph Waldo Emerson

1280. If language be not in accordance with the truth of things, affairs cannot be carried on to success.

—Confucius

381, 1495, 1972, 2298.

LAUGHTER

1281. I want someone to laugh with me, someone to be grave with me, someone to please me and help my discrimination with his or her own remark, and at times, no doubt, to admire my acuteness and penetration.

—Robert Burns

1282. A man without mirth is like a wagon without springs, in which one is caused disagreeably to jolt by every pebble over which it runs.

—Henry Ward Beecher

1283. As man laughs with those that laugh, so he weeps with those that weep; if thou wish me to weep, thou must first shed tears thyself; then thy sorrow will touch me.

—Horace

1284. By nothing do men show their character more than by the things they laugh at.

—Goethe

1285. Man is distinguished from all other creatures by the faculty of laughter.

—Joseph Addison

1118, 1575, 2150.

LAW

1286.　　Ignorance of the law excuses no man; not that all can know the law, but because 'tis an excuse everyone will plead, and no man can tell how to refute him.

—John Selden

1287.　　Two things fill the mind with ever new and increasing wonder and awe—the starry heavens above me and the moral law within me.

—Immanuel Kant

1288.　　Can anyone of you seriously say the Bill of Rights could get through Congress today? It wouldn't even get out of committee.

—F. Lee Bailey

1289.　　Delight, top-gallant delight, is to him who acknowledges no law or lord but the Lord his God, and is only patriot to heaven.

—Herman Melville

1290.　　The law is not an end in itself, nor does it provide ends. It is preeminently a means to serve what we think is right.

—William J. Brennan, Jr.

1291.　　There is no place in the highest heavens above nor in the deepest waters below where the moral law does not reign.

—Confucius

1292.　　The liberty of the individual must be thus far limited: he must not make himself a nuisance to other people.

—John Stuart Mill

1293.　　The less government we have, the better—the fewer laws, and the less confided power.

—Ralph Waldo Emerson

1294.　　The only stable state is the one in which all men are equal before the law.

—Aristotle

1295.　　Liberty is obedience to the law which one has laid down for oneself.

—Jean-Jacques Rousseau

1296. Wise men, though all laws were abolished, would lead the same lives.

—Aristophanes

88, 1021, 1221, 1493, 1842, 2130.

LAWYER

1297. The man who said "Talk is cheap," hasn't tried to hire a lawyer lately.

1298. The man who had just been found "not guilty" for breaking and entering shook hands and said to his lawyer, "You did a great job. I hope we can be friends from now on. I'll drop in on you sometime."

"That's all right with me," the lawyer said, "but be sure to make it in the daytime."

2170.

LAZINESS

1299. Sloth makes all things difficult, but industry all easy; and he that riseth late must trot all day, and shall scarce overtake his business at night; while laziness travels so slowly, that poverty soon overtakes him.

—Benjamin Franklin

1300. Laziness grows on people; it begins in cobwebs and ends in iron chains. The more business a man has to do the more he is able to accomplish, for he learns to economize his time.

—Sir Matthew Hale

LEADERSHIP

1301. The chief executive in the year 2000 will be a complex breed of corporate leader—bold not bland, forceful not fearful, courageous not cowardly. This will mean departing from the serene seas of the boardroom and plunging into the rough and tumble waters of the hearing room and the press room.

—David Rockefeller

1302.   The best executive is the one who has sense enough to pick good men to do what he wants done, and self-restraint enough to keep from meddling with them while they do it.

—Theodore Roosevelt

1303.   It is better to have a lion at the head of an army of sheep, than a sheep at the head of an army of lions.

—Daniel Defoe

1304.   If we falter in our leadership we may endanger the peace of the world, and we shall surely endanger the welfare of the nation.

—Harry S. Truman

1305.   If we are to continue to lead, then we must be prepared to pay the costs that leadership requires.

—Edmund Muskie

1306.   No man has any right to rule who is not better than the people over whom he rules.

—Cyrus, the Elder

1307.   Nations would be terrified if they knew by what small men they were ruled.

—Charles Talleyrand

1308.   Ill can he rule the great that cannot reach the small.

—Edmund Spenser

1309.   And when we think we lead we most are led.

—Lord Byron

1310.   The man of upright life is obeyed before he speaks.

—Confucius

1311.   No man can rule except one that can be ruled.

—Seneca

293, 385, 644, 683, 1105.

LEARNING

1312.   Learning acquired in youth arrests the evil of old age; and if you understand that old age has wisdom for its food, you will so conduct yourself in youth that your old age will not lack for nourishment.

—Leonardo da Vinci

1313. Merely having an open mind is nothing; the object of opening the mind, as of opening the mouth, is to shut it again on something solid.

—Gilbert Keith Chesterton

1314. Wear your learning, like your watch, in a private pocket; and do not pull it out, and strike it, merely to show that you have one.

—Lord Chesterfield

1315. Examinations are formidable even to the best prepared, for the greatest fool may ask more than the wisest man can answer.

—Charles Caleb Colton

1316. I have known ninety-five of the world's great men in my time, and of them eighty-seven were followers of the Bible.

—William E. Gladstone

1317. Though a man may become learned by another's learning, he can never be wise but by his own wisdom.

—Noah Webster

1318. The best lessons in life are learned from negative experiences that are turned into positive ones.

—Art Linkletter

1319. There is no royal road to learning; no short cut to the acquirement of any valuable art.

—Anthony Trollope

1320. As a field, however fertile, cannot be fruitful without cultivation, neither can a mind without learning.

—Cicero

1321. As we acquire more knowledge, things do not become more comprehensible but more mysterious.

—Albert Schweitzer

1322. Learning without thought is labor lost; thought without learning is perilous.

—Confucius

1323. What we have to learn to do, we learn by doing.

—Aristotle

1324.   Learning makes the wise wiser and the fool more foolish.

—*John Ray*

1325.   Learn not only by a comet's rush, but by a rose's blush.

—*Robert Browning*

1326.   There is more to life than increasing its speed.

—*Mahatma Gandhi*

1327.   Live to learn and you will learn to live.

—*Ancient proverb*

634, 650, 652, 663, 693, 1139, 1267, 1343, 1705, 2247.

LECTURE

1328.   About 4:00 A. M. on New Year's day, a highway patrolman stopped a car for speeding. "You look and smell as though you've been to a big New Year's Eve party. Where do you think you are going in such a hurry?"

"Oh," the driver said, "I'm late to a lecture. I should have been there half an hour ago."

"A lecture?" the patrolman said. "Who is going to give a lecture at this time of night?"

"My wife," the man said.

LEISURE

1329.   The men who are really busiest have the most leisure for everything.

—*James Payn*

1330.   Increased means and increased leisure are the two civilizers of man.

—*Benjamin Disraeli*

1331.   Where there is leisure for fiction there is little grief.

—*Samuel Johnson*

2234.

LIBERALS

1332. In my dictionary the first definition of a liberal is "one who is open-minded" and further on down, as a synonym they use the word "tolerant."

Self-proclaimed liberals of today do not qualify to be classified as liberals by either of these definitions. They are neither open-minded nor tolerant of those who do not agree in detail with their political views. The latter are branded as "reactionaries" or "ultra-conservatives."

Were they in truth liberal, they would entertain views not necessarily their own, and at the very least, be open-minded and tolerant rather than labeling them with derogatory adjectives.

—W. R. Hearst, Jr.

LIBERTY

1333. Men are qualified for civil liberties in exact proportion to their disposition to put moral chains on their own appetites. . . Society cannot exist unless a controlling power upon will and appetite is placed somewhere, and the less of it there is within, the more there must be without. It is ordained in the eternal constitution of things that men of intemperate minds cannot be free. Their passions forge their fetters.

—Edmund Burke

1334. I had rather munch a crust of brown bread and an onion in a corner, without ado or ceremony, than feed upon a turkey at another man's table, where I am forced to wipe my mouth every minute, and cannot sneeze or cough, or do other things that are the privileges of liberty and solitude.

—Cervantes

1335. Freedom involves the learning of a lesson, and just as each individual has to learn for himself the basic rudiments of education—how to spell, how to read, how to count, how to think—so each of us has to learn how to be free.

—Steve Allen

1336. Is life so dear or peace so sweet as to be purchased at the price of chains and slavery? Forbid it, Almighty God! I know not what course others may take, but as for me, give me liberty, or give me death.

—Patrick Henry

1337. I would rather belong to a poor nation that was free than to a rich nation that had ceased to be in love with liberty. We shall not be poor if we love liberty.

—Woodrow Wilson

1338. If liberty and equality, as is thought by some, are chiefly to be found in democracy, they will be best attained when all persons alike share in the government to the utmost.

—Aristotle

1339. Four score and seven years ago our fathers brought forth on this continent a new nation, conceived in liberty, and dedicated to the proposition that all men are created equal.

—Abraham Lincoln

1340. Eternal vigilance by the people is the price of liberty, and. . . you must pay the price if you wish to secure the blessing.

—Andrew Jackson

1341. Give me the liberty to know, to utter, and to argue freely according to conscience, above all liberties.

—John Milton

1342. All men have equal rights to liberty, to their property, and to the protection of the laws.

—Voltaire

1343. Liberty without learning is always in peril, and learning without liberty is always in vain.

—John F. Kennedy

1344. The freedom of the press is one of the great bulwarks of liberty.

—George Mason

1345. The tree of liberty grows only when watered by the blood of tyrants.

—Bertrand Barere

1346. A diffusion of knowledge is the only guardian of true liberty.

—James Madison

1347.   Liberty, when it begins to take root, is a plant of rapid growth.

—*George Washington*

560, 815, 1184, 1293, 1676, 1826, 1847, 2211, 2234, 2291.

LIFE

1348.   Life is a tender thing and is easily molested. There is always something that goes amiss. Vain vexations—vain sometimes, but always vexations. The smallest and slightest impediments are the most piercing; and as little letters most tire the eye, so do little affairs most disturb us.

—*Michel Eyquem Montaigne*

1349.   Fill my hour, ye gods, so that I may not say whilst I have done this, "Behold, also, an hour of my life is gone,"—but rather, "I have lived an hour."

—*Ralph Waldo Emerson*

1350.   Life is a child playing around your feet, a tool you hold firmly in your grip, a bench you sit down upon in the evening, in your garden.

—*Jean Anouilh*

1351.   Life has meaning only if one barters it day by day for something other than itself.

—*Saint-Exupery*

1352.   The art of living is to know how to enjoy a little and to endure much.

—*William Hazlitt*

1353.   Such is the little which remains to thee of life. Live as on a mountain.

—*Marcus Aurelius*

1354.   Life is real! Life is earnest!
             And the grave is not its goal.

—*Henry Wadsworth Longfellow*

1355.   Every man's life is a fairy-tale written by God's fingers.

—*Hans Christian Andersen*

192, 226, 363, 500, 857, 925, 1425, 1513, 1977, 2181.

LIGHT
1356.   We can easily forgive a child who is afraid of the dark; the real tragedy of life is when men are afraid of the light.

—*Plato*

1357.   There is no ill which may not be dissipated, like the dark, if you let in a stronger light upon it.

—*Henry David Thoreau*

1358.   Neither do men light a candle, and put it under a bushel, but on a candlestick, and it giveth light unto all that are in the house.

—*Matthew 5:15*

1616, 1723, 1991.

LIMITS
1359.   As we advance in life, we learn the limits of our abilities.

—*James Anthony Froude*

LISTENING
1360.   Eloquence is the art of saying things in such a way that those to whom we speak may listen to them with pleasure.

—*Blaise Pascal*

1361.   Nature has given to men one tongue, but two ears, that we may hear from others twice as much as we speak.

—*Epictetus*

1362.   The most difficult thing of all, to keep quiet and listen.

—*Ancient proverb*

1363.   From listening comes wisdom, and from speaking, repentance.

—*Ancient proverb*

505, 1053, 1108.

LOSS
1364. Prefer a loss to a dishonest gain: the one brings pain at the moment, the other for all time.

—Thomas Carlyle

874, 1115, 2241.

LOVE
1365. Far too often, our lives become overburdened with "trivialities," myriads of small projects which at the time seem so terribly important. Soon, these chores become more important than the truly important things in life—family, faith, lending a helping hand to those who are less fortunate. It takes a real effort to keep from being consumed with the daily comings and goings, but it's a goal which we all should strive toward. We should take the time to hold hands, to say a kind word now and then, to be polite and giving and sharing. More importantly, we should take the time to get back to the basics of life—love.

—Birch Bayh

1366. Without distinction, without calculation, without procrastination, love. Lavish it upon the poor, where it is very easy; especially upon the rich, who often need it most; most of all upon our equals, where it is very difficult, and for whom perhaps we each do least of all.

—Henry Drummond

1367. There is nothing holier in this life of ours than the first consciousness of love—the first fluttering of its silken wings—the first rising sound and breath of that wind which is so soon to sweep through the soul, to purify or to destroy.

—Henry Wadsworth Longfellow

1368. I have a longing for life, and I go on living in spite of logic. Though I may not believe in the order of the universe, yet I love the sticky little leaves that open in the Spring. I love the blue sky.

—Dostoevsky

1369. There is but one virtue: to help human beings to a free and beautiful life; but one sin: to do them indifferent or cruel hurt; the love of humanity is the whole of morality. This is Goodness, this is Humanism, this is the Social Conscience.

—J. William Lloyd

1370.   Alexander, Caesar, Charlemagne, and myself founded empires; but on what foundation did we rest the creations of our genius? Upon force. Jesus Christ founded an empire upon love; and at this hour millions of men would die for Him.

—Napoleon Bonaparte

1371.   The consciousness of being loved softens the keenest pang, even at the moment of parting; yes, even the eternal farewell is robbed of half its bitterness when uttered in accents that breathe love to the last sigh.

—Joseph Addison

1372.   No one else holds or has held the place in the heart of the world which Jesus holds. Other gods have been as devoutly worshipped; no other man has been so devoutly loved.

—John Knox

1373.   Love is an image of God, and not a lifeless image, but the living essence of the divine nature which beams full of all goodness.

—Martin Luther

1374.   Love is like having a fever. . . When a man is in love, he endures more than at other times; he submits to everything.

—Friedrich Nietzsche

1375.   If a single man achieves the highest kind of love, it will be sufficient to neutralize the hate of millions.

—Mahatma Gandhi

1376.   Life is to be fortified by many friendships. To love, and to be loved, is the greatest happiness of existence.

—Sydney Smith

1377.   But love the sense of right and wrong confounds,
           Strong love and proud ambition have no bounds.

—John Dryden

1378.   Things human must be known to be loved; things divine must be loved to be known.

—Blaise Pascal

1379.   Two things only a man cannot hide; that he is drunk, and that he is in love.

—Antiphanes

1380.   The first condition of human goodness is something to love; the second something to reverence.

—George Eliot

1381.   Love consists in this, that two solitudes protect and border and salute each other.

—Rainer Maria Rilke

1382.   The magic of first love is our ignorance that it can ever end.

—Benjamin Disraeli

1383.   It is not the perfect, but the imperfect, who have need of love.

—Oscar Wilde

1384.   Without love and laughter there is no joy; live amid love and laughter.

—Horace

1385.   Love is the master key that opens the gates of happiness.

—Oliver Wendell Holmes

1386.   The only way to speak the truth is to speak lovingly.

—Henry David Thoreau

1387.   We are shaped and fashioned by what we love.

—Goethe

1388.   We pardon in the degree that we love.

—Francois De La Rochefaucauld

1389.   Love means never having to say you're sorry.

—Erich Segal

1390.   The best proof of love is trust.

—Dr. Joyce Brothers

1391.   Take love away from life and you take away its pleasures.

—Moliere

1392.   Respect is what we owe; love, what we give.

—Philip James Bailey

1393.   All loves should simply be stepping stones to the love of God.

—Plato

1394.   When love and skill work together, expect a masterpiece.

—John Ruskin

1395.   If you would be loved, love and be lovable.

—Benjamin Franklin

1396.   Knowledge is strong, but love is sweet.

—Christina Georgina Rossetti

1397.   Honeyed words and flattering looks seldom speak of love.

—Confucius

1398.   Only the hands that give away the flowers of their plucking retain the fragrance thereof.

—Ancient proverb

69, 101, 126, 325, 561, 749, 826, 922, 1026, 1103, 1214, 1667, 1905, 2049, 2241.

LOYALTY

1399.   Loyalty to petrified opinion never yet broke a chain or freed a human soul.

—Mark Twain

1400.   The more I saw of foreign lands, the more I loved my own.

—Dormont De Belloy

1401.   Loyalty is the holiest good in the human heart.

—Seneca

1402.   An ounce of loyalty is worth a pound of cleverness.

—Ancient proverb

10.

LUCK

1403. It's an ill wind that blows when you leave the hairdresser.

—*Phyllis Diller*

1404. Luck affects everything; let your hook always be cast; in the stream where you least expect it, there will be a fish.

—*Ovid*

1405. I must complain the cards are ill shuffled till I have a good hand.

—*Jonathan Swift*

803.

MAIL

1406. Neither snow, nor rain, nor heat, nor gloom of night stays these couriers from the swift completion of their appointed rounds.

—*U. S. Postal Service Motto*
Herodotus 484 B.C.

MAJORITY

1407. It is my principle that the will of the majority should always prevail.

—*Thomas Jefferson*

1408. When one man with courage speaks out—you have a majority.

—*Andrew Jackson*

507, 1558.

MAN

1409. Man is the merriest species of the creation; all above or below him are serious.

—*Joseph Addison*

1410. Thou hast made him a little lower than the angels.

—*Psalms 8:5*

1916, 2095.

MANHOOD
1411.   Manhood, not scholarship, is the first aim of education.

—Ernest Thompson Seton

1412.   Men are like rivers. The water is alike in all of them; but every river is narrow in some places and wide in others; here swift and there sluggish, here clear and there turbid; cold in winter and warm in summer. The same may be said of men. Every man bears within himself the germs of every human quality, displaying all in turn; and a man can often seem unlike himself—yet still remain the same man.

—Leo Tolstoy

1413.   No man can hold another man in the gutter without remaining there himself.

—Booker T. Washington

1414.   I am a man; nothing that concerns mankind is alien to me.

—Terence

MARRIAGE
1415.   A single man has not nearly the value he would have in a state of union. He is an incomplete animal. He resembles the odd half of a pair of scissors.

—Benjamin Franklin

1416.   What joy! I have found the perfect mate. He has a marvelous sense of humor, enthusiasm for the future and a steadfast faith in God. And, oh yes, he loves me.

—Velma Seawell Daniels

1417.   Here's some advice to bachelors; marry a girl from Japan. She'll be kind, obedient, courteous and faithful.   And your mother-in-law will live in Yokohama.

—Henny Youngman

1418.   The best of all possible marriages is a seesaw in which first one, then the other partner is dominant.

—Dr. Joyce Brothers

1419.   Marriage is like panty-hose. It all depends on what you put into it.

—Phyllis Schlafly

1420. The minister had reached that part of the marriage ceremony where he says to the bride, "Do you take this man to be your lawfully wedded husband, to love, honor and obey?"

The bride stood there staring straight ahead, expressionless, and did not answer. The minister thought that perhaps she had not been listening, so he repeated the question and this time said to her, "Did you hear the question?"

"Yes," she said. "I heard you the first time, but I don't want to get involved."

1421. "I'll never forget my wedding day," Jim said. "When the time came, I couldn't find the ring. Boy, did I get an awful fright!"

"You sure did," his friend said, "and you've still got her."

1422. A lady was visiting a zoo and was being shown around by a guide. They came to a cage occupied by a kangaroo.

"Here, lady," he said, "we have a native of Australia."

"Good gracious," she said, "and to think my aunt married one of them."

361, 964, 1556.

MASTERPIECE
1423. A friend may well be reckoned the masterpiece of Nature.

—*Ralph Waldo Emerson*

MEANING
1424. "When I use a word," Humpty-Dumpty said, "it means just what I choose it to mean—neither more nor less."

—*Lewis Carroll*

1425. Life has meaning—to find its meaning is my meat and drink.

—*Robert Browning*

MEDICINE
1426. Adversity is a medicine which people are rather fond of recommending indiscriminately as a panacea for their neighbors. Like other medicines, it only agrees with certain constitutions. There are nerves which it braces, and nerves which it utterly shatters.

—*Justin McCarthy*

MEEKNESS

1427.   Now the man Moses was very meek, above all the men which were upon the face of the earth.

—Numbers 12:3

MEMORY

1428.   The life given us by nature is short; but the memory of a well-spent life is eternal.

—Cicero

1429.   Like a bird singing in the rain, let grateful memories survive in time of sorrow.

—Robert Louis Stevenson

1430.   The best way to keep good acts in memory is to refresh them with new.

—Francis Bacon

1431.   The best qualification of a prophet is to have a good memory.

—Sir George Savile

1432.   The creditor hath a better memory than the debtor.

—James Howell

1433.   Things that were hard to bear are sweet to remember.

—Seneca

1434.   Memory is the treasury of all things and their guardian.

—Cicero

1435.   Memory is the treasure-house of the mind.

—Thomas Fuller

1436.   Several women were chatting at a bridge party. One, who was suspected of being much older than she claimed, said with a sad face, "My, I hate to think of life at forty."

One of her friends couldn't miss the opportunity to say, "Why, what happened to you then?"

252, 1945.

MERCHANT

1437. The craft of the merchant is the bringing of a thing from where it abounds, to where it is costly.

—Ralph Waldo Emerson

MERCY

1438. He that turneth from the road to rescue another, turneth toward his goal; he shall arrive by the footpath of mercy; God will be his guide.

—Henry Van Dyke

1439. He reminds me of the man who murdered both his parents, and then, when sentence was about to be pronounced, pleaded for mercy on the grounds that he was an orphan.

—Abraham Lincoln

1440. Blessed are the merciful: for they shall obtain mercy.

—Matthew 5:7

350, 1227.

MERIT

1441. We can always make ourselves liked provided we act likable, but we cannot always make ourselves esteemed, no matter what our merits are.

—Nicolas Malebranche

2013, 2306.

MESSAGE

1442. The explorer heard the sound of drums coming from deep within the jungle. So in the spirit of discovery he slashed his way through the thicket in search of the drums. At last he came to a clearing where a witch doctor of a strange tribe was beating on a hollow log.

Through his native interpreter, the explorer said to the witch doctor, "Why doctor make boom-boom?"

"We need water—we want water," the witch doctor said.

"So," the explorer said, "witch doctor beat drum for rain?"

The interpreter didn't bother to translate that question. Instead, he turned to the explorer and said, "Don't be silly. He's calling the plumber."
259.

MIDDLE AGE
1443.   A great thing about Middle Age is that one is usually in charge of one's own life more completely than ever before. For the first time you're neither Acting Parent, nor Acted-Upon Child. It is invigorating to be simply an autonomous, free person, setting your own alarm clock, table, goals, standards, patterns.

—Peg Bracken

1444.   The old believe everything, the middle-aged suspect everything, the young know everything.

—Oscar Wilde

1445.   Two housewives who were close friends decided they would go back to work now that their children were grown. They went together to apply for employment at a large manufacturing plant.

They were sitting side by side as they filled in the long and detailed application form. As one of the women came to the little box marked "age" she sat staring out of the window as though in deep thought.

Her friend leaned over and whispered, "Go ahead and put it down. The longer you wait, the worse it gets."

MIND
1446.   A fresh mind keeps the body fresh. Take in the ideas of the day, drain off those of yesterday. As to the morrow, time enough to consider it when it becomes today.

—Bulwer-Lytton

1447.   Great minds have purposes, others have wishes. Little minds are tamed and subdued by misfortune; but great minds rise about them.

—Washington Irving

1448.   A chief event in life is the day in which we have encountered a mind that startled us.

—Ralph Waldo Emerson

1449.   This is a proof of a well-trained mind, to rejoice in what is good and to grieve at the opposite.

—*Cicero*

1450.   The growth of the human mind is still high adventure, in many ways the highest adventure on earth.

—*Norman Cousins*

1451.   My only hope for the world is in bringing the human mind into contact with divine revelation.

—*William E. Gladstone*

1452.   By a tranquil mind I mean nothing else than a mind well ordered.

—*Marcus Aurelius*

1453.   The mind that is anxious about the future is miserable.

—*Seneca*

1454.   No beauty's like the beauty of the mind.

—*Ancient proverb*

1455.   Danger, the spur of all great minds.

—*George Chapman*

1456.   The human mind is our fundamental resource.

—*John F. Kennedy*

1457.   'Tis the mind that makes the body rich.

—*William Shakespeare*

632, 871, 1033, 1149, 1673, 1843, 1974, 2295.

MINISTER

1458.   A minister who often helped his wife with the housework finally protested when she demanded that he help wash the dishes. "This isn't a man's job," he said.

"Yes it is," she said. "Look up II Kings 21:13."

This is what he read, ". . .and I will wipe Jerusalem as a man wipeth a dish, wiping it, and turning it upside down."

MISERY

1459.   To me the expression Ms. really means misery.

—*Phyllis Schlafly*

1570, 1882.

MISFORTUNE

1460.   The beauty of the soul shines out when a man bears with composure one heavy mischance after another, not because he does not feel them, but because he is a man of high and heroic temper.

—*Aristotle*

1461.   Mishaps are like knives, that either serve us or cut us, as we grasp them by the blade or the handle.

—*Herman Melville*

1462.   We exaggerate misfortune and happiness alike. We are never either so wretched or so happy as we say we are.

—*Honore de Balzac*

801.

MISTAKE

1463.   There is no more mistaken path to happiness than worldliness, revelry, and high life.

—*Arthur Schopenhauer*

1464.   The man who makes no mistakes does not usually make anything.

—*Bishop W. C. Magee*

1465.   Mistakes are often the best teachers.

—*James Anthony Froude*

1466.   Every man is a fool in some man's opinion.

—*Ancient proverb*

1467.   He who never made a mistake, never made a discovery.

—*Ancient proverb*

13, 424, 603, 788, 814, 1895, 2263.

MODESTY
1468. Modesty is to merit as shades to figures in a picture; giving it strength and beauty.

—*Jean De La Bruyere*

205, 1531, 1687.

MOMENT
1469. To improve the golden moment of opportunity and catch the good that is in our reach, is the great art of life.

—*Samuel Johnson*

1470. He who seizes on the moment, he is the right man.

—*Goethe*

2063, 2121, 2123.

MONEY
1471. Once when William Randolph Hearst was planning to buy a certain piece of art, he was told that it would probably go at auction at, what his agent considered a prohibitively high price, he said, "That's too bad, but I'm willing to pay anything reasonably extortionate."

—*William Randolph Hearst, Sr.*

1472. It's good to have money and the things that money can buy, but it's good, too, to check up once in a while and make sure you haven't lost the things that money can't buy.

—*George Horace Lorimer*

1473. Money is a new form of slavery, and distinguishable from the old simply by the fact that it is impersonal—that there is no human relation between master and slave.

—*Leo Tolstoy*

1474. Credit buying is much like being drunk. The buzz happens immediately, and it gives you a lift. . .The hangover comes the day after.

—*Dr. Joyce Brothers*

1475.   The darkest hour in any man's life is when he sits down to plan how to get money without earning it.

—Horace Greeley

1476.   I've got all the money I'll ever need if I die by 4 o'clock.

—Henny Youngman

1477.   If you can count your money, you don't have a billion dollars.

—J. Paul Getty

1478.   Would you know what money is, go borrow some.

—George Herbert

1479.   Never spend your money before you have it.

—Thomas Jefferson

1480.   Three generations from shirtsleeves to shirtsleeves.

—Andrew Carnegie

1481.   They who are of the opinion that money will do everything, may very well be suspected to do everything for money.

—Sir George Savile

1482.   Remember that time is money.

—Benjamin Franklin

1483.   With money in your pocket, you are wise and you are handsome and you sing well, too.

—Ancient proverb

419, 625, 774, 806, 856, 874, 1138, 2105, 2110, 2231.

MORNING

1484.   In the morning, when thou art loth to rise, have this thought ready in thy mind: "I am rising to a man's work."

—Marcus Aurelius

MOTIVATION

1485.   I think it rather fine, this necessity for the tense bracing of the will before anything worth doing can be done. I rather like it myself. I

feel it is to be the chief thing that differentiates me from the cat by the
fire.

—Arnold Bennett

1486.   The young man had just been hired as a buyer for a large department store.

"I hope you will enjoy working here," the personnel director
said.

"I'm sure I will," the young man said. "I have always thought
this was one of the greatest department stores in the country and I'll do
my best to be worthy of your confidence in hiring me."

"I am sure you will," the personnel man said. "And you'll succeed if you just keep in mind our slogan for the Buying Department."

"What is the slogan?" the young man asked.

"Buy good—or goodbye," the personnel director said.

MUSIC

1487.   Besides theology, music is the only art capable of affording
peace and joy of the heart like that induced by the study of the science of
divinity. The proof of this is that the Devil, the originator of sorrowful
anxieties and restless troubles, flees before the sound of music almost as
much as he does before the Word of God. This is why the prophets
preferred music before all the other arts, proclaiming the Word in
psalms and hymns.

—Martin Luther

1488.   A friend once asked the great composer Haydn why his
church music was always so full of gladness. He answered: "I cannot
make it otherwise. I write according to the thoughts I feel. When I think
upon my God, my heart is so full of joy that the notes dance and leap
from my pen; and since God has given me a cheerful heart, it will be
pardoned me that I serve Him with a cheerful spirit."

—Henry Van Dyke

1489.   If I had my life to live over again, I would have made a rule to
read some poetry and listen to some music at least once a week; for perhaps the parts of my brain now atrophied would thus have been kept active through use.

The loss of these tastes is a loss of happiness, and may possibly be injurious to the intellect, and more probably to the moral character, by enfeebling the emotional part of our nature.

—*Darwin*

1490.   Jazz will endure as long as people hear it through their feet instead of their brains.

—*John Philip Sousa*

1491.   What is music? This question occupied my mind for hours last night before I fell asleep. The very existence of music is wonderful, I might even say miraculous. Its domain is between thought and phenomena. Like a twilight mediator, it hovers between spirit and matter, related to both, yet differing from each. It is spirit, but it is spirit subject to the measurement of time. It is matter, but it is matter that can dispense with space.

—*Heinrich Heine*

1492.   Music is the art of the prophets, the only art that can calm the agitations of the soul; it is one of the most magnificent and delightful presents God has given us.

—*Martin Luther*

1493.   I knew a very wise man that believes that. . .if a man were permitted to make all the ballads, he need not care who should make the laws of a nation.

—*Andrew Fletcher*

1494.   There is a chord in every heart that has a sigh in it if touched aright.

—*Ouida*

1495.   Music is the only language in which you cannot say a mean or sarcastic thing.

—*John Erskine*

1496.   Men, even when alone, lighten their labor by song, however rude it may be.

—*Quintilian*

1497.   Take a music-bath once or twice a week for a few seasons, and you will find that it is to the soul what the water-bath is to the body.

—*Oliver Wendell Holmes*

1498. When I hear music I fear no danger, I am invulnerable, I see no foe. I am related to the earliest times, and to the latest.

—*Henry David Thoreau*

1499. Music is a means of giving form to our inner feelings without attaching them to events or objects in the world.

—*George Santayana*

1500. Music has been called the speech of angels; I will go further, and call it the speech of God himself.

—*Charles Kingsley*

1501. Music is a revelation; a revelation loftier than all wisdom and all philosophy.

—*Ludwig van Beethoven*

1502. Music quickens time, she quickens us to the finest enjoyment of time.

—*Thomas Mann*

1503. Who hears music, feels his solitude peopled at once.

—*Robert Browning*

1504. Music is to the mind as air is to the body.

—*Plato*

1505. Music is love in search of a word.

—*Sidney Lanier*

1506. Where words fail, music speaks.

—*Hans Christian Andersen*

2202.

NAMES

1507. The biology teacher was trying to get a little class participation, and said, "Some plants have the prefix 'dog,' For instance, there is the 'dogwood' and the 'dogviolet.' Who can name another plant prefixed by the word 'dog?' "

The smart little boy in the back called out and said, "How about 'collie flower?' "

NATIONS

1508.   I would hope that the nations of the world might say that we had built a lasting peace, based not on weapons of war but on international policies which reflect our own most precious values.

—*Jimmy Carter*

2144, 2359.

NATURE

1509.   Nature gives to every time and season some beauties of its own; and from morning to night, as from the cradle to the grave, is but a succession of changes so gentle and easy that we can scarcely mark their progress.

—*Charles Dickens*

1510.   A lake is the landscape's most beautiful and expressive feature. It is earth's eye, looking into which the beholder measures the depth of his own nature.

—*Henry David Thoreau*

1511.   Posterity will some day laugh at the foolishness of modern materialistic philosophy. The more I study nature, the more I am amazed at the Creator.

—*Louis Pasteur*

1512.   Art imitates nature as well as it can, as a pupil follows his master, thus it is a sort of grandchild of God.

—*Dante*

1513.   Nature has granted the use of life like a loan, without fixing any day for repayment.

—*Cicero*

1514.   We think according to nature; we speak according to rules; we act according to custom.

—*Francis Bacon*

1515.   To him who in the love of nature holds communion with her visible forms, she speaks a various language.

—*William Cullen Bryant*

1516.   Nature is the living, visible garment of God.

—*Goethe*

1517.   One touch of nature makes the whole world kin.

—*William Shakespeare*

222, 578, 1423, 1507, 1861, 1870, 1949, 2002.

NECESSITY
1518.   What is the strongest thing? Necessity; for it alone masters all.

—*Thales*

1519.   Necessity never made a good bargain.

—*Benjamin Franklin*

1520.   Necessity has no law.

—*St. Augustine*

NEED
1521.   The great and the little have need one of another.

—*Thomas Fuller*

1522.   The husband was going through his usual routine of complaining about his wife's spending habits. "You're reckless with our money," he said. "Every time you go to the supermarket you come home with something you don't need, like another frying pan or a food chopper or a bake dish or some other kitchen gadget. This has got to stop."

"Don't fuss at me," his wife said. "Look at all the money you waste. You buy a lot of needless junk, too."

"Tell me one thing I've bought that we don't need," he said.

"Okay," she shouted, "what about the stupid fire extinguisher you bought three years ago? We've never used it one time."

1201, 1671.

NEIGHBOR
1523.   Love your neighbor, yet pull not down your hedge.

—*George Herbert*

1524.   Love thy neighbor as thyself.

—Matthew 19:19

1877.

NEST
1525.   Every bird likes its own nest best.

—Ancient proverb

1526.   As a bird that wandereth from her nest, so is a man that wandereth from his place.

—Proverbs 27:8

NEW
1527.   There is no subject so old that something new cannot be said about it.

—Dostoevsky

70, 568.

NEWS
1528.   How beautiful upon the mountains are the feet of him that bringeth good tidings.

—Isaiah 52:7

705.

NEW TESTAMENT
1529.   The New Testament is the best Book the world has ever known or will ever know.

—Charles Dickens

NOBILITY
1530.   A noble heart, like the sun, shows its greatest countenance in its lowest estate.

—Sir Philip Sidney

1743.

NOSTALGIA
1531.   The teenager's grandfather was telling her about the way things used to be. "The girls of today are different," he said.

"How different?" she asked.

"Well," said her grandfather, "you never see a girl of today blush. It was different when I was a young fellow, they blushed in those days."

"Why, Grandfather," she asked, "what in the world did you say to them?"

OATH
1532.   It is not the oath that makes us believe the man, but the man the oath.

—Aeschylus

1659.

OBEDIENCE
1533.   All the things that God would have us to do are hard for us to do—remember that—and hence, He oftener commands us than endeavors to persuade. And if we obey God, we must disobey ourselves, wherein the hardness of obeying God consists.

—Herman Melville

597, 1202, 1310.

OBSERVATION
1534.   Observation more than books, experience rather than persons, are the prime educators.

—Amos Bronson Alcott

1919, 2225.

OCCASIONS
1535.   Occasions do not make a man either strong or weak, but they show what he is.

—Thomas A. Kempis

OFFENSE

1536.   No man lives without jostling and being jostled; in all ways he has to elbow himself through the world, giving and receiving offense.

—Thomas Carlyle

OPEN MIND

1537.   An open mind is all very well in its way, but it ought not to be so open that there is no keeping anything in or out of it.

—Samuel Butler

1313.

OPINION

1538.   I do not care what others say and think about me. But there is one man's opinion which I very much value, and that is the opinion of James Garfield.

—James A. Garfield

1539.   The man who never alters his opinion is like standing water, and breeds reptiles of the mind.

—William Blake

1540.   Free and unbiased exercise of political opinion is the only sure foundation of republican government.

—Martin Van Buren

1541.   Those who never retract their opinions love themselves more than they love the truth.

—Joseph Joubert

1542.   Every new opinion, at its starting, is precisely in a minority of one.

—Thomas Carlyle

1543.   Men will die for an opinion as soon as for anything else.

—William Hazlitt

330, 585, 789, 1399, 1795, 1856, 2018.

OPPORTUNITY

1544.   If we do not watch, we lose our opportunities; if we do not make haste, we are left behind; our best hours escape us, the worst are come.

—Seneca

1545.   The reason so many people never get anywhere in life is because when opportunity knocks, they are out in the back yard looking for four-leaf clovers.

—Walter P. Chrysler

1546.   Man's capacities have never been measured; nor are we to judge of what he can do by any precedents, so little has been tried.

—Henry David Thoreau

1547.   Next to knowing when to seize an opportunity, the most important thing in life is to know when to forego an advantage.

—Benjamin Disraeli

1548.   Freedom bestows on us the priceless gift of opportunity—if we neglect our opportunities we shall certainly lose our freedom.

—Dwight D. Eisenhower

1549.   When opportunity knocks, you'd better have your bags packed.

—Ancient proverb

1550.   A man must make his opportunity as oft as find it.

—Francis Bacon

1551.   Small opportunities are often the beginning of great enterprises.

—Demosthenes

1552.   Seize now and here the hour that is, nor trust some later day.

—Horace

1553.   Nature has given us the seed of knowledge, not knowledge itself.

—Seneca

1554.   No great man ever complains of want of opportunity.

—*Ralph Waldo Emerson*

1555.   He who seizes the right moment is the right man.

—*Goethe*

1556.   Two friends were chatting. "How are you and that new girlfriend getting along—the one you wanted to marry? Did you propose to her yet?"

"Yes, but she turned me down."

"What? Turned you down? You didn't impress her enough. Why didn't you tell her about that 90-year-old rich uncle of yours?"

"I did. Now she's my new rich aunt."

1240, 1469, 1470, 2276.

OPPOSITION
1557.   One-fifth of the people are against everything all the time.

—*John F. Kennedy*

OPPRESSION
1558.   The oppression of a majority is detestable and odious: the oppression of a minority is only by one degree less detestable and odious.

—*William Gladstone*

OPTIMISM
1559.   Because you have occasional low spells of despondence, don't despair. The sun has a sinking spell every night but it rises again all right the next morning.

—*Henry Van Dyke*

1560.   An optimist is someone who thinks that things can't get any worse. A pessimist is an optimist one day later.

—*Bob Orben*

1561.   The man was applying for a loan to finance a new business. "Can you give me a statement?" the banker asked.

"Yes," the applicant said. "I'm optimistic."

728.

ORATORY
1562. Oratory is the power of beating down your adversary's arguments and putting better in their place.

—*Samuel Johnson*

1964, 1970, 2167.

ORIGINALITY
1563. The most original modern authors are not so because they advance what is new, but simply because they know how to put what they have to say, as if it had never been said before.

—*Goethe*

1564. Originality is simply a pair of fresh eyes.

—*T. W. S. Higginson*

893, 1931, 2161.

OTHERS
1565. The bee is more honored than other animals, not because she labors, but because she labors for others.

—*St. John Chrysostom*

1566. When you rise in the morning, form a resolution to make the day a happy one to a fellow-creature.

—*Sidney Smith*

1567. He makes people pleased with him by making them first pleased with themselves.

—*Lord Chesterfield*

1568. We are interested in others when they are interested in us.

—*Publilius Syrus*

1569. Those having torches will pass them to others.

—*Plato*

1854, 2175, 2216.

PAIN
1570. Whoever is spared personal pain must feel himself called up to help in diminishing the pain of others. We must all carry our share of the misery which lies upon the world.

—*Albert Schweitzer*

1571.   A sharp knife cuts the quickest and hurts the least.

—*Katharine Hepburn*

250, 1655.

PARENTS
1572.   Parenthood remains the greatest single preserve of the amateur.

—*Alvin Toffler*

1573.   Honor thy father and mother; that thy days may be long upon the land which the Lord thy God giveth thee.

—*Exodus 20:12*

2000, 2001.

PARKING
1574.   I just solved the parking problem. I bought a parked car.

—*Henny Youngman*

PARADISE
1575.   He deserves Paradise who makes his companions laugh.

—*Mohammed*

PASSION
1576.   Anger is a vulgar passion directed to vulgar ends, and it always sinks to the level of its object.

—*Ernst von Feuchtersleben*

1577.   We may affirm absolutely that nothing great in the world has been accomplished without passion.

—*Georg Wilhelm Friedrich Hegel*

1578.   A man in a Passion rides a mad horse.

—*Benjamin Franklin*

1579.   He that shows a passion, tells his enemy where he may hit him.

—*Ancient proverb*

106, 792, 1195, 1613.

PAST

1580.   Those who cannot remember the past are condemned to repeat it.

—George Santayana

1581.   The Present is the living sum-total of the whole Past.

—Thomas Carlyle

706, 1517, 2118.

PATIENCE

1582.   No great thing is created suddenly, any more than a bunch of grapes or a fig. If you tell me that you desire a fig, I answer you that there must be time. Let it first blossom, then bear fruit, then ripen.

—Epictetus

1583.   The country is undoubtedly back of me. . .and I feel myself under bonds to it to show patience to the utmost. My chief puzzle is to determine where patience ceases to be a virtue.

—Woodrow Wilson

1584.   Endeavor to be patient in bearing the defects and infirmities of others, of what sort soever they be; for thou thyself also hast many failings which must be borne with by others.

—Thomas A. Kempis

1585.   The life of man is made up of action and endurance; the life is fruitful to the ratio in which it is laid out in noble action or in patient perseverance.

—Canon Liddon

1586.   No road is too long to the man who advances deliberately and without undue haste; and no honors are too distant for the man who prepares himself for them with patience.

—Jean De La Bruyere

1587.   How poor are they that have not patience!
What wound did ever heal but by degrees?

—William Shakespeare

1588.   Patience and diligence, like faith, remove mountains.

—William Penn

1589.   A small leak will sink a great ship.

—Thomas Fuller

1590.   Patience is bitter, but its fruit sweet.

—Jean-Jacques Rousseau

1591.   A patient man's a pattern for a king.

—Thomas Dekker

1592.   They also serve who only stand and wait.

—John Milton

1593.   Genius is eternal patience.

—Michelangelo

1594.   The greatest of human virtues is always patience.

—Cato

1595.   Patience is a necessary ingredient of genius.

—Benjamin Disraeli

1596.   Our patience will achieve more than our force.

—Edmund Burke

1597.   What cannot be removed, becomes lighter through patience.

—Horace

1598.   Forebearance is a part of justice.

—Marcus Aurelius

1599.   There is nothing so bitter, that a patient mind cannot find some solace for it.

—Seneca

1600.   Patience is the best remedy for every trouble.

—Plautus

1601.   He that is slow to anger is better than the mighty; and he that ruleth his spirit than he that taketh a city.

—Proverbs 16:32

63, 489, 729, 1092, 1217, 1626.

PATRIOTISM
1602.   Let our object be, our country, our whole country, and nothing but our country. And, by the blessing of God, may that country it-

self become a vast and splendid monument, not of oppression and terror, but of wisdom, of peace, and of liberty, upon which the world may gaze with admiration forever.

—Daniel Webster

1603.   This is the greatest country on the face of the earth. We are rich in human and material resources. Our task is to marshall our resources at home and in concert with our allies to meet the challenges of today and tomorrow.

—Henry M. Jackson

1604.   Call it mysticism if you will, I have always believed that there was some divine plan that placed this nation between the oceans to be sought out and found by those with a special kind of courage and an overabundant love of freedom.

—Ronald Reagan

1605.   Patriotism, to me, is like pregnancy. There is no such thing as being a little bit pregnant or partially patriotic: "You either is or you ain't."

—W. R. Hearst, Jr.

1606.   Breathes there the man with soul so dead,
                Who never to himself hath said,
                This is my own, my native land!

—Sir Walter Scott

1607.   The ideal state is that in which an injury done to the least of its citizens is an injury done to all.

—Solon

1608.   Our whole duty, for the present at any rate, is summed up in the motto: America first.

—Woodrow Wilson

1609.   A politician thinks of the next election; a statesman, of the next generation.

—James Freeman Clarke

90, 119, 138, 140, 1988.

PEACE

1610.   Just as, in fact there can be no peace without order so there can be no order without justice. . .Justice demands that legitmately constituted authority be respected and obeyed by its subjects; that laws be wisely made for the common good and conscientiously observed by all.

—Pope Pius XII

1611.   Try all the ways to peace and welfare you can think of, and you will find that there is no way that brings you to it except the way of Jesus.

—Matthew Arnold

1612.   The decisive desire of men is not for peace, however deep their longing, but for life in dignity, the sense of which burns, however feebly, in every man, however humble his status or obscure his place upon the earth.

—Eric Severeid

1613.   It is easier to lead men to combat and to stir up their passions than to temper them and urge them to the patient labors of peace.

—Andre Gide

1614.   Five great enemies to peace inhabit with us, namely, avarice, ambition, envy, anger, and pride. If these enemies were to be banished, we should infallibly enjoy perpetual peace.

—Petrarch

1615.   Peace, above all things, is to be desired, but blood must sometimes be spilled to obtain it on equable and lasting terms.

—Andrew Jackson

1616.   Order means light and peace, inward liberty and free command over oneself; order is power.

—Henri-Frederic Amiel

1617.   He is the happiest, be he king or peasant, who finds peace in his own home.

—Goethe

1618.   Mankind must put an end to war, or war will put an end to mankind.

—John F. Kennedy

1619. To be prepared for war is one of the most effectual means of preserving peace.

—George Washington

1620. First keep the peace within yourself, then you can also bring peace to others.

—Thoms A. Kempis

1621. To maintain peace in the future it is necessary to be prepared for war.

—Ulysses S. Grant

1622. A wise man in time of peace prepares for war.

—Horace

1623. They shall beat their swords into plough-shares, and their spears into pruning hooks; nation shall not lift up sword against nation, neither shall they learn war any more.

—Isaiah 2:4

1624. Glory to God in the highest, and on earth peace, good will toward men.

—Luke 2:14

1625. America's first goal is and always will be peace with honor. America must remain first in keeping peace in the world. We can remain first in peace only if we are never second in defense.

—Gerald R. Ford

1626. Peace is also fragile. Without prudence it can easily be shattered. Without care and patience and steadiness, its web cannot be spun.

—Edmund Muskie

1627. A couple who had lived and raised a family near a seaside resort had been putting up with visiting relatives, passing acquaintances, and their children's friends. At last they retired and bought a small home on a beautiful lake in a secluded little village.

When they were moving in, the woman said to her husband, "This is a lovely place; so beautiful and peaceful. What will we name it?"

"Name it?" her husband asked, "What do you mean?"

"Oh," his wife said, "people name their homes: like Lakeside Haven or Oaken Paradise or Whispering Breezes."

"I think that's a good idea," her husband said, "and I have the perfect name for this place, NO VACANCY."
421, 904, 1304, 2053.

PEACE OF MIND
1628.   From his cradle to his grave, a man never does a single thing which has any first and foremost object save one—to secure peace of mind, spiritual comfort for himself.

—Mark Twain

PEOPLE
1629.   The ability to deal with people is as purchasable a commodity as sugar or coffee. And I pay more for that ability than for any other under the sun.

—John D. Rockefeller

1630.   You must look into people as well as at them.

—Lord Chesterfield

1829, 1947.

PERFECTION
1631.   People who wait for a perfect time to do something and who insist upon perfection as a minimum goal invariably postpone a project until paralysis sets in and nothing is accomplished.

—Art Linkletter

1632.   The true work of art is but a shadow of the divine perfection.

—Michelangelo

1633.   One of the world's greatest engravers decided to try his hand at counterfeiting. He made up his mind that he would make a perfect copy of a $50 bill. He spent weeks working on the plates. Every line, every dot was copied exactly. Then, he printed a million dollars' worth. But, the first time he tried to cash one, he was arrested by a Secret Service agent.

He said to the agent, "I am one of the world's greatest engravers.

I'm sure nobody can tell the difference between the original and my copy. How could you tell that my bills were counterfeit?''

"It was easy,'' the agent said. ''You made a perfect copy of a counterfeit $50 bill.''
851.

PERFORMANCE
1634.   Attempt only what you are able to perform.

—Cato

2011.

PERSEVERANCE
1635.   It is not he that enters upon any career, or starts in any race, but he that runs well and perseveringly that gains the plaudits of others, or the approval of his own conscience.

—Alexander Campbell

1636.   If you wish success in life, make perseverance your bosom friend, experience your wise counsellor, caution your elder brother, and hope your guardian genius.

—Joseph Addison

1637.   Life is not easy for any of us. But what of that? We must have perseverance and above all confidence in ourselves.

—Marie Curie

1638.   'Tis known by the name of perseverance in a good cause—and of obstinacy in a bad one.

—Laurence Sterne

1639.   Courage and perseverance have a magical talisman, before which difficulties disappear and obstacles vanish into air.

—John Quincy Adams

111, 497.

PERSISTENCE
1640.   Get up when you fall down. We all fall down, but the biographies of those whom the world calls ''successful'' reveal that they get

up when they fall down. Sometimes more than once they've had to pick themselves up and dust themselves off and keep on keeping on.

—Paul Harvey

1641.   Do you remember how small grains of sand are? Yet if enough are placed in a ship, they sink it.

—St. Augustine

1642.   Everything cometh to him who waiteth, so long as he who waiteth worketh like hell while he waiteth.

—Allen Drury

1643.   Nothing is so difficult but that it may be found out by seeking.

—Terence

1644.   The fall of dropping water wears away the stone.

—Lucretius

1645.   The dog that trots about finds a bone.

—George Borrow

1646.   Few things are impossible to diligence and skill.

—Samuel Johnson

1647.   Plodding wins the race.

—Aesop

1648.   The newspaperman was interviewing the old man on his hundredth birthday. "To what do you attribute your longevity?" the newspaperman asked.

"Well, now, young fellow," the old man said, "I was a golfer. I played 18 holes of golf every day until I was 80 and since then I have played nine holes every day. That's what keeps me going."

"But," said the newspaperman, "I had an uncle who played golf every day and he died when he was 62. How do you account for that?"

"He just didn't keep it up long enough," the old golfer said.

2012, 2073.

PERSPECTIVE
1649.   Genius is one percent inspiration and ninety-nine percent perspiration.

—Thomas Edison

PERSUASION

1650.   Rhetoric is the art of leading souls by persuasion.

—Plato

794.

PHILOSOPHY

1651.   True philosophy is that which makes us to ourselves and to all about us, better; and at the same time, more content, patient, calm, and more ready for all decent and pure enjoyment.

—Lavater

1652.   A man who leaves home to mend himself and others is a philosopher; but he who goes from country to country guided by the blind impulse of curiosity, is only a vagabond.

—Oliver Goldsmith

1653.   Wonder is the foundation of all philosophy.

—Michel Eyquem Montaigne

686, 1778.

PLAN

1654.   He who every morning plans the transactions of the day, and follows out that plan, carries a thread that will guide him through the labyrinth of the most busy life. The orderly arrangement of his time is like a ray of light which darts itself through all his occupations. But where no plan is laid, where the disposal of time is surrendered merely to the chance of incidents, all things lie huddled together in one chaos, which admits of neither distribution nor review.

—Victor Hugo

22.

PLEASURE

1655.   All fits of pleasure are balanced by an equal degree of pain or languor; 'tis like spending this year, part of the next year's revenue.

—Jonathan Swift

1656.   The greatest of all pleasures is to give pleasure to one we love.

—Jean De Boufflers

1657.   There is more pleasure in loving, than in being loved.

—*Thomas Fuller*

1658.   Who pleasure gives, shall joy receive.

—*Benjamin Franklin*

260, 1034, 1093, 1360, 1764, 2130.

PLEDGE
1659.   We mutually pledge to each other our lives, our fortunes, and our sacred honor.

—*Thomas Jefferson*

PLIABLE
1660.   Be ever soft and pliable like a reed, not hard and unbending like a cedar.

—*The Talmud*

POETRY
1661.   Poetry should please by a fine excess and not by singularity. It should strike the reader as a wording of his own highest thoughts, and appear almost as a remembrance.

—*John Keats*

1662.   Poetry makes immortal all that is best and most beautiful in the world.

—*Shelley*

886, 1489.

POLITENESS
1663.   Politeness is the ritual of society, as prayers are of the church.

—*Ralph Waldo Emerson*

1664.   Politeness costs nothing, and gains everything.

—*Lady Mary Wortley Montagu*

POLITICIAN
1665.   After a hard campaign for Governor, the politician sat in his campaign headquarters watching the results on television. When it be-

came obvious that he had lost, a young and pretty little newspaper woman came to him with her notebook and pencil in hand and said, "What are your plans, now?"

"I appreciate you asking me" he said. "I don't have anything planned. What are you doing this evening?"
235, 1609, 1695.

POLITICS
1666. There are only two kinds of politics. . .the politics of fear and the politics of trust. One says: you are encircled by monstrous dangers. . .The other says: the world is a baffling and hazardous place, but it can be shaped to the will of men.

—Edmund Muskie

1667. Given the usual pronouncements by politicians and the unrelenting dullness of most political discourse, is it any wonder that so few Americans take the trouble even to vote?

—Edwin Newman

1668. We should not tolerate a packed jury which is to decide on the fate of a single man, but we are content to leave the life of the nation at the mercy of a packed convention.

—James Russell Lowell

POSSESSIONS
1669. Possessions, outward success, publicity, luxury—to me these have always been contemptible. I believe that a simple and unassuming manner of life is best for the body and the mind.

—Albert Einstein

395, 898.

POSTERITY
1670. The Constitution of the United States was made not merely for the generation that then existed, but for posterity—unlimited, undefined, endless, perpetual posterity.

—Henry Clay

1511.

POWER

1671. The great need of the world today is the spiritual power necessary for the overthrow of evil, for the establishment of righteousness, and for the ushering in of the era of perpetual peace; and that spiritual power begins in the surrender of the individual to God. It commences with obedience to the first commandment.

—William Jennings Bryan

1672. Knowledge, in truth, is the great sun in the firmament. Life and power are scattered with all its beams.

—Daniel Webster

1673. There are but two powers in the world, the sword and the mind. In the long run the sword is always beaten by the mind.

—Napoleon Bonaparte

1674. Talent is that which is in a man's power! Genius is that in whose power a man is.

—James Russell Lowell

1675. Eloquence is the power to translate a truth into language perfectly intelligible to the person to whom you speak.

—Ralph Waldo Emerson

1676. The love of liberty is the love of others; the love of power is the love of ourselves.

—William Hazlitt

1677. Everyone loves power, even if they do not know what to do with it.

—Benjamin Disraeli

1678. You can never have a great or a less dominion than that over yourself.

—Leonardo da Vinci

1679. Every addition to true knowledge is an addition to human power.

—Horace Mann

1680. Only he deserves power who every day justifies it.

—Dag Hammarskjold

1681. Threats without power are like powder without ball.

—*Nathan Bailey*

1682. Knowledge is power.

—*Francis Bacon*

245, 341, 607, 813, 1009, 1123, 1701, 1961, 2036, 2234.

PRACTICE

1683. An ounce of practice is worth a pound of precept.

—*Richard D. Blackmore*

1684. Practice makes perfect, as often I've read.

—*Christopher Anstey*

51.

PRAISE

1685. It is a rare and, when just, a noble thing to praise. Few people praise enough. All ought to praise whenever they see something that can be praised. Once in a century a man may be ruined, or for the time made insufferable by praise, but surely once in a minute something generous dies for want of it. I once heard someone say, "The occupation of heaven is praise."

—*John Masefield*

1686. How a little praise warms out of a man the good that is in him, as the sneer of contempt which he feels is unjust chills the order to excel.

—*Bulwer-Lytton*

1687. Praise has different effects, according to the mind it meets with; it makes a wise man modest, but a fool more arrogant, turning his weak brain giddy.

—*Owen Feltham*

1688. It takes a good deal of grace to be able to bear praise. . .praise soon suggests pride, and is there not an unmixed good.

—*Charles Spurgeon*

1689.   Those who are greedy of praise prove that they are poor in merit.

—Plutarch

1690.   By low ambition and the thirst of praise.

—William Cowper

1691.   Let another man praise thee, and not thine own mouth; a stranger, and not thine own lips.

—Proverbs 27:2

320, 1085, 1772.

PRAYER

1692.   Give us, O Lord, steadfast hearts, which no unworthy thought can drag downwards; unconquered hearts, which no tribulation can wear out; upright hearts, which no unworthy purpose may tempt aside. Bestow upon us also, O Lord our God, understanding to know Thee, diligence to seek Thee, wisdom to find Thee, and a faithfulness that may finally embrace Thee.

—St. Thomas Aquinas

1693.   O heavenly Father, who hast filled the world with beauty: open, we beseech Thee, our eyes to behold Thy gracious hand in all Thy works; that rejoicing in Thy whole creation, we may learn to serve Thee with gladness.

—Book of Common Prayer

1694.   Why, if I did not feel in my inmost soul the living light and love of that Christian faith, my works. . .would be the works of a liar and an ape. My art is my prayer.

—Richard Wagner

1695.   I think the Chaplain of the Senate has the right idea. He prays when each session begins and gives thanks when it ends.

—Bob Orben

1696.   I used to pray that God would do this or that. Now I pray that God will make His will known to me.

—Mme. Chiang Kai-Shek

1697. O Holy Spirit, descend plentifully into my heart. Enlighten the dark corners of this neglected dwelling and scatter there Thy cheerful beams.

—St. Augustine

1698. Certain thoughts are prayers. There are moments when, whatever be the attitude of the body, the soul is on its knees.

—Victor Hugo

1699. There is a time to pray and a time to fight. This is the time to fight.

—John Peter Gabriel Muhlenberg

1700. Here, Lord, is my life. I place it on the altar today. Use it as You will.

—Albert Schweitzer

1701. I have found the greatest power in the world is the power of prayer.

—Cecil B. DeMille

1702. More things are wrought by prayer
Than this world dreams of.

—Alfred, Lord Tennyson

1703. Who rises from Prayer a better man, his prayer is answered.

—George Meredith

1704. A grateful thought toward heaven is of itself a prayer.

—Gotthold Lessing

1705. No man ever prayed heartily without learning something.

—Ralph Waldo Emerson

1706. The fewer the words the better the prayer.

—Martin Luther

1707. Ask, and it shall be given you; seek, and ye shall find, knock, and it shall be opened unto you.

—Matthew 7:7

633.

PREJUDICE

1708.   I am, in plainer words, a bundle of prejudice—made up of likings and dislikings.

—*Charles Lamb*

1709.   Prejudice is the child of ignorance.

—*William Hazlitt*

1710.   I can promise to be upright but not to be unprejudiced.

—*Goethe*

1746.

PREPARATION

1711.   The man who is prepared has his battle half fought.

—*Cervantes*

1712.   A man spoke to a fellow sitting next to him at a bar. "What do you do for a living?"

"I work for the carnival. I'm a human cannonball."

"Hey, I never met a human cannonball before. I'll bet your job takes a lot of courage."

"It sure does," the cannonball said, "That's why I'm here right now. I have to get loaded before I can do it."

185, 550, 1169, 1549, 1586, 1619, 1622.

PRESENT

1713.   There is no moment like the present. The man who will not execute his resolutions when they are fresh upon him can have no hope from them afterwards: they will be dissipated, lost, and perish in the hurry and scurry of the world, or sunk in the slough of indolence.

—*Maria Edgeworth*

1714.   Use well the moment; what the hour
Brings for thy use is in thy power;
And what thou best canst understand
Is just the thing lies nearest to thy hand.

—*Goethe*

1715.   Look not mournfully into the Past. It comes not back again. Wisely improve the Present. It is thine. Go forth to meet the shadowy Future, without Fear, and with a manly heart.

—Henry Wadsworth Longfellow

1716.   One of the illusions is that the present hour is not the critical, decisive hour. Write it on your heart that every day is the best day in the year.

—Ralph Waldo Emerson

1717.   Duty and today are ours; results and futurity belong to God.

—Horace Greeley

2128.

PRESSURE
1718.   He who is of a calm and happy nature will hardly feel the pressure of age, but to him who is of an opposite disposition youth and age are equally a burden.

—Plato

PRETENSE
1719.   We are only vulnerable and ridiculous through our pretensions.

—Madame De Giradin

PRICE
1720.   A woman stopped at a roadside and bought some tomatoes and cucumbers and bell peppers. When the bill was added the man said, "That will be $4.60."

   "My, things are getting high," the woman said. "But, I guess I'll just have to pay it. Tell me, did you raise these vegetables yourself?"

   "Yes, I did," the farmer said. "But it's on account of inflation. Yesterday they would have cost you only $4.35."

856, 952, 1340, 1471, 2198, 2201.

PRIDE

1721.   It is well for a man to respect his own vocation whatever it is, and to think himself bound to uphold it, and to claim for it the respect it deserves.

—Charles Dickens

1722.   There is such a thing as a man being too proud to fight.

—Woodrow Wilson

1723.   To be proud of knowledge is to be blind with light.

—Benjamin Franklin

1106, 1253.

PRINCIPLES

1724.   He who shall introduce into public affairs the principles of Christ will change the face of the world.

—Benjamin Franklin

1725.   Men and times change—but principles—never.

—Grover Cleveland

236, 1129, 1407.

PRIZE

1726.   It is they who have the will to act who oftenest win the prizes.

—Xerxes

PROBLEMS

1727.   Snow and adolescence are the only problems that disappear if you ignore them long enough.

—Earl Wilson

195, 868, 2140.

PROCRASTINATION

1728.   While we are procrastinating, life speeds by.

—Seneca

2129.

PROFESSIONAL

1729.   A pro is a man who can do his best at a time when he doesn't particularly feel like it.

—Alistair Cooke

1730.   I am all for professionals. They have created the modern world—but I don't hold that against them.

—John W. Gardner

PROGRESS

1731.   The divine right of kings may have been a plea for feeble tyrants, but the divine right of government is the keystone of human progress, and without it government sinks into police and a nation into a mob.

—Benjamin Disraeli

1732.   Let each of us remember that he will make progress in all spiritual things only insofar as he rids himself of self-love, self-will, self-interest.

—St. Ignatius of Loyola

1733.   You can say this for these ready-mixes—the next generation isn't going to have any trouble making pies exactly like mother used to make.

—Earl Wilson

1734.   It is hard to find a man who has studied for three years without making some progress in virtue.

—Confucius

1735.   Would you realize what Revolution is, call it Progress, and would you realize what Progress is, call it Tomorrow.

—Victor Hugo

1736.   The United States has to move very fast to even stand still.

—John F. Kennedy

1737.   Progress, therefore, is not an accident, but a necessity.

—Herbert Spencer

1738.   Life means progress, and progress means suffering.

—Hendrik Willem Van Loon

1175.

PROMISE

1739.   The Christian cannot promise to do or not to do a given thing at a given time, for he cannot know what the law of love, which is the commanding principle of his life, will demand of him at that time.

—Leo Tolstoy

1740.   A man and his wife were swimming together in the surf at a well-known resort in the Bahamas. Suddenly the fin of a shark appeared nearby and the life guard shouted, "Shark, shark, everybody out of the water."

The woman's husband headed for shore in panic, leaving her to struggle toward the beach as best she could. When she finally joined him on dry land she screamed at him, "That was a terrible thing to do, deserting me like that. I was scared to death. Don't you remember when we were married you told me you would face death for me?"

"Yes," her husband said. "And I would, too. But that shark wasn't dead."

PROPHECY

1741.   I shall always consider the best guesser the best prophet.

—Cicero

1742.   A prophet is not without honour, save in his own country, and in his own house.

—Matthew 13:57

1431.

PROSPERITY

1743.   Prosperity has this property: It puffs up narrow souls, makes them imagine themselves high and mighty, and leads them to look down upon the world with contempt; but a truly noble spirit appears greatest in distress; and then becomes more bright and conspicuous.

—Plutarch

1744.   Friendship makes prosperity brighter, while it lightens adversity by sharing its griefs and anxieties.

—Cicero

1745.   Prosperity is a great teacher; adversity is a greater. Possession pampers the mind; privation trains and strengthens it.

—*William Hazlitt*

338, 848, 853.

PROTECTION
1746.   Knowledge—that is, education in its true sense—is our best protection against unreasoning prejudice and panic-making fear, whether engendered by special interest, illiberal minorities, or panic-stricken leaders.

—*Franklin D. Roosevelt*

1342.

PUBLIC OFFICE
1747.   Public officers are the servants and agents of the people, to execute the laws which the people have made.

—*Grover Cleveland*

1748.   I shall never ask, never refuse, nor ever resign an office.

—*Benjamin Franklin*

PUNISHMENT
1749.   The Bishop gave up golf during Lent. But, the sun came out the Saturday before Easter and he couldn't resist the temptation to "hit a few practice shots." Soon he was half way around the course, playing by himself. A little Angel noticed him and said to the Lord, "Hey, Lord, look down there at the Bishop. He promised to give up golf during Lent and he broke his vow. You should punish him."

"You are right," the Lord said. "I'll do it. Watch me."

While the little Angel looked on, the Bishop teed off on a 450 yard dog-leg and made a hole-in-one.

"Excuse me, Lord," the little Angel said, "But, do you call that punishment?"

"I certainly do," the Lord said. "The Bishop has just made the greatest shot in the history of golf—and he can't tell anybody about it."

974, 1816, 2067.

PURITY
1750. The stream is always purer at its source.

—Blaise Pa cal

1751. Blessed are the pure in heart; for they shall see God.

—Matthew 5:8

PURPOSE
1752. We throw all our attention on the utterly idle question whether A has done as well as B, when the only question is whether A has done as well as he could.

—William Graham Sumner

1753. Firmness of purpose is one of the most necessary sinews of character, and one of the best instruments of success. Without it genius wastes its efforts in a maze of inconsistencies.

—Lord Chesterfield

1754. Live every day of your life as though you expected to live forever.

—Douglas MacArthur

1755. The secret of success is constancy of purpose.

—Benjamin Disraeli

42, 219, 617, 1070, 1447, 1825, 1973.

QUESTION
1756. In everything that we do, we should ask ourselves what is best for:

> First, our God
> Second, the Free World
> Third, our Nation
> Fourth, our Organization
> Fifth, our Fellows and Family
> Finally, Ourselves

—Lt. Gen. John Peter Flynn

1757. There is but one question, and that is the will of God. That settles all other questions.

—William Gladstone

1758.   The big game hunter was telling his adventures to a group of school children during their show-and-tell period. In describing some of his exciting experiences in Africa, he said, "One night I remember being awakened by a great roaring noise. I jumped up and grabbed my gun which I always kept loaded at the foot of my cot. I rushed out and killed a huge lion in my pajamas."

At the close of his presentation he asked if there were any questions.

"Yes," said a little girl on the front row, "how did the lion get into your pajamas?"
1021.

QUIET
1759.   When God intended to reveal any future events or high notions to His prophets, He then carried them either to the deserts or the seashore, that having so separated them from amidst the press of people and business, and the cares of the world, He might settle their mind in a quiet repose, and there make them fit for revelation.

—Izaak Walton

1927.

QUOTATIONS
1760.   Nothing gives an author so much pleasure as to find his works respectfully quoted by other learned authors.

—Benjamin Franklin

2264.

REACH
1761.   Ah, but a man's reach should exceed his grasp
          Or what's a Heaven for?

—Robert Browning

READING
1762.   Reading is to the mind what exercise is to the body. As by the one, health is preserved, strengthened and invigorated: by the other,

virtue (which is the health of the mind) is kept alive, cherished and confirmed.

—Joseph Addison

1763.   Let us tenderly and kindly cherish. . .the means of knowledge. Let us dare to read, think, speak and write.

—John Adams

1764.   The habit of reading is the only enjoyment in which there is no alloy; it lasts when all other pleasures fade.

—Anthony Trollope

1765.   Read not to contradict and confute, nor to believe and take for granted, nor to find talk and discourse—but to weigh and consider.

—Francis Bacon

1766.   I'm not a speed reader. I'm a speed understander.

—Isaac Asimov

44, 77, 266, 277, 634, 2094, 2182.

REALITY
1767.   The only real people are the people who never existed.

—Oscar Wilde

1130.

REASON
1768.   Reason elevates our thoughts as high as the stars, and leads us through the vast space of this mighty fabric; yet it comes far short of the real extent of our corporeal being.

—Samuel Johnson

1769.   Reason is a light that God has kindled in the soul.

—Aristotle

1770.   We no longer depend for Salvation upon either a man or a book. Men help us; books help us; but back of all stands our divine reason.

—Charles W. Eliot

1771.   Reason, the choicest gift bestowed by heaven.

—Sophocles

1772. The most agreeable recompense which we can receive for things which we have done is to see them known, to have them applauded with praises that honor us.

—*Moliere*

227, 572, 721, 1195, 1937, 2163.

RECOGNITION
1773. A young mother had put her two children to bed. She then changed into an oversized sweatshirt that belonged to her husband and put on a pair of his blue jeans and proceeded to shampoo her hair.

During the time she was washing her hair, she could hear the children getting louder and louder and wilder and wilder.

The moment she finished she wrapped a bath towel around her head and rushed into the children's bedroom and screamed at them, "You quiet down. This instant. And I mean it."

They did. A few minutes after she had turned out the light and left the room, the two-year-old whispered to his older brother, "Who was that?"

956, 1085, 1812, 2272.

REFORM
1774. We are reformers in Spring and Summer. In Autumn and Winter we stand by the old. Reformers in the morning; conservatives at night. Reform is affirmative; conservatism, negative. Conservatism goes for comfort; reform for truth.

—*Ralph Waldo Emerson*

1775. Be not the first by whom the new are tried,
Nor yet the last to lay the old aside.

—*Alexander Pope*

688, 1017.

RELIEF
1776. There is a certain relief in change, even though it be from bad to worse; as I have found in traveling in a stage-coach, that it is often a comfort to shift one's position and be bruised in a new place.

—*Washington Irving*

1777.   To pity distress is but human: to relieve it is Godlike.

—Horace Mann

RELIGION
1778.   A little philosophy inclineth a man's mind to atheism, but depth in philosophy bringeth man's mind about to religion.

—Francis Bacon

1779.   When Christ came into my life, I came about like a well-handed ship.

—Robert Louis Stevenson

1780.   A woman went into the Post Office to buy stamps to mail her daughter's wedding invitations.

"I'd like two hundred stamps, please," she said to the clerk.

"What denomination?" he asked.

"Oh, dear," she said. "I didn't know it had come to that. I suppose it would be best if I split them. Give me one hundred Baptist and one hundred Presbyterian."

228, 248.

REPAIR
1781.   When the man answered the phone, the voice on the other end said, "Mr. Jones, this is Les Henderson's garage. Your wife just drove into the garage a few minutes ago to have a new air conditioner hose installed and I was calling to ask if you are going to pay for. . ."

"Yes," Jones said, interrupting the caller. "I'll pay for the hose. Just send me the bill."

"Oh," the voice said, "I'm not calling about the air conditioner hose. Your wife already paid me for that. I want to know if you intend to pay for the side of my garage that she knocked out when she drove into it?"

REPENTANCE
1782.   It is neither Christian nor Military to nag a repentant sinner to his grave.

—Lt. Gen. John Peter Flynn

REPUTATION

1783. The great difficulty is first to win reputation; the next to keep it while you live; and the next to preserve it after you die.

—Benjamin Robert Haydon

1784. It is pleasing to be pointed at with the finger and to have it said, "There goes the man."

—Persius

1785. Conscience and reputation are two things. Conscience is due to yourself, reputation to your neighbor.

—St. Augustine

1786. The show *Oh, Calcutta!* is the kind of thing that could give pornography a bad name.

—Clive Barnes

1787. It is better to lose an eye than one's reputation.

—Ancient proverb

1788. A good name is rather to be chosen than great riches.

—Proverbs 22:1

1508, 1801.

RESEARCH

1789. Knowledge is of two kinds. We know a subject ourselves, or we know where we can find information upon it.

—Samuel Johnson

RESISTANCE

1790. The spirit of resistance to government is so valuable on certain occasions that I wish it to be always kept alive.

—Thomas Jefferson

RESOLUTIONS

1791. Great actions are not always true sons of great and mighty resolutions.

—Samuel Butler

1566.

RESOURCES

1792.   Few men during their lifetime come anywhere near exhausting the resources dwelling within them. There are deep wells of strength that are never used.

—Admiral Richard E. Byrd

1138, 1456.

RESPECT

1793.   Go into the street, and give one man a lecture on morality, and another a shilling, and see which will respect you most.

—Samuel Johnson

1794.   To have a respect for ourselves guides our morals; and to have a deference for others governs our manners.

—Laurence Sterne

1795.   I never make the mistake of arguing with people for whose opinions I have no respect.

—Edward Gibbon

1796.   He removes the greatest ornament of friendship, who takes away from it respect.

—Cicero

340, 1392, 1721.

RESPONSIBILITY

1797.   *Responsibility,* n. A detachable burden easily shifted to the shoulders of God, Fortune, Luck or one's neighbor. In the days of astrology it was customary to unload it upon a star.

—Ambrose Bierce

1798.   A chief is a man who assumes responsibility. He says, "I was beaten." He does not say, "My men were beaten."

—Saint-Exupery

1799.   Many times a day I realize how much my own outer and inner life is built upon the labors of my fellowmen, both living and dead, and how earnestly I must exert myself in order to give in return as much as I have received.

—Albert Einstein

1800. The most important thought I ever had was that of my individual responsibility to God.

—Daniel Webster

1801. We are ourselves responsible for the good and the ill that is said of us.

—Philip II of Macedonia

1802. Great responsibility must go hand in hand with great privileges.

—Theodore Roosevelt

1803. The price of greatness is responsibility.

—Sir Winston Churchill

1804. The buck stops here.

—Harry S. Truman

2, 618, 1174.

RESTRAINT
1805. Certain bounds must be observed in our amusements, and we must be careful not to carry things too far and, swept by our passions, lapse into shameful excess.

—Cicero

REST
1806. There is no rest for a messenger till the message is delivered.

—Joseph Conrad

RESULTS
1807. Things turn out best for the people who make the best of the way things turn out.

—Art Linkletter

1808. The wheel that squeaks the loudest is the one that gets the grease.

—Josh Billings

1809. The result proves the wisdom of the act.

—Ovid

REVERENCE

1810.   Reverence for parents—this standeth written third among the statutes of Justice to whom supreme honor is due.

—*Aeschylus*

REVOLUTION

1811.   When you start a Bible movement, it means revolution—a quiet revolution against darkness and crime.

—*Toyohiko Kagawa*

822.

REWARD

1812.   The highest reward for man's toil is not what he "gets for it," but what he "becomes by it."

—*John Ruskin*

1813.   Friends are the end and the reward of life. They keep us worthy of ourselves.

—*Robert Louis Stevenson*

1814.   The reward of a thing well done, is to have done it.

—*Ralph Waldo Emerson*

1815.   The consciousness of having done a splendid action is itself a sufficient reward.

—*Cicero*

1816.   There are in nature neither rewards nor punishment—there are consequences.

—*Robert Ingersoll*

2022.

RICHES

1817.   The difference between a rich man and a poor man, is this—the former eats when he pleases, and the latter when he can get it.

—*Sir Walter Raleigh*

1818.   A miser grows rich by seeming poor; an extravagant man grows poor by seeming rich.

—*William Shenstone*

1819.   Riches are not from an abundance of worldly goods, but from a contented mind.

—*Mohammed*

1820.   How men toil to lay up riches which they never enjoy.

—*William Jay*

1821.   Riches are chiefly good because they give us time.

—*Charles Lamb*

1822.   Who lives content with little possesses everything.

—*Nicholas Boileau*

692, 717, 831, 2009, 2237.

RIGHT

1823.   I painfully reflect that in almost every political controversy of the last fifty years the leisured classes, the educated classes, the wealthy classes, the titled classes, have been in the wrong. The common people—the toilers, the men of uncommon sense—these have been responsible for nearly all of the social reform measures which the world accepts today.

—*William Gladstone*

1824.   May we pursue the right, without self-righteousness. May we know unity, without conformity. May we grow in strength, without pride in self. May we, in all our dealings with all people of the earth, ever speak truth and serve justice.

—*Dwight D. Eisenhower*

1825.   Right action follows right purpose. We may not at all times be able to divine the future. . .but if our aims are high and unselfish, somehow and in some way the right end will be reached.

—*William McKinley*

1826.   Liberty does not consist in mere declarations of the rights of man. It consists in the translation of those declarations into definite actions.

—*Woodrow Wilson*

1827.   There is one right which man is generally thought to possess, which I am confident he neither does nor can possess—the right to subsistence when his labor will not fairly purchase it.

—*Thomas R. Malthus*

1828.   Wherever there is a human being, I see God-given rights inherent in that being, whatever may be the sex or complexion.

—*William Lloyd Garrison*

1829.   The basis of our political system is the right of the people to make and to alter their constitutions of government.

—*George Washington*

1830.   Never maintain an argument with heat and clamour, though you think or know yourself to be in the right.

—*Lord Chesterfield*

1831.   The true civilization is where every man gives to every other every right that he claims for himself.

—*Robert Ingersoll*

1832.   I prefer to do right and get no thanks, rather than to do wrong and get no punishment.

—*Cato*

1833.   We must support our rights or lose our character, and with it, perhaps, our liberties.

—*James Monroe*

1834.   It may make a difference to all eternity whether we do right or wrong today.

—*James Freeman Clarke*

1835.   To see the right and not do it is want of courage.

—*Confucius*

1836.   One may go wrong in different ways, but right in only one.

—*Aristotle*

1837.   Don't do things by halves. If it is *right*—do it. If it is *wrong*—don't do it.

—*Ancient proverb*

406, 513, 1186, 1377, 1923.

RISK

1838.   One hour of life, crowded to the full with glorious action, and filled with noble risks, is worth whole years of those mean observances of paltry decorum.

—*Sir Walter Scott*

474.

ROMANCE
1839. All history, so far as it is not supported by contemporary evidence, is romance.

—Samuel Johnson

1840. Nothing spoils a romance so much as a sense of humor in the woman.

—Oscar Wilde

RUIN
1841. The ruin of most men dates from some idle moment.

—George S. Hillard

RULES
1842. We have committed the Golden Rule to memory; let us now commit it to life. We have preached Brotherhood for centuries; we now need to find a material basis for brotherhood. Government must be made the organ of Fraternity—a working-form for comrade-love. Think on this—work for this.

—Edwin Markham

1843. If you are ruled by mind you are a king; if by body, a slave.

—Cato

1844. Rules and models destroy genius and art.

—William Hazlitt

1514, 1888.

SACRIFICE
1845. I have nothing to offer but blood, toil, tears and sweat.

—Sir Winston Churchill

1846. The greatest sacrifice is the sacrifice of time.

—Antiphon

1025.

SAFETY
1847. Those, who would give up essential liberty to purchase a little temporary safety, deserve neither liberty nor safety.

—Benjamin Franklin

1848.   The desire for safety stands against every great and noble enterprise.

—Tacitus

1849.   The raft of knowledge ferries the worst sinner to safety.

—Bhagavadgita

296, 2147.

SALES
1850.   I bought a suit that comes from London. It was brought here and sold to a wholesaler. The wholesaler sold it to a retailer and the retailer sold it to me. Think of all those people who are making a living out of something I haven't paid for yet.

—Henny Youngman

SALESMAN
1851.   A rather fussy woman had been trying on shoes for more than an hour and still couldn't decide which pair to buy. The shoe salesman had gone back and forth to the stockroom at least thirty or forty times in search of something that would please her. Finally, he sat in the chair next to her and said, "Excuse me, but do you mind if I rest for a few minutes? Your feet are killing me."

626.

SATISFACTION
1852.   Here is the true, long-term assurance that democracy may flourish in the world. Physical means and skillful organization may see it safely through a crisis, but only if basically the democracy of our day satisfied the mental, moral and physical wants of the masses living under it, can it continue to exist.

—Dwight D. Eisenhower

1853.   Rub out often with your pen, if you will write things worth reading; nor labour that the crowd may admire you, but be satisfied with a few readers.

—Horace

1854.   The greatest comfort of my old age, and that which gives me the highest satisfaction, is the pleasing remembrance of the many benefits and friendly offices I have done to others.

—*Cato*

14, 15, 1024.

SAVING
1855.   It is saving, not getting, that is the mother of riches.

—*Sir Walter Scott*

SCHOLAR
1856.   A scholar is a man with this inconvenience, that, when you ask his opinion of any matter, he must go home and look up his manuscripts to know.

—*Ralph Waldo Emerson*

1857.   The ink of the scholar is more sacred than the blood of the martyr.

—*Mohammed*

1858.   Three women were chatting about their sons who were in college.

"My son is going to be a doctor," the first woman said.

"And my son is studying for the ministry," her friend said.

Then they looked at the other woman and said, "And what is your son going to be when he graduates?"

"An old man," she said.

642.

SCHOOL
1859.   I will never forget my school days. I was the teacher's pet. She couldn't afford a dog.

—*Henny Youngman*

1860.   You send your child to the schoolmaster, but 'tis the schoolboys who educate him.

—*Ralph Waldo Emerson*

165, 630, 649.

SCIENCE
1861.   Science is becoming the hallmark of our age and epoch. The conquest of nature is first of all a conquest of ignorance. Men can control only what they can understand. Science, in itself, is neither blessing nor terror; men make that decision—you and I.

—Eric Severeid

1862.   Science is a first-rate piece of furniture for a man's upper chamber, if he has common sense on the ground floor.

—Oliver Wendell Holmes
223.

SCRIPTURES
1863.   I speak as a man of the world to men of the world, and I say to you: search the Scriptures. The Bible is the Book of all others to read at all ages and in all conditions of human life: not to be read once or twice or thrice through and then laid aside; but to be read in small portions of one or two chapters a day and never to be omitted by some overwhelming necessity.

—John Quincy Adams
129.

SECRET
1864.   Three may keep a secret, if two of them are dead.

—Benjamin Franklin

SECURITY
1865.   Even in the common affairs of life, in love, friendship, and marriage, how little security have we when we trust our happiness in the hands of others!

—William Hazlitt

1866.   Uneasy lies the head that wears a crown.

—William Shakespeare
1848.

SEED

1867.   Wonder—which is the seed of knowledge.

—Francis Bacon

SEEKING

1868.   A man from a small town was visiting the city. After asking directions from several persons with negative results, he spotted a policeman directing traffic at an intersection. Watching traffic carefully, he finally dashed between the passing cars to where the policeman stood.

Almost out of breath he said, "Can you please tell me how to get to the City Memorial Hospital?"

"That's easy," the policeman said. "You stand right where you are for about five minutes and an ambulance will be along and take you there."

SELF

1869.   Every one now believes that there is in a man an animating, ruling, characteristic essence, or spirit, which is himself. This spirit, dull or bright, petty or grand, pure or foul, looks out of the eyes, sounds in the voice, and appears in the manners of each individual. It is what we call personality.

—Charles W. Eliot

1870.   Every artist dips his brush in his own soul, and paints his own nature into his pictures.

—Henry Ward Beecher

1871.   When the fight begins within himself, a man's worth something.

—Robert Browning

898.

SELF-ASSURANCE

1872.   Whistling to keep myself from being afraid.

—John Dryden

SELF-CONFIDENCE
1873.   Self-confidence is the first requisite to great undertakings.

—*Samuel Johnson*

2290.

SELF-CONTROL
1874.   He is most powerful who has power over himself.

—*Seneca*

153.

SELF-DECEPTION
1875.   The greatest self-deception is to believe you will get something for nothing.

—*Arnold "Nick" Carter*

SELF-DEFENSE
1876.   A man had passed his final examination in a karate school of self-defense. Three weeks later he was set upon by a mugger. He quickly used his newly learned skills and had beaten his attacker into a whimpering mass of human flesh.

Within minutes the police had arrived. "We heard the screaming," the patrolman said. "You certainly are to be congratulated on handling yourself so well, but what was that strange cry you were making?"

"Well," the man said, "I have always been taught to be formal with strangers, so instead of yelling 'Hi, Karate!' I just yelled 'Hello Karate!' and pulled his shoulder out of joint."

SELF-DISCIPLINE
1877.   There is an idea abroad among moral people that they should make their neighbors good. One person I have to make good: myself. But my duty to my neighbor is much more nearly expressed by saying that I have to make him happy—if I may.

—*Robert Louis Stevenson*

1878. He conquers twice, who upon victory overcomes himself.

—Francis Bacon

1012.

SELF-HELP
1879. The gods help them that help themselves.

—Aesop

SELF-INTEREST
1880. If you love yourself too much, nobody else will love you at all.

—Ancient proverb

1568, 1732.

SELFISHNESS
1881. Selfishness is not living as one wishes to live; it is asking others to live as one wishes to live. And unselfishness is letting other people's lives alone, not interfering with them. Selfishness always aims at creating around it an absolute uniformity of type. Unselfishness recognizes infinite variety of type as a delightful thing, accepts it, acquiesces in it, enjoys it.

—Oscar Wilde

1882. If you want to be miserable, think about yourself, about what you want, what you like, what respect people ought to pay you, and what people think of you.

—Charles Kingsley

1883. Above all the grace and gifts that Christ gives to his beloved is that of overcoming self.

—St. Francis of Assisi

1046, 2316.

SELF-JUDGMENT
1884. He who accuses himself cannot be accused by another.

—Publilius Syrus

SELF-KNOWLEDGE

1885.   A man can know nothing of mankind without knowing something of himself. Self-knowledge is the property of that man whose passions have their full play, but who ponders over their results.

—Disraeli

1886.   When we cannot find contentment in ourselves it is useless to seek it elsewhere.

—Francois De La Rochefaucauld

1887.   The easiest person to deceive is one's own self.

—Bulwer-Lytton

1888.   Who cannot rule himself, how should he rule others?

—Confucius

1889.   Nobody can give you better advice than yourself.

—Cicero

1890.   He who knows others is worldly, but he who also knows himself is wise.

—Ancient proverb

79, 1124.

SELF-RELIANCE

1891.   Every man who rises above the common level has received two educations: the first from his teachers, the second, more personal and important, from himself.

—Edward Gibbon

1892.   Doubt whom you will, but never doubt yourself.

—Christian Nestell Bovee

1893.   Every man is of importance to himself.

—Samuel Johnson

999, 2135.

SELF-RESPECT

1894.   If you want to be respected by others, the great thing is to respect yourself. Only by that, only by self-respect will you compel others to respect you.

—Dostoevsky

1895.   I can pardon everybody's mistakes except my own.

—Cato

SELF-REVERENCE
1896.   Who then is free? The wise man who is lord over himself; whom neither poverty nor death, nor chains alarm, strong to withstand his passions and despise honors, and who is completely finished and founded off in himself.

—Horace

SERENITY
1897.   Cheerfulness keeps up a kind of daylight in the mind, filling it with a steady and perpetual serenity.

—Joseph Addison

1898.   It is only in contemplative moments that life is truly vital.

—George Santayana

491.

SERIOUSNESS
1899.   I find we are growing serious, and then we are in great danger of being dull.

—William Congreve

SERMON
1900.   That is not the best sermon which makes the hearers go away talking to one another and praising the speaker, but which makes them go away thoughtful and serious, and hastening to be alone.

—Bishop Gilbert Burnet

1901.   You can preach a better sermon with your life than with your lips.

—Oliver Goldsmith

SERVICE
1902.   Service is both the inspiration and the accomplishment of quite everything worthwhile which impels us onward and upward. With

service, which the Nazarene would approve, are associated all our ideals and our finer aspirations.

—*Warren G. Harding*

1903.   So long as we love, we serve. So long as we are loved by others I would almost say we are indispensable; and no man is useless while he has a friend.

—*Robert Louis Stevenson*

1904.   Nor are we to use living creatures like old shoes or dishes and throw them away when they are worn out or broken with service.

—*Plutarch*

1905.   To be glad instruments of God's love in this imperfect world is the service to which man is called.

—*Albert Schweitzer*

1906.   I prefer death to lassitude. I never tire of serving others.

—*Leonardo da Vinci*

1907.   The most acceptable service of God is doing good to man.

—*Benjamin Franklin*

1908.   The superior man is easy to serve and difficult to please.

—*Confucius*

1909.   Who serves his country well has no need of ancestors.

—*Voltaire*

1910.   The highest of distinctions is service to others.

—*George VI*

1911.   Who has not served cannot command.

—*John Florio*

1912.   It is high time that the ideal of success should be replaced by the ideal of service.

—*Albert Einstein*

1913.   Service above Self.

—*Motto, Rotary International*

1914.   A man had been sitting in a restaurant for twenty minutes and had not been served. Finally he caught the eye of a waitress and said, "Please, I would like to get served. I only have one hour for lunch."

"Can't you see I'm busy," the waitress said. "I don't have time to talk to you about your labor problems."
616, 1028, 1475.

SEX
1915. We are foolish, and without excuse foolish, in speaking of superiority of one sex to the other, as if they could be compared in similar things! Each has what the other has not; each completes the other; they are in nothing alike; and the happiness and perfection of both depend on each asking and receiving from the other what the other only can give.

—John Ruskin

SHAME
1916. Man is the only animal that blushes. Or needs to.

—Mark Twain

SHARING
1917. If you have knowledge, let others light their candles at it.

—Margaret Fuller

501, 1365.

SHELTER
1918. Knowledge is a comfortable and necessary retreat and shelter for us in an advanced age; and if we do not plant it while young, it will give us no shade when we grow old.

—Lord Chesterfield

SIGHT
1919. I pity the man who can travel from Dan to Beersheba and cry, " 'Tis all barren!"

—Laurence Sterne

1920. To love someone means to see him as God intended him.

—Dostoevsky

1921. We live by information, not by sight.

—Baltasar Gracian

SILENCE

1922.   There are three kinds of silence. Silence from words is good, because inordinate speaking tends to evil. Silence or rest from desires or passions is still better, because it prompts quickness of spirit. But the best of all is silence from unnecessary and angering thoughts, because that is essential to internal recollection, and because it lays a foundation for a proper regulation and silence in other respects.

—*Madame Guyon*

1923.   I think the first virtue is to restrain the tongue; he approaches nearest to the gods who knows how to be silent, even though he is in the right.

—*Cato*

1924.   It is easy to utter what has been kept silent, but impossible to recall what has been uttered.

—*Plutarch*

1925.   Silence and reserve suggest latent power. What some men think has more effect than what others say.

—*Lord Chesterfield*

1926.   Blessed are they who have nothing to say, and who cannot be persuaded to say it.

—*James Russell Lowell*

1927.   Silence is the element in which great things fashion themselves.

—*Thomas Carlyle*

1928.   Silence is a true friend who never betrays.

—*Confucius*

468, 1955.

SIMPLICITY

1929.   Beauty of style and harmony and grace and good rhythm depend on simplicity.

—*Plato*

1930.   Nothing is more simple than greatness; indeed, to be simple is to be great.

—*Ralph Waldo Emerson*

SINCERITY

1931. The merit of originality is not novelty; it is sincerity. The believing man is the original man.

—Thomas Carlyle

1932. Enthusiasm is the genius of sincerity, and truth accomplishes no victories without it.

—Bulwer-Lytton

1933. Sincerity and truth are the basis of every virtue.

—Confucius

1934. Sincerity needs no witnesses.

—Ancient proverb

633.

SKEPTICISM

1935. Skepticism is the first step on the road to philosophy.

—Denis Diderot

SKILL

1936. When love and skill work together, expect a masterpiece.

—John Ruskin

433, 592, 1394, 1646.

SLAVERY

1937. He who will not reason, is a bigot; he who cannot, is a fool; and, he who dares not, is a slave.

—William Drummond

1938. The slave has but one master; the man of ambition has as many as there are people useful to his fortune.

—Jean De La Bruyere

1939. No man can lift up his head with manly calmness and peace who is the slave of other men's judgments.

—J. W. Alexander

1940. Corrupted freemen are the worst of slaves.

—David Garrick

644, 818, 1473, 2155.

SLEEP
1941.   A man was complaining to a friend about his inability to sleep.

"What do you take when you can't sleep?" he asked his friend.

"I always drink a glass of wine or a Martini at regular intervals," his friend said.

"Will that make you sleep?"

"No," his friend said, "but it makes me satisfied to stay awake."

SMILE
1942.   I love the man that can smile in trouble, that can gather strength from distress, and grow brave by reflection. 'Tis the business of little minds to shrink, but he whose heart is firm, and whose conscience approves his conduct, will pursue his principles unto death.

—Thomas Paine

1943.   What sunshine is to flowers, smiles are to humanity. They are but trifles, to be sure; but, scattered along life's pathway, the good they do is inconceivable.

—Joseph Addison

1944.   A smile is ever the most bright and beautiful with a tear upon it. What is the dawn without the dew? The tear is rendered by the smile precious above the smile itself.

—Walter Savage Landor

1945.   Better by far you should forget and smile,
                   Than that you should remember and be sad.

—Christina Georgina Rossetti

1946.   In came Mrs. Fezziwig, one vast substantial smile.

—Charles Dickens

1947.   A smile is the shortest distance between two people.

—Victor Borge

1237.

SOCIAL SECURITY
1948.   The clerk at the Social Security office said to the worn-out looking man standing at her desk, "I'm sorry but *feeling* 65 isn't good enough. You've got to *be* 65."

SOCIETY
1949. Society is like a lawn, where every roughness is smoothed, every bramble eradicated, and where the eye is delighted by the smiling verdure of a velvet surface. He, however, who would study nature in its wildness and variety, must plunge into the forest, must explore the glen, must stem the torrent, and dare the precipice.

—Washington Irving

331, 851, 2162.

SOLITUDE
1950. I love to be alone. I never found the companion that was so companionable as solitude.

—Henry David Thoreau

1951. Solitude is as needful to the imagination as society is wholesome for the character.

—James Russell Lowell

1900.

SOLUTIONS
1952. The first step in solving a problem is to tell someone about it.

—Lt. Gen. John Peter Flynn

1953. In this little Book will be found the solution to all the problems of the world.

—Calvin Coolidge

1954. If we could be twice young and twice old we could correct all our mistakes.

—Euripides

1955. The little boy was a genuine stinker—a holy terror. "I think we should get him a bicycle," his mother said to her husband.

"Do you think that will improve his disposition?" he asked. "Not really," she said, "but it will spread his meanness over a wider area."

SONG
1956. Oh, give us the man who sings at his work.

—Thomas Carlyle

905, 1054, 1483.

SORROW

1957.   Believe me, every man has his secret sorrows, which the world knows not; and often times we call a man cold when he is only sad.

—Henry Wadsworth Longfellow

1958.   Never bear more than one kind of trouble at a time. Some people bear three—all they have had, all they have now, and all they expect to have.

—Edward Everett Hale

1959.   For in much wisdom is much grief; and he that increaseth knowledge increaseth sorrow.

—Ecclesiastes 1:18

1960.   He that goes a borrowing goes a sorrowing.

—Benjamin Franklin

489, 2177.

SOUL

1961.   If the Father deigns to touch with divine power the cold and pulseless heart of the buried acorn and to make it burst forth from its prison walls, will He leave neglected in the earth the soul of man made in the image of his Creator?

—William Jennings Bryan

1962.   Do you ask where the Supreme God dwells? In the soul. And unless the soul be pure and holy, there is no room in it for God.

—Seneca

1963.   What sculpture is to a block of marble, education is to the soul.

—Joseph Addison

426, 1246.

SPEAKING

1964.   If ever a woman feels proud of her lover, it is when she sees him as a successful public speaker.

—Harriet Beecher Stowe

1965. In Maine we have a saying that there's no point in speaking unless you can improve on silence.

—Edmund Muskie

1966. I never failed to convince an audience that the best thing they could do was go away.

—Thomas Love Peacock

1967. The first is freedom of speech and expression—everywhere in the world. The second is freedom of every person to worship God in his own way—everywhere in the world. The third is the freedom from want. . .everywhere in the world. The fourth is freedom from fear. . .anywhere in the world.

—Franklin D. Roosevelt

1968. Speak properly and in as few words as you can, but always plainly; for the end of speech is not ostentation but to be understood.

—William Penn

1969. The unluckiest insolvent in the world is the man whose expenditure of speech is too great for his income of ideas.

—Christopher Morley

1970. When his words fell soft as snowflakes on a winter's day, then could no mortal man beside vie with Odysseus.

—Homer

1971. The first duty of man is to speak; that is his chief business in this world.

—Robert Louis Stevenson

1972. Language, as well as the faculty of speech, was the immediate gift of God.

—Noah Webster

1973. One ought, every day at least. . .to speak a few reasonable words.

—Goethe

1974. Speech is the index of the mind.

—Seneca

1975.   A man who stuttered had been taking lessons in remedial speech. A friend asked him how he was getting along.

"Fine," the man said. "Listen to what I have learned to say: Peter Piper picked a peck of pickled peppers. If Peter Piper picked a peck of pickled peppers, where is the peck of pickled peppers that Peter Piper picked?"

"That's wonderful," his friend said. "You are doing great."

"Yes, I am," the stutterer said, "b-but it's s-sure h-hard to w-work it into a c-conversation."
505, 1278, 1563, 2058.

SPEED
1976.   Down to Gehenna or up to the Throne,
                             He travels the fastest who travels alone.

—Rudyard Kipling

1977.   There is more to life than increasing its speed.

—Mahatma Gandhi

1978.   A senior citizen was driving on a busy Interstate highway during the afternoon rush hour. He was poking along at his usual speed—35 miles per hour—while people honked at him and made abusive remarks at him for holding up traffic.

After awhile a highway patrolman overtook him and had him pull over to the side of the road. "I suppose you know why I stopped you," the officer said.

"Yes," the man said, "I was the only one you could catch."
393, 1328.

SPENDING
1979.   "One thing you must say about my wife," a man said to his friend, "she's years ahead of her time."

"What do you mean?" his friend asked.

"I mean she's already spent my salary for the next six years."
1522.

SPIRIT

1980.   I should as soon attempt to raise flowers if there were no atmosphere, or produce fruits if there were neither light nor heat, as to regenerate men if I did not believe there was a Holy Spirit.

—Henry Ward Beecher

1981.   You will find as you look back on your life that the moments that stand out above everything else are the moments when you have done things in a spirit of love.

—Henry Drummond

1982.   If wrinkles must be written upon our brows, let them not be written upon the heart. The spirit should not grow old.

—James A. Garfield

223, 1671, 1869.

STATESMANSHIP

1983.   We learned once and for all that compromise makes a good umbrella but a poor roof; that it is a temporary expedient, often wise in party politics, almost sure to be unwise in statesmanship.

—James Russell Lowell

STATISTICS

1984.   Take the statistical view of rascals and fools. There are so many per thousand of the population. You have met your share. If you seem to be meeting more than your share, lie down: you may be tired.

—John W. Gardner

STRENGTH

1985.   When they told me there was treatment but no cure at this time, I dropped to my knees. Two things from out of my past, when I went to church as a child, came back to me. Number one, "Where can I go but to the Lord?" and number two, "I am weak, but He is strong."

The third feeling I had was, "When life comes down to basics, really how little control we all have over our own lives." And it also came to me, even if we live to be 100, how really short life here is. And therefore, it's important to enjoy it and not rush so fast, and take time to smell the roses.

—*Marvella Bayh*

1986.   All of us are concerned—and rightly so—that we not slip into military weakness. . .Yet cutting back our other international programs contributes to another kind of weakness, every bit as dangerous. It cuts back our arsenal of influence.

—*Edmund Muskie*

1987.   He who knows no hardships will know no hardihood. He who faces no calamity will need no courage. Mysterious though it is, the characteristics in human nature which we love best grow in a soil with a strong mixture of troubles.

—*Harry Emerson Fosdick*

1988.   We are a proudly idealistic nation, but let no one confuse our idealism with weakness.

—*Jimmy Carter*

1989.   The block of granite which was an obstacle in the pathway of the weak becomes a stepping-stone in the pathway of the strong.

—*Thomas Carlyle*

1990.   Be like a rocky headland on which the waves break incessantly, but it stands fast and the waters sink to rest.

—*Marcus Aurelius*

1991.   In all my perplexities and distresses, the Bible has never failed to give me light and strength.

—*Robert E. Lee*

1992.   We dare not allow America to become weak and defenseless because if we do, the day could come when we would not be divided into hawks and doves—just pigeons.

—*Ronald Reagan*

1993.   Only by the supernatural is man strong; nothing is so weak as an egotist.

—*Ralph Waldo Emerson*

1994.   A good cause makes a stout heart and a strong arm.

—*Thomas Fuller*

1995. That which does not kill me makes me stronger.

—*Friedrich Nietzsche*

1996. If I have to, I can do anything. I am strong. I am invincible; I am woman.

—*Helen Reddy*

1997. People do not lack strength; they lack will.

—*Victor Hugo*

1998. A wise man is strong; yea, a man of knowledge increaseth strength.

—*Proverbs 24:5*

1999. Whatsoever thy hand findeth to do, do it with thy might.

—*Ecclesiastes 9:10*

74, 488, 1460, 1792, 1824.

STUDENT

2000. The college student wrote a letter home that said, "Dear Mom and Dad, I am so worried about you. I haven't heard from you in more than a month. Please send me a check so I'll know that everything is all right at home."

2001. A college student said to his roommate, "What a lousy trick my dad played on me!"

"What did he do?" his roommate asked.

"I wrote home for $96.00 to buy an unabridged dictionary—and look what he did. He sent me the dictionary."

639.

STUDY

2002. The study of nature is intercourse with the Highest Mind. You should never trifle with Nature.

—*Jean Louis Agassiz*

2003. Crafty men condemn studies; simple men admire them: and wise men use them.

—*Francis Bacon*

1511, 1734.

STYLE

2004. Beauty of style and harmony and grace and good rhythm depend on simplicity.

—*Plato*

1929, 2052, 2174.

SUBLIME

2005. The sublime and the ridiculous are often so nearly related that it is difficult to class them separately. One step above the sublime makes the ridiculous, and one step above the ridiculous makes the sublime again.

—*Thomas Paine*

SUBSTITUTE

2006. We have substitute hair, substitute food, substitute leather and substitute snow. Let's be sure we don't try to substitute for compassion, care and kindness.

—*Will L. Ketner*

SUCCESS

2007. Take life too seriously, and what is it worth? If the morning wake us to no new joys, if the evening bring us not the hope of new pleasure, is it worthwhile to dress and undress? Does the sun shine on me today that I may reflect on yesterday? That I may endeavor to foresee and to control what can neither be foreseen nor controlled—the destiny of tomorrow?

—*Goethe*

2008. If we do our best; if we do not magnify trifling troubles; if we look resolutely, I will not say at the bright side of things, but at things as they really are; if we avail ourselves of the manifold blessings which surround us, we can not but feel that life is indeed a glorious inheritance.

—*John Lubbock*

2009. The man who starts out with the idea of getting rich won't succeed; you must have a larger ambition. There is no mystery in business success. If you do each day's task successfully, stay faithfully within the natural operations of commercial law, and keep your head clear, you will come out all right.

—*John D. Rockefeller*

2010.   If the day and the night are such that you greet them with joy, and life emits a fragrance like flowers and sweet-scented herbs, is more elastic, more starry, more immortal—that is your success.

—*Henry David Thoreau*

2011.   Most people feel that success is winning or achieving or completing something. I feel most successful when I am actually doing it. Competing. Performing. When I am delivering my very best, then that is when I feel successful. The ultimate outcome is anti-climax.

—*Art Fettig*

2012.   Nothing in the world can take the place of persistence. Talent will not; nothing is more common than unsuccessful men with talent. Genius will not; unrewarded genius is almost a proverb. Education will not; the world is full of educated derelicts. Persistence and determination alone are all-powerful.

—*Calvin Coolidge*

2013.   There is but one straight road to success, and that is merit. The man who is successful is the man who is useful. Capacity never lacks opportunity. It can not remain undiscovered, because it is sought by too many anxious to use it.

—*Burke Cockran*

2014.   Success is not a harbor but a voyage with its own perils to the spirit. The game of life is to come up a winner, to be a success, or to achieve what we set out to do. Yet there is always the danger of failing as a human being. The lesson that most of us on this voyage never learn, but can never quite forget, is that to win is sometimes to lose.

—*Richard M. Nixon*

2015.   The best way to achieve success is to get even. I have spent my whole life getting even with the people who said I would wind up as a bad person. The reason they said this was because I was funny when I was a kid, and nobody likes a funny kid. Most of the people who predicted my demise are dead, but that hasn't stopped me—I am still getting even with them.

—*Art Buchwald*

2016.   He that climbs the tall tree has won right to the fruit,
He that leaps the wide gulf should prevail in his suit.

—Sir Walter Scott

2017.   I look on that man as happy, who, when there is the question of success, looks into his work for a reply.

—Ralph Waldo Emerson

2018.   There is not one man in a thousand capable of being a successful rogue, while anyone may succeed as an honest man.

—Elias Howe

2019.   Few things are impracticable in themselves, and it is for want of application, rather than of means, that men fail of success.

—Francois De La Rochefaucauld

2020.   The men who try to do something and fail are infinitely better than those who try to do nothing and succeed.

—Lloyd Jones

2021.   The world is blessed most by men who do things, and not by those who merely talk about them.

—James Oliver

2022.   Success is a journey, not a destiny. It should be enjoyed through the entire trip, not endured until the final reward.

—Art Linkletter

2023.   The greatest misdirection of emotion comes when you resent the success of other people.

—Arnold "Nick" Carter

2024.   As a general rule the most successful man in life is the man who has the best information.

—Benjamin Disraeli

2025.   Not what men do worthily, but what they do successfully, is what history makes haste to record.

—Henry Ward Beecher

2026.   We mount to heaven mostly on the ruins of our cherished schemes, finding our failures were successful.

—Amos Bronson Alcott

2027. I owe all my success in life to having been always a quarter of an hour beforehand.

—Lord Nelson

2028. The whole idea is to somehow get an edge. Sometimes it takes just a little extra something to get that edge. But you have to have it.

—Don F. Shula

2029. I have always observed that to succeed in the world one should appear like a fool but be wise.

—Montesquieu

2030. Let us be thankful for the fools. But for them the rest of us could not succeed.

—Mark Twain

2031. Try not to become a man of success but rather try to become a man of value.

—Albert Einstein

2032. The world tolerates conceit from those who are successful, but not from anybody else.

—John Lauris Blake

2033. Success is simply a matter of luck. Ask any failure.

—Earl Wilson

2034. We can do anything we want to do if we stick to it long enough.

—Helen Keller

2035. Experience has always shown, and reason also, that affairs which depend on many seldom succeed.

—Guicciardini

2036. God is generally on the side of the large battalions against the small.

—Bussy Rabutin

2037. But, chiefly, the mould of a man's fortune is in his own hands.

—Francis Bacon

2038.   Singing and dancing alone will not advance one in the world.

—Jean-Jacques Rousseau

2039.   Providence is always on the side of the last reserve.

—Napoleon Bonaparte

2040.   Success is a rare paint, hides all the ugliness.

—Sir John Suckling

2041.   Be commonplace and creeping, and you attain all things.

—Beaumarchais

2042.   Nothing succeeds like success.

—Alexander Dumas

2043.   A woman was bragging about her children. "Jean is 26 and is a portrait painter in New Orleans; Willard is 24 and writes poetry; Margaret is 22 and is a professional dancer."

"Don't you have a younger son?" her friend asked. "What is he doing?"

"Oh, that's Joey," the proud mother said. "He's just 20. He's nothing but a plumber's helper. But, if it weren't for him, all the rest of us would be starving."

26, 117, 120, 234, 474, 596, 692, 714, 953, 1276, 1300, 1636.

SUFFERING
2044.   It is easier to advise the suffering than to bear suffering.

—Euripides

2177.

SUGGESTION
2045.   To know how to suggest is the great art of teaching.

—Henri Frederic Amiel

SURPRISE
2046.   Not many sounds in life, and I include all urban and all rural sounds, exceed in interest a knock at the door.

—Charles Lamb

SUSPICION
2047.   It is as hard for the good to suspect evil as it is for the bad to suspect good.

—Cicero

2048.   Beneath the rule of men entirely great,
          The pen is mightier than the sword.

—Bulwer-Lytton

130.

SYMPATHY
2049.   No one can deal with the hearts of men unless he has the sympathy which is given by love. . .You must have enough benevolence, not only for yourself, but for others, to pervade and fill them. This is what is meant by living a godly life.

—Henry Ward Beecher

2050.   To cultivate sympathy you must be among living creatures, and thinking about them; and to cultivate admiration, you must be among beautiful things and looking at them.

—John Ruskin

2051.   A man thought he was going to die with a toothache. He asked his friend, "What can I do to relieve the pain?"

     "I'll tell you what I do," his friend said. "When I have a toothache, or a pain, I go to my wife, and she puts her arms around me, and caresses me, and soothes me until finally I forget all about the pain."

     His friend brightened up and said, "Gee, that sounds wonderful! Is she home now?"

868, 1283.

TACT
2052.   It is not sufficient to know what one ought to say, but one must also know how to say it.

—Aristotle

TALENT
2053.   I believe that the Good Lord gave each and every one of us a special talent, a unique talent. And if we can only discover that talent

and polish that talent and go to work and put that talent to work for the good of all mankind then this can be a world full of love and peace and understanding.

—*Art Fettig*

2054.   Talent is the capacity of doing anything that depends on application and industry; it is a voluntary power, while genius is involuntary.

—*William Hazlitt*

2055.   If you have great talents, industry will improve them; if you have but moderate abilities, industry will supply their deficiencies.

—*Sir Joshua Reynolds*

2056.   Doing easily what others find difficult is talent; doing what is impossible for talent is genius.

—*Henri-Frederic Amiel*

2057.   Talents are best nurtured in solitude; character is best formed in the stormy billows of the world.

—*Goethe*

5, 1213, 1674, 2012, 2328.

TALK

2058.   Talking and eloquence are not the same; to speak, and to speak well are two things. A fool may talk, but a wise man speaks.

—*Ben Jonson*

2059.   The French do not go to priests, doctors, or psychiatrists, to talk over their problems. They sit over a cup of coffee or a glass of wine and talk to each other.

—*Eric Severeid*

2060.   As empty vessels make the loudest sound, so they that have the least wit are the greatest babblers.

—*Plato*

2061.   He has a rage for saying something when there's nothing to be said.

—*Samuel Johnson*

2062. Were we as eloquent as angels, yet we should please some men, some women, and some children much more by listening, than by talking.

—*Charles Caleb Colton*

2063. He knew the precise psychological moment when to say nothing.

—*Oscar Wilde*

283, 469, 949, 1297, 2253, 2282.

TAXI

2064. After a man had ridden halfway across town in a taxi he discovered he had left his wallet at home and didn't have a dime with him. As he came within two blocks of his destination, he tapped on the glass between him and the driver and said, "Please stop at that liquor store just ahead. I want to run in and get some matches. I want to look for a $20.00 bill I just dropped on the floor back here."

The driver did as he was asked. The man went into the liquor store, picked up a packet of free matches. But when he came out of the store, the taxi had driven off.

TEACHER

2065. They who educate children well, are more to be honored than they who produce them; for these only gave them life, those the art of living well.

—*Aristotle*

963, 1191, 1507, 1859, 2045.

TEENAGER

2066. A woman was chatting with her neighbor over a morning cup of coffee. "We had a trying time at the house last night. Our teenage daughter had a temper fit and started to run away. But, lucky for all of us she didn't get any farther than the front door."

"What happened?" the friend asked.

"The telephone rang," the teenager's mother said.

TELEVISION

2067. A newspaper reporter was writing a feature story about prison life and was interviewing one of the prisoners. "Do you watch much television here?"

"Only the daytime shows," the inmate said. "At night we're locked in our cells and don't see any television."

"That's too bad," the reporter said, "But I do think it is nice that the warden lets you watch it in the daytime."

"What do you mean, nice?" the inmate said. "That's part of the punishment."

TEMPER

2068. Good temper, like a sunny day, sheds a brightness over everything. It is the sweetener of toil and the soother of disquietude.

—Washington Irving

2069. The only time to lose your temper is when it's deliberate.

—Richard M. Nixon

TEMPERANCE

2070. Temperance puts wood on the fire, meal in the barrel, flour in the tub, money in the purse, credit in the country, contentment in the house, clothes on the children, vigor in the body, intelligence in the brain, and spirit in the whole constitution.

—Benjamin Franklin

2071. If temperance prevails, then education can prevail; if temperance fails, then education must fail.

—Horace Mann

2072. The town drunk had finally signed the pledge and swore never to touch another drop of booze. After a week or two the craving became more than he could stand. So, he went into the local bar and said to the bartender, "I'd like a glass of orange juice, please."

"One plain orange juice coming up," the bartender said.

"By the way," the thirsty felllow said, "I wouldn't get sore at you if you slipped a jigger or two of gin in it without me knowing it."
572, 1177, 1463.

TENACITY

2073.   When you get into a tight place and everything goes against you, till it seems as though you could not hold on a minute longer, never give up then, for that is just the place and time that the tide will turn.

—Harriet Beecher Stowe

TENDERNESS

2074.   An infinitude of tenderness is the chief gift and inheritance of all truly great men.

—John Ruskin

TEXAS

2075.   "Son," said a Texan to his little boy, "I just overheard you asking that new neighbor what state he was from. Now, there is something you should understand. If somebody comes from Texas, he'll tell you, and if he isn't you shouldn't embarrass him."

THANKSGIVING

2076.   We have been a most favored people. We ought to be a most grateful people. We have been a most blessed people. We ought to be a most thankful people.

—Calvin Coolidge

2077.   Hearts, like doors, will open with ease
                  To very, very little keys,
                  And don't forget that two of these
                  Are "I thank you" and "If you please."

—Nursery Rhyme

2078.   A thankful heart is not only the greatest virtue, but the parent of all the other virtues.

—Cicero

2079.   I have good health, good thoughts, and good humor, thanks to God Almighty.

—William Byrd

2080.   A youngster at the school cafeteria complained to the woman in charge about the bread, "It's terrible," he said.

"Young man," she said, "you ought to be thankful. If George Washington had had that bread at Valley Forge, he and his men would have eaten it with relish."

"We could do that, too, maybe," said the boy, "but there isn't any relish on our table."

690, 1054, 1060.

THINK

2081.   The only way in which one human being can properly attempt to influence another is encouraging him to think for himself, instead of endeavoring to instill ready-made opinions into his head.

—Sir Leslie Stephen

2082.   Those who have few things to attend to are great babblers; for the less men think, the more they talk.

—Montesquieu

2083.   Very little is needed to make a happy life. It is all within yourself, in your way of thinking.

—Marcus Aurelius

2084.   Think in the morning. Act in the noon. Eat in the evening. Sleep in the night.

—William Blake

2085.   If you are not a thinking man, to what purpose are you a man at all?

—Samuel Taylor Coleridge

2086.   And to cease to think is but little different from ceasing to be.

—Benjamin Franklin

2087.   Thinking, trying, toiling, and trusting in God, is all of my biography.

—John Wanamaker

2088.   What is the hardest task in the world? To think.

—Ralph Waldo Emerson

2089.   Nurture your mind with great thoughts.

—Benjamin Disraeli

56, 431, 1763, 2341.

THOUGHT

2090. Our great thoughts, our great affections, the truths of our life, never leave us. Surely they cannot separate from our consciousness, shall follow it whithersoever that shall go, and are of their nature divine and immortal.

—William Makepeace Thackery

2091. If any imagine they will find thought in many books, certainly they will be disappointed. Thought dwells by the stream and the sea, by the hill and in the woodland, in the sunlight and free wind.

—Richard Jefferies

2092. The contemplation of celestial things will make a man both speak and think more sublimely and magnificently when he comes down to human affairs.

—Cicero

2093. A man is not idle because he is absorbed in thought. There is a visible labour and there is an invisible labour.

—Victor Hugo

2094. Reading furnishes the mind only with materials of knowledge; it is thinking makes what we read ours.

—John Locke

2095. Man is but a reed, the weakest thing in nature; but he is a thinking reed.

—Blaise Pascal

2096. Not a brick was made but some man had to *think* of the making of that brick.

—Thomas Carlyle

2097. I have always thought the actions of men the best interpreters of their thoughts.

—John Locke

2098. Our knowledge is the amassed thought and experience of innumerable minds.

—Ralph Waldo Emerson

2099. He never is alone that is accompanied with noble thoughts.

—John Fletcher

2100.   'Twas her thinking of others made you think of her.

— *Elizabeth Barrett Browning*

378, 648, 1322, 1488, 1698, 1704, 1768, 1925, 2350.

THOUGHTFULNESS

2101.   We are all of us fellow-passengers on the same planet and we are all of us equally responsible for the happiness and well-being of the world in which we happen to live.

— *Hendrik Willem Van Loon*

2102.   What do we live for, if it is not to make life less difficult for each other?

— *George Eliot*

2103.   Behave toward everyone as if receiving a great guest.

— *Confucius*

2104.   "Harry," the man's wife said at the breakfast table one morning. "You will notice that I mended that hole in your pocket last night after you went to bed. Don't you think I'm a thoughful and considerate wife?"

"I sure do," her husband said, "and I appreciate it. But tell me one thing. How did you discover that I had a hole in my pocket?"

1068.

THRIFT

2105.   Knowing how to make money and also how to keep it—either of these gifts might make a man rich.

— *Seneca*

2106.   Believe me when I tell you that thrift of time will repay you in after-life, with a usury of profit beyond your most sanguine dreams; and that waste of it will make you dwindle alike in intellectual and moral stature, beyond your darkest reckoning.

— *William Gladstone*

1855.

TIME

2107.　In motion pictures about fighters, either the major motion pictures invariably promised or the minor motion pictures nobody acknowledges making, it is impossible for any fight to go the distance.

—Edwin Newman

2108.　You are young, my son, and as the years go by, time will change, and even reverse many of your present opinions. Refrain therefore awhile from setting yourself up as a judge of the highest matters.

—Plato

2109.　Time to me is so precious that with great difficulty can I steal one hour in eight days, either to satisfy myself or to gratify my friends.

—John Knox

2110.　Unfaithfulness in the keeping of an appointment is an act of clear dishonesty. You may as well borrow a person's money as his time.

—Horace Mann

2111.　Time is painted with a lock before, and bald behind, signifying, thereby that we must take time by the forelock, for when it is once past there is no recalling it.

—Jonathan Swift

2112.　Time is what we want most, but what alas! we use worst.

—William Penn

2113.　There's a time for some things, and a time for all things; a time for great things, and a time for small things.

—Cervantes

2114.　The greatest friend of truth is Time, her greatest enemy is Prejudice, and her constant companion is Humility.

—Charles Caleb Colton

2115.　The bird of time has but a little way to flutter—
And the bird is on the wing.

—Omar Khayyam

2116.　Ordinary people think merely how they shall *spend* their time; a man of any intellect tries to *use* it.

—Shopenhauer

2117.   Do not act as if you had a thousand years to live. It is later than you think.

—Marcus Aurelius

2118.   Neither can the wave that has passed be called back; nor can the hour which has gone by return.

—Ovid

2119.   I recommend you take care of the minutes, for the hours will take care of themselves.

—Lord Chesterfield

2120.   Time is money. . .And very good money, too, to those who reckon interest by it.

—Charles Dickens

2121.   Who makes quick use of the moment, is a genius of prudence.

—Johann Kaspar Lavater

2122.   Time is infinite movement without one moment of rest.

—Leo Tolstoy

2123.   Do not delay, the gold moments fly!

—Henry Wadsworth Longfellow

2124.   The inaudible and noiseless foot of Time.

—William Shakespeare

2125.   A man who does nothing never has time to do anything.

—Ancient Proverb

149, 403, 1476, 1582, 1713, 1846, 1985, 2027, 2228, 2351.

TODAY

2126.   Finish each day and be done with it. You have done what you could. Some blunders and absurdities no doubt crept in; forget them as soon as you can. Tomorrow is a new day; begin it well and serenely and with too high a spirit to be cumbered with your old nonsense. The day is all that is good and fair. It is too dear with its hopes and invitations to waste a moment on yesteryears.

—Ralph Waldo Emerson

2127.   You better live your best and act your best and think your best today; for today is the sure preparation for tomorrow and all the other tomorrows that follow.

—Harriet Martineau

2128.   Seize the present; trust the future as little as you may.

—Horace

2129.   Have you something to do tomorrow, do it today.

—Benjamin Franklin

732, 1089, 1149, 1716, 1725, 2007.

TOIL

2130.   If you want knowledge, you must toil for it; if food, you must toil for it; and if pleasure, you must toil for it; toil is the law.

—John Ruskin

2131.   A truly American sentiment recognizes the dignity of labor and the fact that honor lies in honest toil.

—Grover Cleveland

1820.

TOMORROW

2132.   Even if I knew that tomorrow the world would go to pieces, I would still plant my apple tree.

—Martin Luther

2133.   Tomorrow to fresh woods, and pastures new.

—John Milton

50, 732, 1089, 1102, 1735.

TRADE

2134.   All government—indeed, every human benefit and enjoyment, every virtue and every prudent act—is founded on compromise and barter.

—Edmund Burke

2135.   Commerce is the great civilizer. We exchange ideas when we exchange fabrics.

—Robert Ingersoll

2136.   No nation was ever ruined by trade.

—Benjamin Franklin

1437.

TRANQUILLITY
2137.   It is neither wealth nor splendor, but tranquillity and occupation which give happiness.

—Thomas Jefferson

TRANSIENCE
2138.   Already, within the main centers of change, in California and Cambridge, Massachusetts, in New York and London and Toyko, millions are living the life of the future. What makes them different? Certainly they are richer, better educated, more mobile. But what specifically marks them is the fact that they "live faster."

To survive in such communities, however, the individual must become infinitely more adaptable than ever before. Above all he must understand *transience*. Transience is the new "temporariness" in everyday life. It can be defined as the rate at which our relationships—with things, places, people and information—turn over.

—Alvin Toffler

TREASURE
2139.   Where your treasure is, there will your heart be also.

—Matthew 6:21

TRIAL
2140.   Life is a test and this world a place of trial. Always the problems—or it may be the same problem—will be presented to every generation in different forms.

—Sir Winston Churchill

2141.   Trial is the true test of mortal man.

                                                        —Pindar

TRIUMPH
2142.   There are some defeats more triumphant than victories.

                                        —Michel Eyquem Montaigne

TROUBLES
2143.   I have told you of the man who always put on his spectacles when about to eat cherries, in order that the fruit might look larger and more tempting. In like manner I always make the most of my enjoyments, and, though I do not cast my eyes away from troubles, I pack them into as small a compass as I can for myself, and never let them annoy others.

                                                —Robert Southey

848, 2343.

TRUST
2144.   It is a maxim founded on the universal experience of mankind that no nation is to be trusted farther than it is bound by its interest.

                                            —George Washington

2145.   Government is a trust, and the officers of the government are trustees; and both the trust and the trustees are created for the benefit of the people.

                                                    —Henry Clay

2146.   The man who trusts men will make fewer mistakes than he who distrusts them.

                                                        —Cavour

2147.   Put your trust in God, my boys, and keep your powder dry.

                                                —Oliver Cromwell

420, 422, 702, 1390, 1666.

TRUTH

2148. I do not know what I may appear to the world, but to myself I seem to have been only like a boy playing on the seashore, and diverting myself in now and then finding a prettier shell, or a smoother pebble than ordinary, whilst the great ocean of truth lay all undiscovered before me.

—Sir Isaac Newton

2149. If your work of art is good, if it is true, it will find its echo and make its place—in six months, in six years, or after you are gone.

—Gustave Flaubert

2150. Man is the only animal that laughs and weeps; for he is the only animal that is struck with the difference between what things are, and what they ought to be.

—William Hazlitt

2151. The superstitution that the hounds of truth will rout the vermin of error seems, like a fragment of Victorian lace, quaint, but too brittle to be lifted out of the showcase.

—William F. Buckley, Jr.

2152. I am nothing, but truth is everything. I know I am right, because I know that liberty is right, for Christ teaches it, and Christ is God.

—Abraham Lincoln

2153. When you have closed your doors, and darkened your room, remember never to say that you are alone, for you are not alone; God is within, and your genius is within—and what need have they of light to see what you are doing?

—Epictetus

2154. Love the truth but pardon error.

—Voltaire

2155. All I know is, it is better to tell the truth than to lie, better to be free than a slave, better to have knowledge than be ignorant.

—H. L. Mencken

2156. It was for the love of the truths of the great and good Book that our fathers abandoned their native shore for the wilderness.

—Zachary Taylor

2157.   Today's "fact" becomes tomorrow's "misinformation."
—Alvin Toffler

2158.   Our minds possess by nature an insatiable desire to know the truth.
—Cicero

2159.   Truth is the secret of eloquence and of virtue, the basis of moral authority; it is the highest summit of art and life.
—Henri-Frederic Amiel

2160.   One should never trust a woman who tells one her real age. A woman who would tell that would tell anything.
—Oscar Wilde

2161.   What is originality? It is being one's self, and reporting accurately what we see and are.
—Ralph Waldo Emerson

2162.   The spirit of truth and the spirit of freedom—they are the pillars of society.
—Henrik Ibsen

2163.   We know the truth, not only by reason, but also by the heart.
—Blaise Pascal

2164.   The first and last thing required of genius is the love of truth.
—Goethe

2165.   So absolute good is truth, truth never hurts the teller.
—Robert Browning

2166.   The man who finds a truth lights a torch.
—Robert Ingersoll

2167.   An orator's virtue is to speak the truth.
—Plato

2168.   You shall know the truth, and the truth shall make you free.
—John 8:32

2169.   Whether he be a sinner or no, I know not: one thing I know, that, whereas I was blind, now I see.
—John 9:25

2170.   A Boy Scout had been called as a witness in court. The lawyer who was cross-examining him said, "Did anyone tell you what to say in court?"

"Yes, sir," the Boy Scout said.

"I thought so," the lawyer said. "Who was it?"

"My Scoutmaster," the boy said.

"Aha," the lawyer cried, "and what did he tell you?"

"He said the lawyers would get me mixed up if I wasn't careful, but that if I just told the truth, I would be all right."

104, 207, 365, 674, 969, 1052, 1233, 1541, 1675, 1824.

TWINS
2171.   I have a friend who has a twin sister. There's one strange thing about them. He's 45 years old and she's only 35.

2172.   The little six-year old was telling all of her friends about the great excitement at her house. "My mother just came home from the hospital with two little boys. They're twins," she explained.

"Who do they look like?" one of her friends asked.

"They look like each other," the proud little girl said.

UNCERTAINTY
2173.   Nothing is so uncertain or unpredictable as the feelings of a crowd.

—Livy

UNDERSTANDING
2174.   The first rule of all writing—that rule to which every other is subordinate—is that the words used by the writer shall be such as most fully and precisely convey his meaning to the great body of his readers. All considerations about the purity and dignity of style ought to bend to this consideration.

—Thomas Macaulay

2175.   The improvement of the understanding is for two ends; first, for our own increase of knowledge; secondly, to enable us to deliver and make out that knowledge to others.

—John Locke

2176. Despise not any man, and do not spurn anything; for there is no man that has not his hour, nor is there anything that has not its place.

—Author unknown

2177. If we could read the secret history of our enemies we should find in each man's life sorrow and suffering enough to disarm all hostility.

—Henry Wadsworth Longfellow

2178. When we are understood, it is proof that we speak well; and all your learned gabble is mere nonsense.

—Moliere

2179. Know well that a hundred holy temples of wood and stone have not the value of one understanding heart.

—Zoroaster

2180. The great object in trying to understand history is to get behind and grasp ideas.

—Lord Acton

2181. Life can only be understood backwards but it can only be lived forwards.

—Soren Kierkegaard

2182. It is a tie between men to have read the same book.

—Ralph Waldo Emerson

2183. To know what we know, and know what we do not know, that is understanding.

—Confucius

2184. What we do not understand we do not possess.

—Goethe

2185. Happy is the man that findeth wisdom, and the man that getteth understanding.

—Proverbs 3:13

2186. A man drove up to a friend's house and as he was getting out of his car his friend's fierce looking dog rushed within two or three feet of him and began barking as loud as he could.

The man was obviously frightened but his friend said, "Hey, he won't bite. He's just excited at seeing a stranger. You know the old proverb about a barking dog never bites."

"Yes," said the man. "I know the proverb, and you know the proverb, but are you sure the dog knows the proverb?"
549, 1009, 1766, 1861, 2053, 2286, 2299.

UNITY

2187.   Honest differences of views and honest debate are not disunity. They are the vital process of policy making among free men.

—Herbert Hoover

2188.   Yes, we must indeed all hang together, or most assuredly, we shall all hang separately.

—Benjamin Franklin

2189.   In essentials unity, in nonessentials liberty, in all things charity.

—St. Augustine

2190.   Behold how good and how pleasant it is for brethren to dwell together in unity.

—Psalms 133:1

674, 1824.

UNIVERSE

2191.   God gave man an upright countenance to survey the heavens, and to look upward to the stars.

—Ovid

2192.   That's one small step for man, one giant leap for mankind.

—Neil Armstrong

329, 514.

UNIVERSITY

2193.   The true University of these days is a collection of books.

—Thomas Carlyle

638.

UNSELFISHNESS

2194.   The only gift is a portion of thyself.

—Ralph Waldo Emerson

VACATION

2195. A vacation is what you take when you can no longer take what you've been taking.

—*Earl Wilson*

VALUES

2196. It is critical that we transmit the values by which we live to the younger generation. Clearly, each generation must be concerned about the succeeding ones. I think it is especially incumbent upon the family to transmit values and provide a thread of continuity through the turmoil of change. Naturally, young people eventually determine their own values. But all of us have an obligation at least to expose them to our own experience, learning, and aspirations.

—*David Rockefeller*

2197. A cynic is a man who knows the price of everything, and the value of nothing.

—*Oscar Wilde*

2198. Anybody can cut prices, but it takes brains to make a better article.

—*Philip D. Armour*

2199. What is all our knowledge worth? We do not even know what the weather will be tomorrow.

—*Berthold Auerbach*

2200. The aim of education is the knowledge not of fact, but of values.

—*Dean William Ralph Inge*

2201. "What?" the woman shopper said to the manager of the meat department, "do you mean to tell me your turkeys are 69¢ a pound? They're on sale at the other supermarkets for only 52¢ a pound."

The manager was a bit irked at the woman and said, "If you can buy turkeys so cheap over there, why don't you do it?"

"Because they are out of turkeys this morning, that's why," she said.

"Oh, I can do better than he can," the manager said. "Come back

some day when I'm out of turkeys and I'll price them to you at only 39¢ a pound."
2031.

VARIETY

2202.   I don't see why people want new plays all the time. What would happen to concerts if people wanted new music all the time?

—Clive Barnes

VERACITY

2203.   Any fool may write a most valuable book by chance, if he will only tell us what he heard and saw with veracity.

—Thomas Gray

VICTORY

2204.   It is defeat that turns bone to flint, and gristle to muscle, and makes men invincible, and forms those heroic natures that are now in ascendancy in the world. Do not then be afraid of defeat. You are never so near to victory as when defeated in a good cause.

—Henry Ward Beecher

2205.   You ask, what is our aim? I can answer in one word: Victory—victory at all costs, victory in spite of all terror, victory however long and hard the road may be; for without victory there is no survival.

—Sir Winston Churchill

2206.   So to conduct one's life as to realize oneself—this seems to me the highest attainment possible to a human being. It is the task of one and all of us, but most of us bungle it.

—Henrik Ibsen

2207.   I count him braver who overcomes his desire than him who overcomes his enemies; for the hardest victory is victory over self.

—Aristotle

2208.   They dared beyond their strength, hazarded beyond their judgment and in extremities were of excellent hope.

—Thucydides

2209. The ideal man bears the accidents of life with dignity and grace, making the best of circumstances.

—Aristotle

2210. The vanquished never yet spake well of the conqueror.

—Samuel Daniel

731, 1104, 1878, 2142.

VIGILANCE
2211. The condition upon which God has given liberty to man is eternal vigilance.

—John Philpot Curran

1340.

VIOLENCE
2212. Violence is the last refuge of the incompetent.

—Isaac Asimov

VIRTUE
2213. There are three marks of superior man: being virtuous, he is free from anxiety; being wise, he is free from perplexity; being brave, he is free from fear.

—Confucius

2214. The strength of a man's virtue should not be measured by his special exertions, but by his habitual acts.

—Blaise Pascal

2215. Knowledge is, indeed, that which, next to virtue, truly and essentially raises one man above another.

—Joseph Addison

2216. Search others for their virtues, thyself for thy vices.

—Benjamin Franklin

2217. The whole praise of virtue lies in action.

—Cicero

2218. Who can find a virtuous woman? for her price is far above rubies.

—Proverbs 31:10

2219.   Whatsoever things are true, whatsoever things are honest, whatsoever things are just, whatsoever things are pure, whatsoever things are lovely, whatsoever things are of good report; if there be any virtue, and if there be any praise, think on these things.

—Phillippians 4:8

38, 121, 124, 205, 1077, 1078, 1594, 1734, 1923, 2167.

VISION
2220.   A feeble man can see the farms that are fenced and tilled, the houses that are built. The strong man sees the possible houses and farms. His eye makes estates as fast as the sun breeds clouds.

—Ralph Waldo Emerson

2221.   Nobody, I think, ought to read poetry, or look at pictures or statues, who cannot find a great deal more in them than the poet or artist has actually expressed.

—Nathaniel Hawthorne

2222.   The dwarf sees farther than the giant, when he has the giant's shoulders to mount on.

—Samuel Taylor Coleridge

2223.   Vision is the art of seeing things invisible.

—Jonathan Swift

2224.   Where there is no vision, the people perish.

—Proverbs 29:18

890.

VOYAGE
2225.   In sea voyages, where there is nothing to be seen but sky and sea, men make diaries; but in land travel, wherein so much is to be observed, for the most part they omit it.

—Francis Bacon

2226.   Life's a voyage that's homeward bound.

—Herman Melville

WAR
2227. To eliminate ignorance, poverty, and disease, is a precondition to eliminating war.

—Warren G. Magnuson

360, 421, 1618, 1619.

WASTE
2228. Does thou love life? Then do not squander time, for that is the stuff life is made of.

—Benjamin Franklin

WATER
2229. Everywhere water is a thing of beauty, gleaming in the dewdrop; singing in the summer rain; shining in the icegems till the leaves all seem to turn to living jewels; spreading a golden veil over the setting sun; or a white gauze around the midnight sun.

—John Bartholomew Gough

1644.

WEAKNESS
2230. You cannot run away from weakness; you must some time fight it out or perish; and if that be so, why not now, and where you stand?

—Robert Louis Stevenson

1986, 1993.

WEALTH
2231. Money never made a man happy yet, nor will it. There is nothing in its nature to produce happiness. The more a man has, the more he wants. Instead of filling a vacuum, it makes one. If it satisfied one want, it doubles and trebles that want another way. That was a true proverb of the wise man, rely on it: "Better is a little with the fear of the Lord, than great treasure and trouble therewith."

—Benjamin Franklin

2232.   There is no real wealth but the labor of man. Were the mountains of gold and the valleys of silver, the world would not be one grain of corn the richer; nor one comfort would be added to the human race.

—Percy Bysshe Shelley

2233.   When I didn't have any, I believed that money was the measure of a person's wealth. Now I know that self-esteem and having true friends are more important.

—Art Fettig

2234.   Wealth may be an excellent thing, for it means power, it means leisure, it means liberty.

—James Russell Lowell

2235.   The true worth of a man is to be measured by the objects he pursues.

—Marcus Aurelius

2236.   He that loses wealth loses much:
            But he that loses courage loses all.

—Cervantes

2237.   Wealth, with wisdom added, is the best gift of fortune.

—Pindar

450, 1013, 1477, 1819, 1821, 2247, 2310.

WEATHER
2238.   When two Englishmen meet, their first talk is of the weather.

—Samuel Johnson

2239.   The clerk in the supermarket said to the shopper, "No, we haven't had any in a long time, now."

The manager who was passing by heard what the clerk said and he broke into the conversation and said, "Oh, yes, we have, lady. This is a new clerk and he doesn't know how we keep our stock records and inventory. We have plenty in the warehouse and will get some over this afternoon. If you come back after lunch we'll have plenty. Now, tell me, just what it was that he said we haven't had in a long time."

"Rain," the lady said as she turned and walked away.

WICKED

2240. The wicked flee when no man pursueth.

—Proverbs 28:1

WIN

2241. To love and win is the best thing; to love and lose is the next best.

—William Makepeace Thackeray

930, 1726, 2410.

WISDOM

2242. Though every old man has been young, and every young one hopes to be old, there seems to be a most unnatural misunderstanding between those two stages of life. This unhappy want of commerce arises from arrogance or exultation in youth, and irrational despondence or self-pity in age.

—Sir Richard Steel

2243. He is not to be called a true lover of wisdom who loves it for the sake of gain. And it may be said that the true philosopher loves every part of wisdom, and wisdom every part of the philosopher, inasmuch as she draws all to herself, and allows no one of his thoughts to wander to other things.

—Dante

2244. The wise of the earth have said in their hearts always, "God is, and there is none beside Him;" and the fools of all the earth have said in their hearts always, "I am, and there is none beside me."

—John Ruskin

2245. The wise man must remember that while he is a descendant of the past, he is a parent of the future; and that his thoughts are as children born to him, which he may not carelessly let die.

—Herbert Spencer

2246. There is a difference between happiness and wisdom; he that thinks himself the happiest man is really so but he who thinks himself the wisest man is generally the greatest fool.

—Francis Bacon

2247.   The true wealth of a nation lies not in its gold or silver, but in its learnings, wisdom, and in the uprightness of its sons.

—*Kahlil Gibran*

2248.   A wise man is cured of ambition by ambition itself; his aim is so exalted that riches, office, fortune, and favour cannot satisfy him.

—*Jean De La Bruyere*

2249.   It is wise to get knowledge and learning from every source—from a sot, a pot, a fool, a winter-mitten, or an old slipper.

—*Francois Rabelais*

2250.   He that can bear a reproof, and mend by it, if he is not wise, is in a fair way of being so.

—*Benjamin Franklin*

2251.   To know how to grow old is the master work of wisdom, and one of the most difficult chapters in the great art of living.

—*Henri-Frederic Amiel*

2252.   A man's wisdom is most conspicuous where he is able to distinguish among dangers and make the choice of the least.

—*Niccolo Machiavelli*

2253.   The wise man, before he speaks, will consider well what he speaks, to whom he speaks and where and when.

—*St. Ambrose*

2254.   A single conversation across the table with a wise man is better than ten years' study of books.

—*Henry Wadsworth Longfellow*

2255.   It is impossible to account for the creation of the universe, without the agency of a Supreme Being.

—*George Washington*

2256.   It is the province of knowledge to speak, and it is the privilege of wisdom to listen.

—*Oliver Wendell Holmes*

2257.   Authority without wisdom is like a heavy axe without an edge, fitter to bruise than polish.

—*Anne Bradstreet*

2258. I don't think much of a man who is not wiser today than he was yesterday.

—Abraham Lincoln

2259. The farther backward you can look, the farther forward you are likely to see.

—Sir Winston Churchill

2260. It is not knowing much, but what is useful, that makes a wise man.

—Thomas Fuller

2261. To write well, express yourself like the common people, but think like a wise man.

—Aristotle

2262. There is nothing more beautiful in this world than a healthy wise old man.

—Lin Yutang

2263. The wise course is to profit from the mistakes of others.

—Terence

2264. One must be a wise reader to quote wisely and well.

—Amos Bronson Alcott

2265. Never seem wiser, nor more learned, than the people you are with.

—Lord Chesterfield

2266. As for me, all I know is that I know nothing.

—Socrates

2267. Happy is he who gains wisdom from another's mishap.

—Publilius Syrus

2268. Before God we are all equally wise—equally foolish.

—Albert Einstein

2269. Not many men have both good fortune and good sense.

—Livy

2270. Sciences may be learned by rote, but wisdom not.

—Laurence Sterne

2271. Only the wisest and the stupidest of men never change.

—Confucius

2272. It takes a wise man to recognize a wise man.

—Xenophanes

2273. A loving heart is the truest wisdom.

—Charles Dickens

2274. Knowledge comes, but wisdom lingers.

—Alfred, Lord Tennyson

2275. There's a hell of a lot of difference between a wise man and a wise guy.

—John Cameron Swayze
278, 454, 1115, 1241, 1312, 1890, 1998, 2029, 2185, 2213.

WISH
2276. Opportunity, sooner or later, comes to all who work and wish.

—Lord Stanley

2277. The owner of a small town ice cream parlor was cleaning out his attic and found an old brass teakettle. Thinking it would make a beautiful antique if it were polished, he set out to clean it up. The moment he began to rub it, a genie appeared.

"I'm a genie," he said. "You have liberated me and now I am your servant forever. I can fulfill any wish you make. What would you like?"

"I don't know," the man said. "I want a lot of things. But first, I'd like to sit and think about my good fortune and then decide."

"That's a good idea," the genie said. "Why don't you wish for a vacation. I'll give you tickets for a Caribbean cruise and you and your wife can relax and you can do a lot of thinking."

"That sounds great," the man said, "but who would run the ice cream parlor while I am gone?"

"No problem," the genie said. "I'll take care of it myself."

So the man wished for a vacation. He was given his tickets and away he and his wife went. The genie kept his word. Monday morning he was on hand and opened the store exactly on time—9:00 o'clock. A few minutes later a man came in and sat at the counter and said, "Please make me a chocolate soda with whipped cream topping and a cherry on top."

And the genie said, "Okay, you are now a chocolate soda with whipped cream topping and a cherry on top."

WITNESS

2278.   History is the witness of the times, the torch of truth, the life of memory, the teacher of life, the messenger of antiquity.

—Cicero

2279.   There is no witness so terrible, no accuser so potent, as the conscience that dwells in every man's breast.

—Polybius

WOMAN

2280.   A modest woman, dressed out in all her finery, is the most tremendous object of the whole creation.

—Oliver Goldsmith

2281.   It was we, the people; not we, the white male citizens; nor yet we, the male citizens; but we the whole people who formed the Union. . .not to give the blessing of liberty, but to secure them. . .to the whole people—women as well as men.

—Susan B. Anthony

2282.   They say women talk too much. If you have worked in Congress you know that the filibuster was invented by men.

—Clare Boothe Luce

2283.   A woman's advice is not worth much, but he who doesn't heed it is a fool.

—Pedro Calderon

2284.   Women are never disarmed by compliments; men always are.

—Oscar Wilde

2285.   Most women would rather cuddle a baby than a typewriter or a machine.

—Phyllis Schlafly

2286.   However dull a woman may be, she will understand all there is in love; however intelligent a man may be, he will never know but half of it.

—Author unknown

2287.   Certainly, men and women are different. At the supper table if you ask a man, "Where did you get this cake?" he'll tell you, "At the supermarket." Ask his wife and she'll say, "What's the matter with it?"

Or, ask a woman how she bruised her toe and she'll say, "I kicked a chair." Ask her husband and he'll say, "Somebody left a chair in the middle of the room."

131, 362, 437, 643, 819, 1059, 1915, 2160, 2218, 2292.

WOMEN'S LIB

2288.   Man is not the enemy here, but the fellow victim. The real enemy is women's denigration of themselves.

—Betty Friedan

2289.   Women are like tea bags, you don't know their real strength until they get in hot water.

—Phyllis Schlafly

2290.   I'm for women's lib, but I am confident enough that I don't mind walking three paces behind Jerry.

—Betty Ford

2291.   I never had to become a feminist; I was born liberated.

—Grace Slick

2292.   I'd like to thank God, because *She* makes everything possible.

—Helen Reddy

WONDER

2293.   Is it any wonder that to this day this Galilean is too much for our small hearts?

—H. G. Wells

2294.   Wonders are many, and none is more wonderful than Man.

—*Sophocles*

1653, 1868.

WORD

2295.   For forty years I have loved the Word of God. I feel the blessed pages under my hand with special thankfulness as a rod and a staff to keep firm my steps through the valley of the shadow of depression and world calamity. Truly the Bible—the teaching of our Savior—is the only way out of the dark. If the wealth of things which we have in abundance has not knocked on our selfish hearts and opened them to the central message of Jesus, "Love ye one another," perhaps these days of widespread suffering will be the pointed instrument that will "stab spirit broad awake."

—*Helen Keller*

2296.   I conceive that words are like money—not the worse for being common, but that it is the stamp of custom alone that gives them circulation or value.

—*William Hazlitt*

2297.   Man does not live by words alone, despite the fact that sometimes he has to eat them.

—*Adlai Stevenson*

2298.   Words are like money; there is nothing so useless, unless when in actual use.

—*Samuel Butler*

2299.   The words *you know* and *I mean* are strewn like loose gravel through ordinary conversation, causing slippage in meaning.

—*Norman Cousins*

2300.   Without knowing the force of words, it is impossible to know men.

—*Confucius*

2301.   Words, like glasses, observe everything which they do not make clear.

—*Joseph Joubert*

2302.   One good word quenches more heat than a bucket of water.

—*Ancient proverb*

2303.   Four things do not come back: The spoken word, the sped arrow, the past life, and the neglected opportunity.

—*Ancient proverb*

2304.   Is not my word like as a fire? saith the Lord; and like a hammer that breaketh the rock in pieces?

—*Jeremiah 23:29*

1132, 1397, 1424, 1706, 1922, 1968, 1973.

WORK

2305.   Give us, oh, give us, the man who sings at his work! He will do more in the same time—he will do it better—he will persevere longer. One is scarcely sensible of fatigue whilst he marches to music. The very stars are said to make harmony as they revolve in their spheres. Wonderous is the strength of cheerfulness, altogether past calculation in its powers of endurance. Efforts to be permanently useful, must be uniformly joyous, a spirit all sunshine, graceful from very gladness, beautiful because bright.

—*Thomas Carlyle*

2306.   Inasmuch as most good things are produced by labor, it follows that all such things ought to belong to those whose labor has produced them. But it has happened in all ages of the world that some had labored, and others, without labor, have enjoyed a large proportion of the fruits. This is wrong, and should not continue. To secure to each laborer the whole product of his labor as nearly as possible is a worthy object of any good government.

—*Abraham Lincoln*

2307.   My share of the work of the world may be limited, but the fact that it is work makes it precious. Darwin could work only half an hour at a time; yet in many diligent half-hours he laid anew the foundations of philosophy. Green, the historian, tells us the world is moved not only by the mighty shoves of the heroes, but also by the aggregate of the tiny pushes of each honest worker.

—*Helen Keller*

2308. When men are rightly occupied, their amusement grows out of their work, as the color petals out of a fruitful flower; when they are faithfully helpful and compassionate, all their emotions are steady, deep, perpetual and vivifying to the soul as is the natural pulse to the body.

—John Ruskin

2309. I studied the lives of great men and famous women; and I found that the men and women who got to the top were those who did the jobs they had in hand, with everything they had of energy, enthusiasm and hard work.

—Harry S. Truman

2310. Whatever there is of greatness. . .in any country, is due to labor. The laborer is the author of all greatness and wealth. Without labor there would be no government, and no leading class, and nothing to preserve.

—Ulysses S. Grant

2311. Poverty is uncomfortable, as I can testify; but nine times out of ten the best thing that can happen to a young man is to be tossed overboard and compelled to sink or swim for himself.

—James A. Garfield

2312. He who would do some great thing in this short life must apply himself to work with such a concentration of his forces as, to idle spectators, who live only to amuse themselves, looks like insanity.

—Francis Parkman

2313. The law of worthy life is fundamentally the law of strife. It is only through labor and painful effort, by grim energy and resolute courage, that we move on to better things.

—Theodore Roosevelt

2314. It is only those who do not know how to work that do not love it. To those who do, it is better than play—it is religion.

—J. W. Paterson

2315. America's competitive spirit, the work ethic of this people, is alive and well. The dignity of work, the value of achievement, the morality of self-reliance—none of these is going out of style.

—Richard M. Nixon

2316.   How much that the world calls selfishness is only generosity with narrow walls—a too exclusive solicitude to maintain a wife in luxury, or make one's children rich.

—T. W. S. Higginson

2317.   I congratulate poor young men upon being born to that ancient and honorable degree which renders it necessary that they should devote themselves to hard work.

—Andrew Carnegie

2318.   Be glad of life because it gives you the chance to love and to work and to play and to look up at the stars.

—Henry Van Dyke

2319.   In the ordinary business of life, industry can do anything which genius can do, and very many things which it cannot.

—Henry Ward Beecher

2320.   It is necessary to work, if not from inclination, at least from despair. Everything considered, work is less boring than amusing oneself.

—Charles Baudelaire

2321.   Let the farmer forevermore be honored in his calling; for they who labor in the earth are the chosen people of God.

—Thomas Jefferson

2322.   Work is not a curse; it is the prerogative of intelligence, the only means to manhood, and the measure of civilization.

—Calvin Coolidge

2323.   Mountain-climbing is when you pay $100 a day to do something that if you had to do it, you'd want to be paid $100 a day.

—Bob Orben

2324.   Some people are suffering from lack of work, some from lack of water, many more from lack of wisdom.

—Calvin Coolidge

2325.   Quite a few people are already working a four-day week. Trouble is, it takes them five or six days to do it.

—Earl Wilson

2326.   Industry, economy, honesty and kindness form a quartette of virtues that will never be improved upon.

—James Oliver

2327.   We have too many people who live without working, and we have altogether too many who work without living.

—Charles B. Brown

2328.   If the power to do hard work is not talent, it is the best possible substitute for it.

—James A. Garfield

2329.   Some people have a perfect genius for doing nothing, and doing it assiduously.

—Thomas C. Haliburton

2330.   The victory of success is half won when one gains the habit of work.

—Sarah A. Bolton

2331.   A man has only so much knowledge as he puts to work.

—St. Francis of Assisi

2332.   A man is a worker. If he is not that, he is nothing.

—Joseph Conrad

2333.   There is no easy road from the earth to the stars.

—Seneca

2334.   Everything comes to him who hustles while he waits.

—Thomas Edison

2335.   Work banishes those three great evils, boredom, vice and poverty.

—Voltaire

2336.   Genius begins great works; labor alone finishes them.

—Joseph Joubert

2337.   Everyone is the sum of his own works.

—Cervantes

2338.   That load becomes light which is cheerfully borne.

—Ovid

2339.   Whatsoever thy hand findeth to do, do it with thy might.

—Ecclesiastes 9:10

2340.   Two men were talking about their jobs. "The company where I work is putting in a computer system and it is going to put a lot of people out of work. Have they started that over where you work?"

"Oh," said his friend, "We've been on computers for more than five years but they can't replace me. Nobody has been able to figure out exactly what I do."

595, 623, 733, 802, 1016, 1277, 1300, 1484, 1642, 1827, 2017.

WORLD
2341.   People who develop the habit of thinking of themselves as world citizens are fulfilling the first requirement of sanity in our time. . .More and more, the choice for the world's people is between becoming world warriors or world citizens.

—Norman Cousins

2342.   I look upon all the world as my parish.

—John Wesley

905.

WORRY
2343.   Worry is interest paid on trouble before it becomes due.

—Dean William Ralph Inge

2344.   It is not work that kills, but worry.

—Ancient proverb

WORSHIP
2345.   What greater calamity can fall upon a nation than the loss of worship?

—Thomas Carlyle

814, 1010, 1372, 1967.

WORTH
2346.   A man's worth is no greater than the worth of his ambition.

—Marcus Aurelius

164, 856.

WRATH

2347. Nursing her wrath to keep it warm.

—Robert Burns

2348. Beware the fury of a patient man.

—John Dryden

2349. A man deep-wounded may feel too much pain to feel much anger.

—George Eliot

WRITING

2350. To write well is to think well, to feel well, and to render well; it is to possess at once intellect, soul, and taste.

—Georges Louis Buffon

2351. That writer does the most, who gives his reader the most knowledge, and takes from him the least time.

—Charles Caleb Colton

2352. When once the itch of literature comes over a man, nothing can cure it but the scratching of a pen.

—Samuel Lover

744, 1190, 2174.

WRONG

2353. A man should never be ashamed to own he has been in the wrong, which is but saying, in other words, that he is wiser today than he was yesterday.

—Alexander Pope

2354. I can retain neither respect nor affection for a government which has been moving from wrong to wrong in order to defend its immorality.

—Mahatma Gandhi

103, 673, 1377, 1832.

YOUTH

2355. A man is still young so long as women can make him happy or unhappy. He reaches middle age when they can no longer make him unhappy. He is old when they cease to make him either happy or unhappy.

—*Author unknown*

2356.   Forty is the old age of youth; fifty is the youth of old age.

—*Victor Hugo*

2357.   As I approve of a youth that has something of the old man in him, so I am no less pleased with an old man that has something of the youth.

—*Cicero*

2358.   Make wisdom your provision for the journey from youth to old age, for it is more certain support than all other possessions.

—*Bias of Priene*

2359.   Men and nations can only be reformed in their youth; they become incorrigible as they grow old.

—*Jean-Jacques Rousseau*

97, 370, 1312, 1444, 1954, 2242.

ZEAL
2360.   I find the great thing in this world is not so much where we stand, as in what direction we are moving.

—*Oliver Wendell Holmes*

2361.   Through zeal knowledge is gotten, through lack of zeal knowledge is lost; let a man who knows this double path of gain and loss thus place himself that knowledge may grow.

—*Buddha*

HUMOROUS OPENERS
The first thirty seconds of your speech following your introduction can often be the most critical half-minute of your entire presentation. If you are ready with your first sentence, if you are full of confidence, if you are relaxed, if you have rehearsed your opening remarks, you will be off to a strong start. You should move into your speech like the well-trained soldier who steps off to the first beat of the drum.

Humor can be the key to a dramatic opening. It can attract the attention of your audience instantly, it helps you build rapport with them, it relaxes them, and incidentally, it helps relax you.

Even if you are speaking on a serious subject, a hearty belly laugh can help establish you as the focal point of the meeting and create an air of expectancy for what is to follow.

Here are a few examples:

2362. I'm happy to be here this evening. My plane arrived on time and I had no delays. I even checked into the hotel in time to take a nap. The airlines in America are great. The other day I had a speech in San Francisco. I had breakfast in Atlanta, lunch in Denver, dinner in San Francisco. Of course, my baggage was in Dallas.

2363. I hope all of you are comfortable. But, not too comfortable. The other night I was speaking, and one man in the audience did get too comfortable. He got so comfortable that he went sound asleep. He moved the dishes out of his way, put his head down on the table and took a nap. His wife was embarrassed. I saw her trying to kick him under the table, but she couldn't reach that far. Finally, she picked up a spoon and tapped him on the head with it. That woke him up. He sat up and rubbed his head and said to her, "Honey, you're going to have to hit me harder than that. I can still hear him."

2364. The other night I was speaking at a banquet, and right in the middle of my speech the public address system went dead. I tried to talk without it, but I noticed a fellow in the back with his hand up to his ear straining to hear me. He said, "Louder." So, I raised my voice and tried again. But, he kept saying, "Louder." I kept raising my voice until I was shouting at him. Finally, I was yelling so loud that it bothered a man sitting down front. He couldn't stand it any more, so he jumped up and called out to the man in the back, "What's the matter back there, can't you hear him?

"No, not a word," the man in the back shouted.

The man in front yelled back, "In that case, buddy, move over. I'm coming back to sit with you."

2365. The man who introduced me called me an expert. I'm reminded of the old definition of an expert, "Anyone who is fifty miles away from home with a brief case in his hand." And my daughter says an expert "is like the bottom of a double-boiler. It shoots off a lot of steam, but it never really knows what's cooking."

2366.   Several weeks ago I was speaking to an oil dealers' convention in Pittsburgh. The man who introduced me tried to impress the audience with my importance. He introduced me as the man who had just made $800,000 in an oil deal down in Texas. Of course, that wasn't exactly true. It wasn't an oil deal, it was a real estate deal. It wasn't in Texas, it was in Florida. Not only that, he got his figures mixed up. It wasn't $800,000, it was $800. Besides, it wasn't a profit, it was a loss.

2367.   Not long ago after I had spoken at a rather large dinner meeting, I was milling around with the crowd in the lobby of the hotel. I wasn't exactly eavesdropping, but I did overhear a woman say to her husband, "Oh, that speaker tonight. I'm so full of his message that I can hardly speak."

And her husband said, "I know exactly how you feel, I got a bellyful of him myself."

2368.   The other night after I had made my speech, I was standing with the president of the association at the door of the dining room shaking hands with the people as they were leaving. Everyone had something nice to say about my speech until that last man who finally shook my hand. As he did, he said, "I think that was the worst speech I ever heard and whoever invited you to speak tonight should be put out of the organization."

Of course, my feelings were hurt. But the president was the one who got upset. He was terribly embarrassed and said to me, "Don't pay any attention to what that fellow said. He's considered to be a half-wit. He's never had an original thought in his life. All he does is stand around listening to what other people say and then he repeats it everywhere he goes."

2369.   One time back in my home town, there was a judge trying a divorce case. He had never had a case like this one. The woman had been married only one day. He was questioning her about her problem. "I can't understand why you want a divorce. You married the most eligible man in town. He was the best-looking man in town. He was rich. He didn't smoke. He didn't drink. All of your friends have been telling you those things about him for months and months. Then you married him yesterday and today you want a divorce. I can't understand it. What is your problem?"

"Well, judge, I guess that's my problem," the woman said. "That man was just naturally over-introduced."

2370. That introduction reminds me of the three hardest things in the world to do. The first is trying to climb over a barbed-wire fence when it is leaning toward you. The second is trying to kiss a pretty girl when she is leaning away from you. The third is trying to live up to all of those complimentary things that Mr. Chairman has just said about me.

2371. This is a great hotel, isn't it? This is the first time I've been here. When I checked in I was so impressed that I was afraid I wouldn't tip the bellman properly, so when he took my bags to my room, I just asked him. I said, "What is the average tip here?"

And he said, "Six dollars."

Well, I didn't want to look cheap, so I gave him the six dollars. But, I said to him, "If six dollars is the average tip here, and with all of the conventions that come here, you must be getting rich."

"No," he said, "All the time I've worked here, this is the first average I was ever able to get."

2372. Wow! After listening to all of those wonderful things that Mr. Chairman has just said, I know exactly how a waffle feels when somebody smothers it with honey.

2373. Thank you, Mr. Chairman, for that gracious and flattering introduction. About the only thing you didn't say about me was that I was born in a log cabin. And you were right. I wasn't born in a log cabin. But my family did move into one as soon as they could afford it.

2374. Recently I was invited to speak to a group of ranchers down in Texas. I had been speaking about two minutes when a great big fellow on the back row stood up and pulled out a pistol and pointed it toward the lectern. That's the sort of thing that will scare anybody, and I said to the chairman. "What have I done wrong? What's the matter?"

And the chairman said, "Don't worry about him. He's not going to hurt you. But, I sure do pity the fellow who just introduced you."

2375. [The speaker touches the microphone and says:] I'm glad this thing is steady. The other night when I started to speak, the microphone dropped down. I pushed it up, but it dropped down again. After that had happened three or four times, the program chairman jumped up with a dime in his hand and began to tighten a set screw. As he worked on it, he said to the audience, "Don't worry, folks. Nothing's the matter except I think our speaker has a screw loose."

HUMOROUS CLOSERS

Bringing the curtain down on a speech is not an easy matter. It's much harder to conclude a speech than it is to start one. Your speech begins when the chairman says, "I now present. . ." There you are and off you go.

But ending a speech is a do-it-yourself proposition. You do not have a chairman handy to say, "Now our honored guest will quit talking and sit down. . ."

There are many ways to end a speech—some on a serious note and some with humor. Someone has estimated that more than twenty thousand after-luncheon, after-dinner and in-between speeches are made in America every day. In most of those cases, the audience would be pleased if the speech ended on a note of levity.

If you want people to remember you and what you said, the old vaudeville rule still stands—"always leave them laughing."

Here are a few stories that will help your speech end with a solid round of applause as well as with a roar of laughter:

2376. I want to thank you for listening this evening. My speech really isn't over yet, but I'm going to stop now because I have to catch a plane that takes off in exactly 56 minutes.

2377. Now, I have come to that part of my speech that is the same as asking a pretty girl for a date. If she says she'll think it over—it already is.

2378. There's a modern proverb that says if you want to put a permanent finish on your car, you can do it by racing the train to the railroad crossing. And if you want to put a finish to my talk, all you have to do is start clapping.

2379. I would like to close by saying "Carbolic acid." I heard a speaker say that one time and afterward I asked him what he meant by it. And he said, "I always end my speeches that way. I used to say 'adios' which is goodbye in Spanish. And sometimes I'd say 'au revoir' which is goodbye in French. I even tried 'auf Wiedersehen.' That means goodbye in German. But, I discovered that most people don't understand those languages. So, now I say 'Carbolic acid.' That means goodbye in any language."

2380. At this point, I wonder if I'm not like the country boy who was walking through the woods with his girl friend one Sunday afternoon. He put his arm around her and looked into her pretty blue eyes and said, "Honey, I love you more than anything in the world. Will you marry me?"

She didn't hesitate a second. "Oh, yes, I'll marry you."

They continued to walk through the woods and neither one of them said anything. After about fifteen or twenty minutes of complete silence, the young lady turned to her boyfriend and said. "Honey, why don't you say something?"

He looked again into her pretty blue eyes and said, "It seems to me that I've probably said too much as it is."

2381. I hope I haven't taken too much of your time today. I hope my speech wasn't like an old friend of mine who is eighty-six. He's always dreamed of living to be a hundred years old. Last summer he went for his annual checkup and the doctor told him that he would have to give up drinking and smoking.

"And then will I live to be a hundred?" he asked the doctor.

"I can't guarantee that," the doctor said, "but it will sure seem like it."

2382. [This is a real laugh-getter when you have spoken at a formal dinner where everyone is wearing evening dress.] It was a pleasure speaking to such fine company tonight. I feel like the drunk who was staggering down the street late at night on his way home. His minister happened to pass in his car, and he stopped and picked up the drunk and drove him home. When they arrived in front of the drunk's house the drunk said to the minister. "Thanks for the ride home. Now come up to the front door with me. I want my wife to see who I was out with tonight."

2383. I thank you for inviting me to be a part of your meeting. I want to thank you, too, for laughing at my efforts to tell a story or two. My wife told me the other night that all of my stories are farfetched. I asked her what she meant by farfetched and she said, "Because most of them were brought to this country on the *Mayflower*."

2384.   Thank you for letting me speak to you today. I hope it was as good as a speech I made last week. Because after that one, when I had finished and sat down, everybody said it was the best thing I had ever done.

2385.   Now, I think I had better stop before I get hoarse. That's embarrassing for a speaker. Three weeks ago I had laryngitis. It began rather mildly at the office in the morning, but by the time I was ready to go home I could hardly whisper. I thought it might be a good idea to stop by a doctor's office. A friend told me about a good throat specialist who lived right on my way home. So I stopped at his house and rang the doorbell. In about half a minute the door was opened by the doctor's wife. So, I whispered to her and said, "Is the doctor home?"

And she whispered back and said, "No, he's out of town. Come on in."

2386.   Thank you for letting me speak to you today. I have tried to stick to my subject and not wander too far. When I was at the university we had an absent-minded professor. One evening he dropped in on his old friend, a doctor. They had a pleasant visit, including a game of chess, and before long a couple of hours had passed. As the professor was putting on his coat to leave, the doctor, said, "The family's all well, I suppose?"

"Good heavens," the professor said, "That reminds me why I came to see you. My wife is lying in the middle of our living room having some sort of convulsion."

2387.   [This one will help you end a question and answer period.] I would like to stand here all day answering questions and talking about my favorite subject. But I think I should take the same advice that the mother cabbage gave to her offspring.

Once there was a little baby cabbage who said to his mother, "Mommy, I'm worried about something. As I sit in this row of cabbages and grow and grow and grow day after day, how will I know when to stop growing?"

"The rule to follow," the mamma cabbage said, "is to quit when you are ahead."

2388.   From some of the things I have talked about today, you may think we have a lot of problems facing us. I thought of the troubles of a friend of mine. The other morning, before he could get out of his house and head for work, he had four long-distance calls. Everyone seemed to have a problem. And everybody wanted him to get on a plane that day and come help out. He finally told his wife to forget about his breakfast. He rushed out of the house as fast as he could. Then, when he stepped into the garage he discovered his car wouldn't start. So he called a taxi to take him to work. While he was waiting for the taxi, he got another call—this time from Chicago—about another problem. Finally, the taxi came and my friend rushed out, piled in the back seat and yelled, "All right, let's get going."

"Where do you want me to take you?" the taxi driver asked.

"I don't care where we go," the man shouted. "I've got problems everywhere."

2389.   I guess I have covered everything in my speech except the weather so before I sit down I might as well talk about that for a moment.

Back home on the farm, one time when I was a boy, we had a blizzard. Of course, when we had that kind of weather, the schools would shut down. So they closed the schools for three days. Then, on the first day that school was open, the teacher noticed a little fellow on the front row with his head on his desk, sound asleep. She woke him up and said, "What's the matter? Why are you so sleepy? Are you sick?"

And the little boy said, "No, I'm not sick. It was the chicken thieves last night. You know, they've been stealing our chickens for a long time and Pa said the next time they came around he was going to get himself a couple of dead chicken thieves. And last night in the middle of the night he heard 'em. So Pa jumped out of bed and ran for the chicken house. He didn't even take time to put on his trousers. He ran out in his nightshirt. He grabbed his shotgun by the back door and loaded both barrels. He put his fingers on both triggers and he tiptoed out through all that snow to the chicken house. He heard 'em inside and he was easing that door open real careful-like with his gun pointed inside. Well, you know that old dog of ours named Towser? He came up behind Pa with his cold nose. And we were up all night long picking and cleaning chickens."

Authors Who Are Quoted

A

Acton, Lord John Emerich (1834–1902), English historian.
2180.

Adams, John (1735–1826), Second President of the United States.
645, 1763.

Adams, John Quincy (1767–1848), Sixth President of the United States.
497, 1077, 1088, 1639, 1863.

Adams, Thomas (1612–1653), English clergyman and author.
108.

Addison, Joseph (1672–1719), English essayist and poet.
102, 160, 172, 265, 355, 399, 451, 455, 628, 989, 1026, 1121, 1230, 1285, 1371, 1409, 1636, 1762, 1897, 1943, 1963, 2215.

Adler, Felix (1851–1933), American educator and reformer.
240.

Aeschylus (525–456 B.C.), Greek poet.
840, 1037, 1532, 1810.

Aesop (620–560 B.C.), Greek fabler.
68, 296, 407, 992, 1647, 1879.

Agassiz, Jean Louis (1807–1873), American naturalist and author.
2002.

Alcott, Amos Bronson (1799–1888), American educator.
1534, 2026, 2264.

Alcott, Louisa May (1832–1888), American author.
181, 275.

Aldrich, Thomas Bailey (1836–1907), American poet, novelist.
709.

Alexander the Great (356–323 B.C.), King of Macedonia.
402, 687.

Alexander, J. W. (1856–1915), American painter.
1939.

Allen, James Lane (1845–1925), American novelist.
490.

Allen, Steve (Contemporary), American author, actor, composer.
699, 1117, 1335.

Altgeld, John Peter (1847–1902), Governor of Illinois.
111.

Amiel, Henri-Frederic (1821–1881), Swiss professor.
574, 792, 820, 1236, 1616, 2045, 2056, 2159, 2251.

Andersen, Hans Christian (1805–1875), Danish author of fairy tales.
1355, 1506.

Anouilh, Jean (Contemporary), French dramatist.
1350.

Anstey, Christopher (1724–1805), English essayist.
1684.

Anthony, Susan B. (1820–1906), American feminist; leader in woman suffrage movement.
2281.

Antiphanes (360 B. C.), Greek dramatist.
543, 1379.

Antiphon (5th century B.C.), Greek orator and statesman.
1846.

Aquaviva (1543–1615), Roman Jesuit leader.
916.

Aristophanes (448?–380? B.C.), Athenian dramatist.
1296.

Aristotle (384–322 B. C.), Greek philosopher.
49, 149, 377, 415, 578, 765, 844, 892, 1020, 1224, 1268, 1294, 1323, 1338, 1460, 1769, 1836, 2052, 2065, 2207, 2209, 2261.

Armour, Philip D. (1832–1901), American businessman.
2198.

Armstrong, Neil A. (Contemporary), American astronaut, first man to set foot on the moon.
2192.

Arnold, Matthew (1822–1888), English poet.
414, 664, 886, 997, 1611.

Ascham, Roger (1515–1568), English scholar and writer.
379.

Asimov, Isaac (Contemporary), American author.
790, 1766, 2212.

Asner, Edward (Contemporary), American author.
360.

Astor, John Jacob (1763–1848), American capitalist and philanthropist.
1013.

Auerbach, Berthold (1812–1882), German novelist.
2199.

Aungerville, Richard (1287–1345), English clergyman.
261.

Aurelius, Marcus Antoninus (121–180 A. D.), Roman Emperor.
67, 239, 329, 348, 479, 801, 917, 1188, 1353, 1452, 1484, 1598, 1990, 2083, 2117, 2235, 2346.

Ausonius (4th century A. D.), Roman poet.
1185.

B

Bacon, Francis (1561–1626), English philosopher and essayist.
70, 96, 105, 123, 250, 268, 508, 608, 745, 847, 1430, 1514, 1550, 1682, 1765, 1778, 1867, 1878, 2003, 2037, 2225, 2246.

Bailey, F. Lee (Contemporary), American lawyer, author.
1221, 1288.

Bailey, Nathan (Died 1742), English lexicographer.
1681.

Bailey, Philip James (1816–1902), English poet.
610, 797, 1392.

Baker, Howard H., Jr. (Contemporary), United States senator.
627.

Balzac, Honore de (1799–1850), French author.
549, 1214, 1462.

Barere, Bertrand (1755–1841), French statesman.
1345.

Barham, Richard Harris (1788–1845), English churchman and humorist.
321.

Barnes, Clive (Contemporary), American drama critic.
522, 1786, 2202.

Barrie, Sir James Matthew (1860–1937), Scottish novelist and playwright.
358, 502, 1031.

Barrow, Isaac (1630–1677), English theologian, mathematician.
273.

Barthelemy, August Marseille (1796–1867), French poet and politician.
334.

Barton, Bruce (1886–1967), American advertising executive, author.
467.

Baudelaire, Charles (1821–1867), French poet.
2320.

Baxter, Richard (1615–1691), English preacher, author.
764.

Bayh, Birch (Contemporary), United States senator.
1365.

Bayh, Marvella, Deceased wife of Senator Birch Bayh.
1985.

Beaumarchais, Pierre Caron de (1732–1799), French dramatist and pamphleteer.
227, 2041.

Beecher, Henry Ward (1813–1887), American clergyman, writer, editor.
16, 243, 368, 530, 657, 782, 796, 860, 885, 1064, 1125, 1243, 1282, 1870, 1980, 2025, 2049, 2204, 2319.

Beethoven, Ludwig van (1770–1827), German composer.
755, 1501.

Bellow, Saul (Contemporary), American novelist.
890, 1190.

Belloy, Dormont de (1727–1775), French dramatist.
1400.

Bennett, Charles E. (Contemporary), United States congressman.
555.

Bennett, Arnold (1867–1931), English writer.
311, 634, 1022, 1485.

Bhagavadgita, A sacred Hindu text.
1849.

Bias of Priene (570 B.C.), Greek philosopher.
2358.

Bierce, Ambrose (1842–1914?), American writer, disappeared in Mexico in 1913.
1797.

Billings, Josh (1818–1885), American humorist.
1250, 1808.

Bismarck, Prince Otto E. L. von (1815–1898), German military and political leader.
649.

Black, Jeremiah S. (1810–1883), Justice of the United States Supreme Court.
1226.

Blackmore, Richard D. (1825–1900), English novelist.
1683.

Blake, John Lauris (1778–1857), American clergyman and author.
2032.

Blake, William (1757–1827), English poet and engraver.
249, 1539, 2084.

Bohn, Henry George (1796–1884), English publisher.
471, 854.

Boileau, Nicholas (1636–1711), French poet and critic.
1822.

Bolingbroke (1367–1413), Henry IV, King of England.
1061.

Bolton, Sarah Knowles (1841–1916), American author.
2330.

Bonard (1805–1867), French admiral.
729.

Bonnat (1833–1922), French painter.
1162.

Borge, Victor (Contemporary), Danish-born concert pianist, comedian.
1947.

Borrow, George (1803–1881), English linguist, author.
1645.

Boufflers, Jean de (1738–1815), French writer, soldier.
1656.

Bovee, Christian Nestell (1820–1904), American lawyer.
40, 435, 517, 1205, 1892.

Bowles, William Lisle (1762–1850), English poet, critic.
824.

Bracken, Peg (Contemporary), American author, humorist.
1443.

Bradley, General Omar N. (1893–1981), American military leader.
1105.

Bradstreet, Anne (1612–1672), English poet, American colonist.
2257.

Braun, Wernher von (1912–1977), German-born American rocket engineer.
223.

Brennan, William J. Jr. (Contemporary), Justice of the Supreme Court of the United States.
1290.

Brooks, Phillips (1835–1893), American clergyman.
8, 706, 1062, 1067, 1128.

Brothers, Dr. Joyce (Contemporary), American psychologist, author, television personality.
603, 749, 1209, 1390, 1418, 1474.

Brougham, Henry Peter (1778–1868), Scottish jurist.
644.

Brown, Charles B. (1771–1810), American writer.
2327.

Browne, Sir Thomas (1605–1682), English physician, author.
175, 1254.

Browning, Elizabeth Barrett (1806–1861), English poet.
2100.

Browning, Robert (1812–1889), English poet.
571, 777, 1325, 1425, 1503, 1761, 1871, 2165.

Bruyere, Jean de la (1645–1696), French moralist.
263, 403, 998, 1034, 1468, 1586, 1938, 2248.

Bryan, William Jennings (1860–1925), American statesman.
364, 1671, 1961.

Bryant, William Cullen (1794–1878), American poet.
1515.

Buchwald, Art (Contemporary), American newspaper columnist, author, satirist.
2015.

Buck, Pearl (1892–1973), American novelist; Nobel Prize in literature in 1938.
595, 813.

Buckley, William F. Jr. (Contemporary), American editor, man of letters.
639, 2151.

Budgell, E. (1686–1737), English writer.
838.

Buffon, Georges Louis (1707–1788), French naturalist.
2350.

Bulwer-Lytton, George E. L. (1803–1873), English novelist, dramatist.
132, 346, 470, 703, 1208, 1446, 1686, 1887, 1932, 2048.

Bunyan, John (1628–1688), English preacher, author.
1242.

Burbank, Luther (1849–1926), American horticulturist.
308.

Burke, Edmund (1729–1797), English statesman.
72, 536, 681, 1333, 1596, 2134.

Burnet, Bishop Gilbert (1643–1715), Scottish-born Bishop of Salisbury, historian.
1900.

Burns, Robert (1759–1796), Scottish poet.
114, 1080, 1281, 2347.

Burr, Aaron (1756–1836), Third Vice-president of the United States.
47.

Burroughs, John (1837–1921), American naturalist, author.
196.

Burton, Sir Richard (1821–1890), English Orientalist.
445.

Burton, Robert (1577–1640), English clergyman, scholar, writer.
1092.

Butler, Samuel (1835–1902), English scholar, novelist.
1537, 1791, 2298.

Byrd, Admiral Richard E. (1888–1957), American polar explorer.
1792.

Byrd, William (1647–1744), American planter, satirist.
2079.

Byron, Lord (1788–1824), English poet.
711, 1309.

C

Calderon, Pedro (1600–1681), Spanish poet and playwright.
2283.

Camden, William (1551–1623), English writer.
1058.

Campbell, Alexander (1788–1866), American religious leader.
1635.

Carlyle, Thomas (1759–1881), English writer.
52, 73, 269, 323, 401, 493, 573, 580, 606, 623, 653, 674,
746, 926, 995, 1081, 1126, 1135, 1167, 1180, 1364, 1536,
1542, 1581, 1927, 1931, 1956, 1989, 2096, 2193, 2305,
2345.

Carnegie, Andrew (1835–1919), American industrialist.
48, 1480, 2317.

Carnegie, Dale (1888–1955), American author, lecturer.
829.

Carroll, Lewis (1832–1898), English author, mathematician.
217, 1424.

Carter, Arnold "Nick" (Contemporary), American public
speaker, motivator.
1875, 2023.

Carter, James Earl (Jimmy) (Contemporary), Thirty-ninth President of the United States.
683, 982, 1508, 1988.

Carver, George Washington (1864?–1943), American agricultural
chemist, educator.
204.

Cato, Marcus Porcius (95-46 B.C.), Roman statesman.
53, 1085, 1103, 1594, 1634, 1832, 1843, 1854, 1895, 1923.

Catullus (First century B. C.), Roman poet.
899.

Cavour, Count Camillo Benso di (1810–1861), Italian political
leader.
424, 2146.

Cecil, Lord David (Contemporary), English biographer.
1259.

Cervantes, Miguel de (1547–1616), Spanish poet, playwright.
218, 386, 394, 533, 577, 778, 786, 806, 1060, 1334, 1711,
2113, 2236, 2337.

Chapman, George (1559?–1634), English poet.
972, 1455.

Charron, Pierre (1541–1603), French theologian.
351.

Chateaubriand, Francois (1768–1848), French author, political leader.
378.

Chesterfield, Lord (1694–1773), English statesman, writer.
106, 389, 392, 396, 693, 1157, 1314, 1567, 1630, 1753, 1830, 1918, 1925, 2119, 2265.

Chesterton, Gilbert Keith (1874–1936), English essayist, novelist.
492, 1313.

Chiang Kai-Shek, Mme. (Contemporary), Wife of Chinese statesman.
1696.

Christina, (1626–1689), Queen of Sweden.
591.

Chrysler, Walter P. (1875–1940), American automobile manufacturer.
1545.

Churchill, Charles (1731–1764), English poet and satirist.
1200.

Churchill, Sir Winston (1874–1965), English statesman.
38, 417, 498, 638, 878, 1803, 1845, 2140, 2205, 2259.

Cicero, Marcus Tullius (106–43 B.C.), Roman statesman.
95, 182, 262, 330, 341, 420, 537, 561, 572, 589, 609, 660, 788, 859, 876, 906, 970, 988, 1003, 1075, 1095, 1141, 1160, 1229, 1320, 1428, 1434, 1449, 1513, 1741, 1744, 1796, 1805, 1815, 1889, 2047, 2078, 2092, 2158, 2217, 2278, 2357.

Clarendon, Lord (1609–1674), English statesman.
1113.

Clarke, James Freeman (1810–1888), American theologian, author.
1609, 1834.

Claudius, Appius (10 B.C.–54 A.D.), Roman emperor.
804.

Clay, Henry (1777–1852), American statesman.
1670, 2145.

Clement of Alexandria (190–203 A.D.), Christian theologian.
929.

Clement of Rome (30–100), Bishop of Rome.
1202.

Cleveland, Grover (1837–1908), Twenty-second President of the
United States.
10, 1725, 1747, 2131.

Cleveland, John (1613–1658), English poet.
215.

Cockran, Burke (1854–1923), American lawyer and politician.
2013.

Coleridge, Samuel Taylor (1772–1834), English poet and critic.
688, 927, 1027, 1071, 2085, 2222.

Colton, Charles Caleb (1780–1832), English clergyman, writer.
77, 166, 353, 836, 1245, 1315, 2062, 2114, 2351.

Confucius (551–479 B.C.), Chinese philosopher.
256, 381, 456, 463, 513, 648, 713, 908, 1143, 1244, 1280,
1291, 1310, 1322, 1397, 1734, 1835, 1888, 1908, 1928,
1933, 2103, 2183, 2213, 2271, 2300.

Congreve, William (1670–1729), English dramatist.
1069, 1098, 1899.

Conrad, Joseph (1857–1924), English novelist.
1107, 1806, 2332.

Cook, Captain James (1727–1779), English explorer.
107.

Cooke, Alistair (Contemporary), English journalist, TV narrator.
524, 1729.

Coolidge, Calvin (1872–1933), Thirtieth President of the United
States.
15, 228, 303, 793, 1010, 1127, 1953, 2012, 2076, 2322,
2324.

Cousins, Norman (Contemporary), American author.
258, 544, 1070, 1450, 2299, 2341.

Cowper, William (1731–1800), English poet.
818, 1066, 1253, 1690.

Cromwell, Oliver (1599–1658), English military, political and religious leader.
602, 784, 2147.

Cumberland, Bishop (1631–1718), English religious leader.
58.

Curie, Marie (1867–1934), French chemist, discovered radium.
1637.

Curran, John Philpot (1750–1817), Irish orator, judge.
2211.

Curtis, George William (1842–1892), American essayist, editor.
278.

Cryus, "The Elder" (600?–529 B.C.), King of Persia.
1306.

D

Dana, Charles Anderson (1819–1897), American journalist, editor.
655.

Daniel, Samuel (1562–1619), English poet, historian.
2210.

Daniels, Velma Seawell (Contemporary), American author.
1203, 1416.

Dante, Alighieri (1265–1321), Italian poet.
527, 1267, 1512, 2243.

Darwin, Charles Robert (1809–1882), English naturalist.
1489.

D'Avenant, Sir William (1606–1668), English dramatist, poet.
305.

Davy, Sir Humphrey (1778–1829), English chemist.
1237.

Downs, Hugh (Contemporary), American broadcaster.
91.

Drummond, Henry (1851–1897), Scottish clergyman.
12, 922, 1028, 1366, 1981.

Drummond, William (1585–1649), Scottish poet.
1937.

Drury, Allen (Contemporary), American author.
692, 1642.

Dryden, John (1631–1700), English critic, dramatist, poet.
206, 297, 434, 1377, 1872, 2348.

Dumas, Alexander (1824–1895), French author.
2042.

E

Edgeworth, Maria (1767–1849), English novelist.
1713.

Edison, Thomas Alva (1847–1931), American inventor.
1262, 1649, 2334.

Edwards, Tryon (1809–1894), American clergyman and compiler.
1206, 1252.

Einstein, Albert (1879–1955), German-born American physicist.
815, 969, 1669, 1799, 1912, 2031, 2268.

Eisenhower, Dwight D. (1890–1969), Thirty-fourth President of
the United States.
566, 730, 809, 920, 1548, 1824, 1852.

Eliot, Charles W. (1834–1926), American educator, author.
1770, 1869.

Eliot, George (1819–1880), Pen name of Mary Ann Evans, English novelist.
411, 569, 1011, 1220, 1380, 2102, 2349.

Eliot, T. S. (1888–1965), American-born English poet, critic,
playwright.
582.

Fillmore, Millard (1800–1874), Thirteenth President of the United States.
822.

Fitch, William C. (1865–1909), American playwright.
483.

Flaubert, Gustave (1821–1880), French novelist.
2149.

Fletcher, Andrew (1655–1716), Scottish patriot.
1493.

Fletcher, John (1579–1625), English dramatist.
2099.

Florio, John (1553?–1625), English lexicographer, translator.
1911.

Flynn, General John Peter (Contemporary), Lt. General USAF, retired. Senior United States POW, Hanoi 1967–1973.
1756, 1782, 1952.

Fontaine, Jean de la (1621–1695), French poet.
1193.

Ford, Betty (Contemporary), wife of Gerald Ford, Thirty-eighth President of the United States.
362, 2290.

Ford, Gerald R. (Contemporary), Thirty-eighth President of the United States.
811, 1625.

Ford, Henry (1863–1947), American industrialist.
13, 1207.

Fosdick, Harry Emerson (1878–1969), American preacher, author.
328, 725, 1048, 1987.

Foster, John (1770–1843), English essayist.
889.

France, Anatole (1844–1924), French novelist, poet.
1038, 1192, 1255.

Franklin, Benjamin (1706–1790), American statesman, inventor, writer.

122, 363, 514, 520, 654, 685, 689, 842, 971, 1115, 1139,
1187, 1299, 1395, 1415, 1482, 1519, 1578, 1658, 1723,
1724, 1748, 1760, 1847, 1864, 1907, 1960, 2070, 2086,
2129, 2136, 2188, 2216, 2228, 2231, 2250.

Friedan, Betty (Contemporary), American author, leader in women's rights movement.
819, 2288.

Froude, James Anthony (1818–1894), English historian.
4, 231, 1359, 1465.

Fuller, Buckminster (Contemporary), American architect, inventor.
195, 1138.

Fuller, Margaret (1810–1850), American editor, feminist leader.
1917.

Fuller, Thomas, M.D. (1654–1734), English writer, physician.
61, 152, 397, 405, 503, 510, 528, 587, 845, 1005, 1435,
1521, 1589, 1657, 1994, 2260.

G

Galen (130?–201? A.D.), Greek anatomist, physiologist.
1040.

Galileo (1564–1642), Italian scientist, philosopher.
607.

Galsworthy, John (1867–1933), English novelist, playwright.
894, 1223.

Gandhi, Mahatma (1869–1948), Hindu nationalist, spiritual leader.
734, 1326, 1375, 1977, 2354.

Gardner, John W. (Contemporary), American psychologist, political leader.
686, 978, 1730, 1984.

Garfield, James A. (1831–1881), Twentieth President of the United States.
474, 913, 1131, 1538, 1982, 2311, 2328.

Garrick, David (1717–1779), English author, theater manager.
1189, 1940.

Garrison, William Lloyd (1805–1879), American abolitionist editor, lecturer.
670, 1828.

Gaynor, William J. (1848–1913), American jurist, public official.
1008.

George VI (1895–1952), King of Great Britain and Northern Ireland.
1910.

George, David Lloyd (1863–1945), British Prime Minister.
21, 760.

George, Henry (1839–1897), American economist.
449.

Gesner, Konrad von (1516–1565), Swiss naturalist.
1054.

Getty, J. Paul (1892–1976), American businessman.
1477.

Gibbon, Edward (1737–1794), English historian.
1795, 1891.

Gibbons, James Cardinal (1834–1921), American, Cardinal in Roman Catholic Church.
718.

Gibran, Kahlil (1883–1931), Syrian poet, painter.
898, 1201, 2247.

Gide, Andre (1869–1951), French novelist.
1613.

Girard, Stephen (1750–1831), American merchant, banker, philanthropist.
802.

Girardin, Delphine de (1804–1855), French poet, playwright.
1719.

Gladstone, William E. (1809–1898), English Prime Minister.
1316, 1451, 1558, 1757, 1823, 2106.

Goethe, Johann, Wolfgang von (1749–1832), German playwright, poet.
126, 255, 475, 535, 575, 632, 666, 826, 832, 985, 1042, 1163, 1284, 1387, 1470, 1516, 1555, 1563, 1617, 1710, 1714, 1973, 2007, 2057, 2164, 2184.

Goldsmith, Oliver (1728–1774), English poet, dramatist, novelist.
264, 1094, 1652, 1901, 2280.

Gompers, Samuel (1850–1924), British-born American labor leader.
791.

Gough, John Bartholomew (1817–1886), English temperance orator.
2229.

Gracian, Baltasar (1601–1658), Spanish priest, writer.
743, 1921.

Granada, Luis de (1504–1588), Spanish writer, orator.
97.

Grant, Ulysses S. (1822–1885), Eighteenth President of the United States.
1621, 2310.

Gray, Thomas (1716–1771), English poet.
2203.

Greeley, Horace (1811–1872), American journalist, political leader.
1475, 1717.

Grellet, Stephen (1773–1855), Quaker minister, missionary, philanthropist.
1235.

Guicciardini (1483–1540), Italian statesman, author.
2035.

Guyon, Madame (1648–1717), French writer.
1922.

H

Haeckel, Ernst (1834–1919), German biologist, philosopher.
306.

Hale, Edward Everett (1822–1909), American author.
1174, 1958.

Hale, Sir Matthew (1609–1676), English jurist.
1300.

Haliburton, Thomas C. (1796–1865), Canadian writer.
2329.

Hall, Bolton (1854–1938), American lawyer, lecturer.
775.

Hamilcar, Barca (270–228 B.C.), Carthaginian general, statesman.
597.

Hamilton, Alexander (1755–1804), American lawyer, statesman.
327.

Hamilton, Gail (Mary Abigail Dodge) (1830–1896), American author.
2.

Hammarskjold, Dag (1905–1961), Swedish statesman, United Nations Secretary General 1953–1961.
618, 1680.

Harding, Warren G. (1865–1923), Twenty-ninth President of the United States.
120, 1902.

Hare, August William (1792–1834), English religious leader.
260.

Harrison, Benjamin (1833–1901), Twenty-third President of the United States.
344, 773.

Harrison, William Henry (1773–1841), Ninth President of the United States.
980.

Harte, Bret (1836–1902), American author.
803.

Harvey, Paul (Contemporary), ABC news commentator.
1640.

Hatfield, Mark O. (Contemporary), United States senator.
219.

Herodotus (5th century B.C.), Greek historian.
1406.

Hesiod (8th century B.C.), Greek poet.
1136.

Higginson, T. W. S. (1823–1911), American clergyman, author.
690, 1564, 2316.

Hillard, George S. (1808–1879), American lawyer, author.
1841.

Hobbes, Thomas (1588–1679), English philosopher.
724.

Holland, J. G. (1819–1881), American journalist, editor.
912.

Holmes, Oliver Wendell (1841–1935), Justice of the Supreme
Court of the United States.
406, 747, 1051, 1385, 1497, 1862, 2256, 2360.

Homer (8th century B.C.), Greek poet.
425, 1055, 1970.

Hoover, Herbert (1874–1964), Thirty-first President of the United
States.
563, 999, 1129, 1175, 2187.

Horace (65–8 B.C.), Roman poet.
216, 292, 374, 523, 772, 1087, 1231, 1283, 1384, 1552,
1597, 1622, 1853, 1896, 2128.

Howe, Elias (1819–1867), American inventor.
2018.

Howell, James (1594–1666), English writer.
1432.

Hubbard, Elbert (1856–1915), American author.
511.

Hughes, Thomas (1822–1896), English novelist, reformer, jurist.
170, 827.

Hugo, Victor (1802–1855), French novelist, playwright, poet.
203, 244, 489, 986, 996, 1030, 1101, 1134, 1186, 1654,
1698, 1735, 1997, 2093, 2356.

Hunt, Leigh (1784–1859), English poet, essayist.
78, 1041, 1151.

Huxley, Thomas Henry (1825–1895), English writer, naturalist.
174, 615, 1249.

I

Ibsen, Henrik (1828–1906), Norwegian dramatist.
380, 817, 2162, 2206.

Inge, Dean William Ralph (1860–1954), English clergyman, writer.
2200, 2343.

Ingersoll, Robert G. (1833–1899), American lawyer, speaker.
383, 499, 1816, 1831, 2135, 2166.

Irving, Washington (1783–1859), American author.
187, 1447, 1776, 1949, 2068.

Isocrates (436–338 B.C.), Athenian orator.
413.

J

Jackson, Andrew (1767–1845), Seventh President of the United States.
807, 1340, 1408, 1615.

Jackson, Henry M. (Contemporary), United States senator.
1603.

James, Henry (1843–1916), American novelist.
1133.

James, William (1842–1910), American philosopher.
169, 226.

Jay, William (1769–1853), English clergyman, writer.
1820.

Jefferies, Richard (1848–1887), English writer.
192, 1059, 2091.

Jefferson, Thomas (1743–1826), Third President of the United States.
90, 619, 631, 659, 835, 1033, 1219, 1407, 1479, 1659, 1790, 2137, 2321.

Johnson, Andrew (1808–1875), Seventeenth President of the United States.
779.

Johnson, Lyndon B. (1908–1973), Thirty-sixth President of the United States.
646.

Johnson, Samuel (1709–1784), English essayist, poet.
36, 158, 168, 183, 295, 457, 516, 521, 592, 637, 828, 1000, 1032, 1093, 1257, 1331, 1469, 1562, 1646, 1768, 1789, 1793, 1839, 1873, 1893, 2061, 2238.

Jones, Lloyd (Contemporary), American research analyst.
2020.

Jonson, Ben (1573–1637), English poet, dramatist.
74, 110, 2058.

Joubert, Joseph (1754–1824), French moralist, essayist.
1154, 1265, 1541, 2301, 2336.

Junius, pen name of unknown English writer who wrote articles attacking the king during 1769–1772.
1171.

K

Kagawa, Toyohiko (1866–1960), Japanese religious leader.
1811.

Kant, Immanuel (1724–1804), German philosopher.
246, 1287.

Keats, John (1795–1821), English poet.
207, 1661.

Keble, John (1792–1866), English clergyman, poet.
710.

Keller, Helen (1880–1968), American author, lecturer; deaf and blind from infancy.
242, 2034, 2295, 2307.

Kempis, Thomas A. (1380–1471), German ecclesiastic.
19, 44, 904, 1535, 1584, 1620.

Kennedy, John F. (1917–1963), Thirty-fifth President of the
United States.
221, 616, 1073, 1264, 1343, 1456, 1557, 1618, 1736.

Ketner, Will L. (Contemporary), American political leader, public
speaker.
1112, 1164, 1178, 2006.

Khayyam, Omar (1050?–1123? A.D.), Persian poet, astronomer.
2115.

Kierkegaard, Soren (1813–1855), Danish philosopher, theologian.
2181.

Kingsley, Charles (1819–1875), English author.
200, 259, 354, 454, 1072, 1089, 1500, 1882.

Kipling, Rudyard (1865–1936), English author.
614, 1976.

Knox, John (1505–1572), Scottish religious leader, reformer, author.
1179, 1372, 2109.

Kock, Paul de (1793–1871), French author.
839.

L

Lamartine de Alphonse (1790–1869), French poet.
302.

Lamb, Charles (1775–1834), English essayist.
257, 928, 1119, 1708, 1821, 2046.

Landor, Walter Savage (1775–1864), English poet, essayist, novelist.
1944.

Lang, Andrew (1844–1912), Scottish poet, scholar.
270.

Langford, John Alford (1823–1903), English religious historian.
271.

Lanier, Sidney (1842–1881), American poet.
1505.

Lavater, Johann Kaspar (1741–1801), Swiss poet, theologian.
640, 1651, 2121.

Lee, Robert E. (1807–1870), Commander-in-chief of the Confederate Army.
1991.

Leo XIII, Pope (750–816)
307.

Leonardo da Vinci (1452–1519), Italian artist, inventor, scientist.
1168, 1312, 1678, 1906.

Lescynski, Stanislaus J. (1677–1766), King of Poland.
129, 230.

Lessing, Gotthold (1729–1781), German dramatist, critic.
1704.

Lewis, C. S. (1898–1963), English novelist.
722, 1110.

Lewis, Sinclair (1885–1951), American novelist.
140.

Lichtenberg, Georg Christoph (1742–1799), German satirical writer.
130, 622, 1156.

Liddon, Canon (1824–1890), English theologian.
1585.

Lin Yutang (1895–1970), Chinese scholar, writer.
458, 2262.

Lincoln, Abraham (1809–1865), Sixteenth President of the United States.
554, 707, 721, 795, 812, 1035, 1227, 1339, 1439, 2152, 2258, 2306.

Linkletter, Art (Contemporary), American author, lecturer, broadcaster.
1318, 1631, 1807, 2022.

Linnaeus (1707–1778), Swedish botanist.
883.

Livingstone, David (1813–1873), Scottish medical missionary, explorer.
805.

Livy (59 B.C.–17 A.D.), Roman historian.
430, 1184, 2173, 2269.

Lloyd, J. William (1627–1717), English theologian.
1369.

Locke, John (1632–1704), English philosopher.
54, 696, 2094, 2097, 2175.

Longfellow, Henry Wadsworth (1807–1882), American poet.
17, 117, 343, 581, 905, 1091, 1210, 1228, 1354, 1367, 1715, 1957, 2123, 2177, 2254.

Lorimer, George Horace (1867–1939), American editor, publisher.
1472.

Lover, Samuel (1797–1868), Irish painter, novelist.
2352.

Lowell, Amy (1874–1925), American poet.
579.

Lowell, James Russell (1819–1891), American poet.
46, 171, 473, 620, 712, 789, 884, 1668, 1674, 1926, 1951, 1983, 2234.

Lubbock, John (1834–1913), English author, statesman.
2008.

Luce, Clare Boothe (Contemporary), American author, playwright, political leader, woman of letters.
318, 974, 2282.

Luckman, Charles (Contemporary), American architect.
1149.

Lucretius (96?–55 B.C.), Roman poet, philosopher.
588, 1644.

Luther, Martin (1483–1546), German monk, founder of Protestantism.
150, 198, 338, 921, 1086, 1373, 1487, 1492, 1706, 2132.

Lyly, John (1554?–1616), English novelist, dramatist.
446.

Mc

McCarthy, Justin (1861–1936), Irish politician, historian.
1426.

McIver, Charles D. (1860–1906), American college president.
643.

McKinley, William (1843–1901), Twenty-fifth President of the
United States.
339, 1002, 1825.

M

MacArthur, General Douglas (1880–1964), American military
leader.
487, 1754.

Macaulay, Thomas (1800–1859), English historian, statesman.
157, 349, 388, 751, 981, 2174.

Macdonald, George (1824–1905), Scottish novelist, poet.
94, 279.

Machiavelli, Niccolo (1469–1527), Italian statesman, politician.
326, 2252.

Madison, James (1751–1836), Fourth President of the United
States.
419, 694, 810, 1346.

Maeterlinck, Count Maurice (1862–1949), Belgian poet, naturalist.
1021.

Magee, Bishop W. C. (1821–1891), English religious leader.
1464.

Magnuson, Warren G. (Contemporary), United States senator.
2227.

Malebranche, Nicolas de (1638–1715), French metaphysical philosopher.
1441.

Moyers, Bill (Contemporary), American journalist, author. TV commentator.
564, 1007.

Muhlenberg, John Peter Gabriel (1746–1807), American clergyman.
1699.

Muskie, Edmund (Contemporary), American political leader.
1130, 1305, 1626, 1666, 1965, 1986.

N

Napoleon Bonaparte (1769–1821), Emperor of France.
71, 213, 245, 373, 559, 821, 1001, 1153, 1370, 1673, 2039.

Nelson, Lord (1758–1805), British admiral.
2027.

Newman, Edwin (Contemporary), American journalist, philologist.
1278, 1667, 2107.

Newton, Sir Isaac (1642–1727), English mathematician, scientist.
247, 2148.

Niebuhr, Reinhold (1892–1971), American theologian.
491.

Nietzche, Friedrich (1844–1900), German philosopher, poet.
3, 850, 1374, 1995.

Nixon, Richard M. (Contemporary), Thirty-seventh President of the United States.
440, 1047, 2014, 2069, 2315.

O

Oliver, James (1823–1908), American inventor.
2021, 2326.

Orben, Bob (Contemporary), American humorist.
545, 625, 783, 1560, 1695, 2323.

Ouida (Pen name of Louise de la Ramee) (1839–1908), English novelist.
1494.

Overbury, Sir Thomas (1581–1613), English poet, essayist.
143.

Overstreet, Harry Allen (1875–1970), American philosopher, psychologist.
1009.

Ovid (43 B.C.–17 A.D.), Roman poet.
237, 558, 1404, 1809, 2118, 2191, 2338.

Owen, Dr. John (1616–1683), English clergyman, writer.
1251.

P

Paine, Thomas (1737–1809), British-born political leader and theoretician in the American Revolution.
816, 1079, 1942, 2005.

Palmer, Arnold (Contemporary), American professional golfer.
930.

Parkman, Francis (1823–1893), American historian, author.
2312.

Pascal, Blaise (1623–1662), French philosopher, scientist, writer.
1239, 1248, 1360, 1378, 1750, 2095, 2163, 2214.

Pasteur, Louis (1822–1895), French chemist.
1511.

Pater, Walter (1839–1894), English essayist, novelist, critic.
525.

Paterson, J. W. (1744–1808), American Army general, patriot.
2314.

Paul, VI, Pope (1897–1978).
1106.

Payn, James (1830–1898), English novelist.
1329.

Pliny the Younger (62–113 A.D.), Roman statesman.
51, 1096.

Plutarch (46–120 A.D.), Greek biographer, philosopher.
39, 794, 1225, 1689, 1743, 1904, 1924.

Polybius (205?–125? B.C.), Greek historian.
442, 2279.

Pope, Alexander (1688–1744), English poet, satirist.
119, 141, 148, 673, 798, 1083, 1775, 2353.

Pythagoras (6th century B.C.), Greek philosopher.
14, 1195.

Q

Quintilian (40–100 A.D.), Roman orator, writer.
124, 1057, 1496.

Quintus, Curtius Rufus (2nd century A.D.), Roman historian.
763.

R

Rabelais, Francois (1494?–1553), French satirist, physician.
552, 2249.

Rabutin, Bussy (1618–1693), French writer.
2036.

Raleigh, Sir Walter (1552?–1618), English navigator, colonizer, writer.
1817.

Ray, John (1627–1705), English naturalist.
299, 1324.

Reagan, Ronald (Contemporary), Fortieth President of the U.S.
37, 814, 1604, 1992.

Reddy, Helen (Contemporary), American singer, entertainer, (born in Australia).
1996, 2292.

Reynolds, Sir Joshua (1723–1792), English portrait painter.
179, 1158, 2055.

Richter, Jean Paul (1763–1825), German humorist, novelist.
75, 151.

Rickenbacker, Capt. Eddie (1890–1973), American aviator.
496.

Rilke, Rainer Maria (1875–1926), German poet, writer.
1381.

Rochefaucauld, François, Duc de la (1613–1680), French writer.
42, 69, 116, 164, 320, 429, 459, 495, 532, 896, 1183,
1213, 1388, 1886, 2019.

Rockefeller, David (Contemporary), American financier.
1169, 1301, 2196.

Rockefeller, John D. (1839–1937), American industrialist, philanthropist.
1629, 2009.

Rogers, Will (1879–1935), American humorist, actor, author.
390, 1146, 1261.

Roosevelt, Eleanor (1884–1962), American humanitarian, wife of
President Franklin D. Roosevelt.
488.

Roosevelt, Franklin D. (1882–1945), Thirty-second President of
the United States.
624, 732, 762, 1018, 1746, 1967.

Roosevelt, Theodore (1858–1919), Twenty-sixth President of the
United States.
43, 185, 708, 984, 1302, 1802, 2313.

Rossetti, Christina Georgina (1830–1894), English poet.
1396, 1945.

Rothschild, Meyer A. (1743–1812), German banker.
799.

Rousseau, Jean Jacques (1712–1778), French author.
416, 663, 1177, 1241, 1295, 1590, 2038, 2359.

Ruskin, John (1819–1900), English essayist.
197, 201, 241, 629, 887, 1023, 1029, 1161, 1217, 1394,
1812, 1915, 1936, 2050, 2074, 2130, 2244, 2308.

Russell, Bertrand (1872–1970), English philosopher, reformer.
1247.

S

Saint Ambrose (340?–397 A.D.), Bishop of Milan, author, composer.
2253.

Saint Augustine (354–430 A.D.), Religious leader, author.
621, 723, 1520, 1641, 1697, 1785, 2189.

Saint Bernard of Clairvaux, French churchman; founded Cistercian Abbey in 1115.
222.

Saint-Exupery (1900–1944), French aviator, author.
1351, 1798.

Saint Francis of Assisi (1182?–1226), Italian monk; founder of Franciscan order.
357, 1883, 2331.

Saint Ignatius of Loyola (1491–1556), Spanish ecclesiastic, soldier.
1732.

Saint Jerome (340?–420 A.D.), Latin scholar; prepared the Vulgate.
728.

Saint John Chrysostom (345?–407 A.D.), Patriarch of Constantinople.
542, 1565.

Saint Thomas Aquinas (1225–1274), Italian Dominican monk, philosopher, theologian.
1692.

Sakharow, Andrei (Contemporary), Russian nuclear physicist.
1124.

Sallust (Gaius Sallustius Crispus) (86–34 B.C.), Roman historian.
81.

Sandford, James (1572–?), English translator of arts and sciences.
770.

Santayana, George (1863–1952), Spanish-born American philosopher, poet.
727, 1499, 1580, 1898.

Sappho (7th century B.C.), Greek poet.
973.

Savile, Sir George (Lord Halifax) (1633–1695), English statesman, writer.
1431, 1481.

Schiller, Johann Christop von (1759–1805), German poet, dramatist.
1199.

Schlafly, Phyllis (Contemporary), Political leader, organizer of
the anti-ERA movement.
1419, 1459, 2285, 2289.

Schopenhauer, Arthur (1788–1860), German philosopher.
701, 1463, 2116.

Schweitzer, Albert (1875–1965), French philosopher.
375, 733, 1123, 1197, 1321, 1570, 1700, 1905.

Scott, Sir Walter (1771–1832), Scottish poet, novelist.
89, 481, 546, 617, 1606, 1838, 1855, 2016.

Segal, Erich (Contemporary), American author.
1389.

Selden, John (1584–1654), English jurist.
1286.

Seneca, Lucius Annaeus (4 B.C.–65 A.D.), Roman philosopher.
1, 24, 79, 99, 184, 236, 352, 395, 423, 548, 553, 774, 987,
1204, 1240, 1311, 1401, 1433, 1453, 1544, 1553, 1599,
1728, 1874, 1962, 1974, 2105, 2333.

Seton, Denest Thompson (1860–1946), English writer, illustrator
in the United States.
1411.

Severeid, Eric (Contemporary), American author, TV commentator, man of letters.
331, 369, 1612, 1861, 2059.

Shakespeare, William (1564–1616), English playwright, poet.
109, 147, 460, 512, 679, 704, 849, 990, 1099, 1218, 1256,
1457, 1517, 1587, 1866, 2124.

Shaw, George Bernard (1856–1950), Irish-born English dramatist, critic, essayist.
1173.

Sheen, Fulton J. (1895–1979), American Roman Catholic clergyman, writer, teacher.
1046.

Shelley, Percy Bysshe (1792–1822), English poet.
1152, 1662, 2232.

Shenstone, William (1714–1763), English poet.
1818.

Sheridan, Richard B. (1751–1816), English dramatist.
144.

Shula, Don F. (Contemporary), American football coach.
2028.

Sidney, Sir Philip (1554–1586), English soldier, poet, essayist.
293, 846, 1530.

Skobeleff, General Mikhail Dmitrievich (1843–1882), Russian military leader.
145.

Slick, Grace (Contemporary), American singer, entertainer.
2291.

Smith, Adam (1723–1790), Scottish economist, philosopher.
304.

Smith, Alexander (1830–1867), Scottish designer, man of letters.
748.

Smith, Sidney (1771–1845), English clergyman, essayist.
333, 1260, 1376, 1566.

Socrates (470?–399 B.C.), Greek philosopher, teacher.
238, 2266.

Solon (6th century B.C.), Athenian statesman, poet.
650, 1607.

Sophocles (496–406 B.C.), Greek dramatist.
60, 1771, 2294.

Sousa, John Philip (1854–1932), American band leader, composer.
1490.

Southey, Robert (1774–1843), English poet.
744, 837, 2143.

Swayze, John Cameron (Contemporary), American journalist, news commentator.
2275.

Swedenborg, Emanuel (1688–1772), Swedish scientist, theologian.
448.

Swift, Jonathan (1667–1745), Irish religious leader.
113, 146, 441, 776, 1405, 1655, 2111, 2223.

Syrus, Publilius (1st century A.D.), Roman essayist, playwright.
82, 312, 372, 426, 547, 853, 918, 1568, 1884, 2267.

T

Tacitus (Late 1st, early 2nd centuries A.D.), Roman historian.
1848.

Taft, William Howard (1857–1930), Twenty-seventh President of the United States.
668.

Talleyrand, Charles (1754–1838), French statesman, diplomat.
1307.

Taylor, Zachary (1784–1850), Twelfth President of the United States.
2156.

Tennyson, Alfred, Lord (1809–1892), English poet.
509, 1004, 1702, 2274.

Terence (185–159 B.C.), Roman author.
600, 1414, 1643, 2263.

Thackeray, William Makepeace (1811–1863), English novelist.
702, 726, 800, 1118, 2090, 2241.

Thales (640?–546? B.C.), Greek philosopher, geometrician.
1518.

Themistocles (527–460 B.C.), Athenian political leader.
11.

Thoreau, Henry David (1817–1862), American essayist, naturalist.
277, 611, 680, 753, 841, 925, 1357, 1386, 1498, 1510, 1546, 1950, 2010.

Thucydides (5th century B.C.), Greek historian.
2208.

Tibullus, Albius (54–19 B.C.), Roman poet.
1102.

Toffler, Alvin (Contemporary), American author.
675, 880, 1572, 2138, 2157.

Tolstoy, Leo (1828–1910), Russian novelist, philosopher.
332, 768, 1109, 1412, 1473, 1739, 2122.

Toynbee, Arnold (1889–1975), English historian, educator.
376.

Trollope, Anthony (1815–1882), English novelist.
1319, 1764.

Truman, Harry S. (1884–1972), Thirty-third President of the United States.
719, 808, 1108, 1304, 1804, 2309.

Twain, Mark (Samuel Clemens) (1835–1910), American humorist, writer.
155, 432, 494, 526, 585, 684, 705, 758, 830, 1017, 1148, 1399, 1628, 1916, 2030.

V

Van Buren, Martin (1782–1862), Eighth President of the United States.
1540.

Van Dyke, Henry (1852–1933), American clergyman, educator, author.
924, 1159, 1438, 1488, 1559, 2318.

Van Gogh, Vincent (1853–1890), Dutch painter.
325.

Van Loon, Hendrik Willem (1882–1944), Dutch-born American author.
1738, 2101.

Vauvenargues, Marquis de (1715–1747), French moralist, essayist.
115, 671, 893.

Vega, Lope de (1562–1635), Spanish dramatist, poet.
462.

Victoria, Queen (1819–1901), Queen of United Kingdom of Great Britain and Ireland.
350.

Virgil (70–19 B.C.), Roman poet.
234, 431.

Voltaire (1694–1778), French poet, dramatist, satirist, historian.
128, 142, 177, 283, 923, 1140, 1342, 1909, 2154, 2335.

W

Wagner, Richard (1813–1883), German poet, composer.
1694.

Walpole, Sir Hugh (1884–1941), English novelist.
500.

Walton, Izaak (1593–1683), English man of letters.
156, 1056, 1759.

Wanamaker, John (1838–1922), American merchant, philanthropist.
2087.

Washington, Booker T. (1856–1915), American educator.
1025, 1413, 1709.

Washington, George (1732–1799), First President of the United States.
267, 324, 447, 596, 833, 1078, 1232, 1347, 1619, 1829, 2144, 2255.

Watts, Isaac (1674–1748), English theologian, hymnist.
229, 1063.

Webster, Daniel (1782–1852), American political leader, diplomat.
340, 422, 452, 560, 1602, 1672, 1800.

Webster, John (1580–1625), English dramatist.
41.

Webster, Noah (1758–1843), American lexicographer.
1317, 1972.

Wells, H. G. (1866–1946), English author.
443, 2293.

Wesley, John (1703–1791), English theologian, founder of Methodism.
682, 968, 2342.

Whately, Archbishop (1787–1863), Anglican Archbishop of Dublin.
1016.

Whitehead, Alfred North (1861–1947), English mathematician, philosopher.
1132.

Wilde, Oscar (1854–1900), Irish poet, dramatist, wit.
103, 163, 740, 752, 976, 1166, 1383, 1444, 1767, 1840, 1881, 2063, 2160, 2197, 2284.

Wilson, Earl (Contemporary), American columnist, humorist.
1165, 1727, 1733, 2033, 2195, 2325.

Wilson, Woodrow (1856–1924), Twenty-eighth President of the United States.
56, 139, 347, 562, 662, 780, 1337, 1583, 1608, 1722, 1826.

X

Xenophanes (570–480 B.C.), Greek philosopher, poet.
2272.

Xerxes (519?–465 B.C.), King of Persia.
1726.

Y

Young, Edward (1683–1765), English poet, playwright.
  127, 233, 1044.

Youngman, Henny (Contemporary), American comedian.
  50, 1417, 1476, 1574, 1850, 1859.

Z

Zoroaster (6th century B.C.), Persian prophet, founder of Zoroas-
  trianism.
  2179.

Thematic Index

Another way to find a story.
Look among these 327 subjects to find a story
not listed under a main category.
The number indicates the number of the story—not the page number.